HEART SMART®

COOKBOOK

**by Henry Ford Heart and Vascular Institute
and The Detroit Free Press**

Andrews and McMeel
A Universal Press Syndicate Company
Kansas City

Library of Congress Cataloging-in-Publication Data

Heart smart cookbook / by Henry Ford Heart and Vascular Institute and
    the Detroit Free Press.
              p.   cm.
    Includes index.
    ISBN 0-8362-8059-8 : $14.95
    1. Coronary heart disease—Prevention. 2. Coronary heart disease-
    -Diet therapy—Recipes. 3. Low-fat diet—Recipes. I. Henry Ford
    Heart and Vascular Institute. II. Detroit Free Press.
    RC565.C6H365 1994   94-4620
    641.5'6311—dc20   CIP

First Printing, March 1994
Third Printing, October 1995

Contents

What Is Heart Smart?

Henry Ford Heart and Vascular Institute

Heart Smart® is a community-oriented health promotion program of the Henry Ford Heart and Vascular Institute of Henry Ford Hospital. Through cooperative efforts with organizations, businesses, retail food outlets and corporations, it tries to help the consumer become aware of how choices in food and lifestyle can affect health.

The Heart Smart® program is diverse. At various company cafeterias and some major restaurants, Heart Smart® symbols indicate healthful food choices. Heart Smart® recipes are featured weekly in the Food section of the *Detroit Free Press* and on Kay Lowry's "Eat to Live" segments on WJBK-TV2. Heart Smart® is a registered trademark of the Henry Ford Health System.

For more information about the Heart Smart® program, call (313) 874-4134, 9 a.m. to 5 p.m. weekdays.

Foreword

During the past 10 years, we've become increasingly conscious that we have the power to prevent health problems caused by our lifestyles. Today, one can barely read a newspaper or magazine without being exposed to information about healthy living. In fact, some people may find themselves overloaded with health-related information, some of which can be conflicting, and much of which has not been subjected to scientific study.

This book is intended to help you cut through all that, to provide you with simple suggestions and recipes that will help you gradually and permanently make the change for a healthier lifestyle.

Of the 10 leading causes of death in the United States, nine are clearly related to lifestyle. Five of the 10 are associated with diet: heart disease, cancer, cerebral vascular disease (primarily stroke), diabetes and other atherosclerosis. These five disorders account for nearly 70 percent of the deaths annually in this country.

Most heart attacks and strokes are caused by atherosclerosis, a disease in which cholesterol and other fatty substances clog the inner lining of the arteries. This process begins in childhood and progresses at variable rates, depending not only on one's heredity, but also on one's lifestyle. The three major risk factors for atherosclerosis are cigarette smoking, high blood cholesterol levels and high blood pressure. Research has shown that a combination of exercise and a diet low in saturated fat can significantly reduce your chances of developing a heart attack.

We hope this book will make it easier for you to make the right choices toward a Heart Smart® lifestyle today.

Sidney Goldstein, M.D.
Division Head, Cardiovascular Medicine

Kenneth L. Rhoads, M.D.
Senior Staff Cardiologist

Henry Ford Heart and Vascular Institute

 Heart Smart® Cookbook

Acknowledgments

Henry Ford Health System and The Detroit Free Press would like to thank those who supported and assisted us in producing this book.

Editor: Nunzio Lupo, Detroit Free Press
Project Coordinator: Fay Fitzgerald, Heart® Smart Program

Copy editors: Barbara Arrigo, Will St. John, Patricia Foley, Detroit Free Press

Graphic Design: Hank Szerlag, Detroit Free Press

Cover Illustration: Hank Szerlag, Detroit Free Press

Illustrations: Roger Hicks, Detroit Free Press

Writers: Meda Harrison Bower, registered dietitian, Heart Smart® Program, Henry Ford Hospital; **Fay Fitzgerald,** coordinator, Heart Smart® Program; **Tracy Holmes,** registered dietitian, Heart Smart® Program; **Pat Siloac**, registered dietitian, Heart Smart® Program; **Christine Kassab,** corporate director, media relations, Henry Ford Health System; **Mindy Biglin,** Freelance Writer, Henry Ford Health System.

A special thank you to: Ann Baker, Annette Habecker, Corinna Johnson, Gwen Klein and Laura Ritter for their contributions to the Heart Smart® Program and the Heart Smart® Cookbook.

Special Support: Sidney Goldstein, division head, cardiovascular medicine, Henry Ford Hospital; **Debra Hussong**, corporate director, special projects and promotions, Henry Ford Health System; **Steven Keteyian**, director, Levine Health Enhancement Center, Henry Ford Hospital; **Hildreth Macy**, associate director, dietetics, Henry Ford Hospital; **Linda Taylor,** corporate director, Publications, Henry Ford Health System; **David Robinson**, Detroit Free Press; **Jeanne Sarna**, director, Detroit Free Press Tower Kitchen.

Manuscript preparation: Chris Kierzkowski, Marilyn Nack, Debbie Stevenson, Michelle Welter, Henry Ford Hospital.

Part I

Living the Heart Smart® Lifestyle

Eating for Health

Let's face it: You know you can eat better. Even with the evidence linking diet and health, many of you still eat too much fat and too little fiber.

Improving your diet isn't really so difficult. Today's cuisines already call for bountiful fresh fruits and vegetables, savory lean meats, legumes and whole grains. So with no extra fuss in the kitchen, you can easily adapt new ingredients and cooking methods to the dietary guidelines provided by the U.S. Department of Agriculture and the U.S. Department of Health and Human Services. These guidelines are for healthy people, age 2 or older.

Eat a Variety of Foods

The best way to get all your nutrients is to eat a variety of foods. Your daily menu should include foods from each of the following food groups:

• Vegetables. To stock up on Vitamin A, try including dark green vegetables, such as spinach and broccoli, and deep orange vegetables, such as carrots and winter squash. Serve them crunchy and fresh with low-fat dips, or cook them until tender-crisp and serve without added fat or salt. Dried beans are an excellent source of protein and fiber. Include them in your diet several times a week as an alternative to meat.

• Fruits. Rich in vitamins and minerals, fruits also are high in fiber. Citrus fruits, such as oranges and grapefruit, and melons and berries provide the Vitamin C you need daily.

• Whole Grains, Breads and Cereals. These are good sources of protein, carbohydrates, vitamins, minerals and fiber. Six to 11 half-cup servings a day will provide ample energy for work and play.

• Milk Products. Milk and yogurt are excellent sources of calcium and protein. In fact, without milk products, it is difficult to consume enough calcium for healthy bones and teeth. Skim milk products make it easier to get the calcium and protein you need without consuming the highly saturated fat found in whole milk products.

• Meat, Poultry and Fish. All three are excellent sources of protein, which you need for muscle and tissue development. But many of you eat much more protein than you need. Six ounces of lean meat, poultry or fish each day is enough. As an alternative, try using more legumes such as dried beans or peas. They make an excellent and inexpensive source of low-fat protein.

Maintain Healthy Weight

Being too fat or too thin poses health problems. To maintain your present weight, the calories you consume must equal the calories you burn in daily activities and exercise. To lose weight and keep it off, you must consume fewer calories than you expend and make changes in your eating habits that you can incorporate easily into your lifestyle. Losing, returning to old eating habits and regaining the weight are not good for you. This process can make it even more difficult for you to lose the weight again.

Choose a Diet Low in Fat, Saturated Fat and Cholesterol

Medical studies link a diet high in fat, especially saturated fat, with heart disease and some forms of cancer. Dietary cholesterol also should be limited because it can cause an increase in blood cholesterol levels and, therefore, heart disease.

Choose a Diet With Plenty of Vegetables, Fruits and Grain Products

These foods are high in complex carbohydrates and fiber. The average person's diet includes 11 grams to 14 grams of fiber a day instead of the 30 grams recommended by the American Cancer Society. A high-fiber diet decreases your risk of colon cancer. If you increase your fiber intake, do so slowly or you might experience cramps and bloating. Let your body adjust and drink lots of water.

Use Sugar Only in Moderation

The problem with sugar is that it is a concentrated source of calories, and too many calories can lead to obesity. For children, high sugar snacks can set a pattern that can carry on into adulthood.

Use Salt or Sodium Only in Moderation

Most people need much less salt than the typical 4,000 milligrams to 5,000 milligrams they consume a day. The estimated daily requirement for sodium is 500 milligrams, and that is obtained naturally in foods without any added salt. The diet recommended by the American Heart Association provides 2,000 milligrams to 3,000 milligrams a day or less. Eating less salt may be beneficial to people with high blood pressure.

Drink Alcoholic Beverages in Moderation

Habitual, heavy alcohol consumption is linked to liver disease, high blood pressure and some types of cancer. Drink alcohol prudently: less than 1 ounce a day with periodic days of abstinence.

Reading the Label:
It's All in the Fine Print

If you want to treat your heart right, start by shopping right. Take a few seconds to look over the nutrition and ingredient lists on the packaged foods you buy. It's one of the healthiest things you can do.

When you read labels, be prepared for a shock. You might find that many foods are much higher in fat, sugar and sodium than you dreamed. Many health foods — say granola bars and some yogurts — are loaded with heart-stopping fats and nutritionally bankrupt sugars.

The only way you can be absolutely sure of what you're getting is to learn how to make sense of the information on the label. It's not as hard as you might think. Once you know how to zero in on key information, you'll find it's quick and easy to make Heart Smart® choices.

Identifying Unhealthy Ingredients.

Each ingredient in packaged food is listed in order by weight, which means that the first items listed are the main ingredients.

By looking at the first two or three ingredients, you can tell whether a product belongs in the grocery cart or back on the shelf. Ingredients to avoid include saturated fats — animal or vegetable — plus sugars and sodium. Weeding out these three troublemakers from your groceries requires a sharp eye, however, because they go by many different names. The list at the end of

this chapter will help you learn their code names.

As you read your way through the supermarket, you'll notice some packages don't have nutrition and ingredient labels. For example, catsup is made with mandatory ingredients according to specific government standards. Manufacturers aren't required to list the standardized catsup ingredients, but they must list any optional ingredients.

The U.S. Food and Drug Administration requires nutrition labeling only for:

• Foods supplemented with nutrients.

• Foods that carry specific nutritional claims, such as "half the fat."

• Foods intended for special dietary needs.

If a product doesn't provide nutritional information, choose another brand that does, or write to the manufacturer for it. Some products list a toll-free number — usually a 1-800 number — you can call.

Finding Fat

If you learn only one thing about reading labels, it should be how to figure the percentage of fat in products. Cutting down on fats, particularly saturated fats, is the key to reducing diet-related disease and obesity.

The American Heart Association recommends that 30 percent or less of each day's total calories come from fat, including no more than 10 percent from saturated fat. The more skilled you become at choosing low-fat foods, the closer you'll come to this heart-healthy goal. Because claims on some labels are misleading, you have to be the one to count fat calories.

For example, take a label that boasts "90 percent fat-free." What that means is that the product is 10 percent fat by weight. That information is meaningless, because your body counts calories, not weight.

To avoid falling into promotional fat traps, read the fine print on the label. There, you'll find fat listed in grams. Because you need to know what percentage of the calories in the food comes from fat, you'll have to do some simple math. Often, you'll be able to do it in your head — or at least make an educated guesstimate — right at the grocery store.

Start by memorizing this fat fact: Each gram of fat equals nine calories.

(Incidentally, that's more than twice the calories in a gram of protein or a gram of carbohydrates, which have four each. That's part of the reason why eating fatty foods makes you fat.)

To figure how many calories in a product are from fat, simply multiply the number of fat grams from the label by nine.

For example, one cup of skim milk contains 1 gram of fat.

1 x 9 = 9 calories from fat

Next, figure the percentage of the total calories that come from fat. Find the total number of calories per serving on the label, and divide the number of fat calories by the total amount of calories; then multiply by 100. In the case of skim milk, we know that one cup has 85 calories.

9 / 85 = .10588 x 100 = 10.588%

So, in our example, the percentage of fat in one cup of skim milk is nearly 10.6 percent.

If you don't bring a pocket calculator to the grocery store but know your multiplication tables, you can make a guesstimate. If a frozen dinner entree has 300 calories and 10 grams of fat, you'll know that close to one-third of the calories come from fat. (9x10=90 calories from fat; if it were 100 calories from fat, that would be exactly one-third of the 300 calories total.)

Armed with this simple formula, you can determine the true fat content of many packaged foods. You will then be able to select low-fat foods with confidence and cut the fat in your diet.

To arrive at the suggested 30 percent of calories overall from fat, plan meals so that high-fat foods are balanced by low-fat choices over the course of the day.

Although it's not required, many food producers voluntarily include information about saturated and polyunsaturated fat on their labels. If they do, compare the difference between these two types of fat. Keep in mind that less saturated fat is better for your heart and blood vessels.

Polyunsaturated fats and monounsaturated fats are healthier choices. Vegetable oils are usually polyunsaturated and contain no cholesterol. Fats from animals generally are higher in saturated fat and do have cholesterol.

Words to Live By (Avoid Them)

Fats — Use sparingly or avoid products that contain the following as leading ingredients:

Animal fat
Butter
Cocoa butter
Coconut oil
Cream
Egg and egg yolk solids
Hydrogenated vegetable oil
Lard
Milk chocolate
Palm oil or palm kernel oil
Powdered whole milk solids
Shortening

Sugar — Be on guard for these ingredients, which all really mean sugar:

Brown sugar
Corn syrup
Dextrose
Fructose
Honey
Lactose
Malt
Maltose
Molasses
Sucrose

Sodium — Watch out for these words, which indicate sodium and salt:

Garlic salt
Onion salt
Seasoned salt
Monosodium glutamate
Brine
Sodium nitrite

Shopping Smart

Shopping for heart-healthy foods can be downright confusing. Often, it's because food manufacturers want it that way. They make questionable claims or provide incomplete or even inaccurate nutrition information on labels. But you needn't surrender. With a little education, it's easy to pick your way through the supermarket choosing foods low in fat, cholesterol and sodium.

Here's what to look for in each department of the grocery store.

Produce

Most fruits and vegetables are low in fat and cholesterol and high in vitamins, minerals and fiber. When buying fresh produce, check for bruises and soft spots. Prevent spoilage at home by buying enough only for one week at a time. Remember that darker vegetables generally provide more nutrition. Dark green vegetables such as spinach and bright orange vegetables such as carrots are good sources of Vitamin A. Avoid pre-cut vegetables, because many nutrients are lost when vegetables are exposed to light.

Dairy

Dairy products are excellent sources of protein, calcium, Vitamin A, the B vitamins and Vitamin D. However, many products made from whole milk also are high in saturated fat and cholesterol. Whole milk contains 2 teaspoons of butterfat per cup; 2-percent low-fat milk contains 1 teaspoon of butterfat per cup. Even better, skim milk contains all the protein and calcium of whole milk, but less than an eighth of a teaspoon of fat per cup. Don't be confused by the name buttermilk; it is usually made from skim milk and is, therefore, low in fat.

Fortunately, there are low-fat substitutes for nearly all high-fat dairy products. Look for products listing skim milk, instead of whole milk or cream, as the first ingredient. For example, mozzarella cheese is usually made from skim milk. Also, beware of non-dairy substitutes for cream and sour cream. They often contain oils high in saturated fat, such as coconut or palm oil. In most recipes, it is possible to substitute evaporated skim milk for cream and nonfat or low-fat yogurt for sour cream.

Delicatessen

Most processed meats are high in fat and sodium, which makes it difficult to include them in a Heart Smart® diet.

However, new products are available that represent more healthful choices. Because most of these new products are made from poultry — chicken or turkey — they can be lower in saturated fat, while still high in total fat. When comparing the total fat content of processed meats, don't be misled by products labeled "98 percent fat free." This percentage is based on weight, including water, rather than on the percentage of calories that come from fat. For example, a hot dog might be labeled "82 percent fat free," but 75 percent of its calories come from fat. Look for products that list grams of fat per ounce. Processed meats containing 3 grams of fat or less per ounce contain half the fat of traditional processed meat.

Most processed meats are high in sodium because they are made with salt and sodium nitrites. Typically, processed meats contain 300 milligrams to 600 milligrams of sodium per ounce. Look for reduced versions containing 200 milligrams of sodium or less per ounce.

Meat and Poultry

Shoppers trying to make low-cholesterol, low-fat food choices might feel pangs of guilt at the meat counter. And for good reason: Many cuts of red meat are high in fat, particularly saturated fat. Organ meats, such as liver, are especially high in cholesterol. The American Heart Association recommends eating small portions of lean beef, pork, lamb and veal. A four-ounce serving of lean red meat provides 10 grams to 12 grams of fat and 100 milligrams to 112 milligrams of cholesterol, both well within Heart Association guidelines.

Poultry is a high-quality protein source that is lower in fat and saturated fat, especially if the skin is removed. As an alternative to beef, try using a low-fat ground turkey in your recipes. With chili and spaghetti sauce, for instance, no one will know. Also, when buying a roasting turkey, avoid self-basting turkeys, because they often are injected with oils that are high in saturated fat.

Fish and Shellfish

Fish is a low-fat, high protein food, a great choice for a Heart Smart® meal. Even the fattier varieties such as mackerel and salmon contain fish oil that can provide health benefits.

Although shellfish are high in cholesterol, they do not contain as much cholesterol as originally thought. You can include shellfish in your Heart Smart® diet once or twice a week.

Legumes (Dried Beans, Peas, Lentils)

Legumes are excellent nutritional bargains. Their high protein content makes them a low-fat substitute for meat, and they're also high in fiber.

By themselves legumes represent incomplete protein, compared with meat, which is a complete protein. But if your diet includes rice and whole grains, your body will match up the amino acids in the legumes with the amino acids in the grains, and put them to use as a complete protein.

Tofu, or soybean curd, is a very good source of vegetable protein. It has no taste and picks up the flavor of the ingredients with which it is mixed, making it ideal for soups, casseroles and dips.

Bread

Whole wheat, rye and multi-grain breads are excellent sources of both complex carbohydrates and fiber.

White bread is low in fiber, because the

Heart Smart® Cookbook

refining process removes the bran — the wheat's outer coating — and the germ — the kernel that is the seed of the new plant. As much as 90 percent of the fiber is lost in refining.

When looking at the list of ingredients on a bread label, whole wheat flour should be the first ingredient listed. If the bread contains 2 or more grams of fiber per slice, it is a good source of dietary fiber.

Cereal

Cereals can be one of the best sources of fiber and are often fortified with vitamins and minerals. Read labels carefully to avoid cereals high in sugar and sodium. Watch out for granola-type cereals because they can contain nuts, which are high in fat, and they also may have saturated fats, such as palm oil and coconut oil.

Pasta

Pasta is an excellent source of complex carbohydrates and can be the star of a low-calorie, low-fat meal. Pasta also is high in protein, and when made from whole grains, a good source of fiber.

A pasta meal won't be high in fat unless you use a high-fat sauce. Those prepared with butter and heavy cream are prime offenders. Watch the ingredients on canned or bottled tomato sauces; some get 50 percent or more of their calories from fat.

Vegetable Oils and Margarines

All vegetable oils contain about 120 calories per tablespoon and are pure fat. Polyunsaturated and monounsaturated oils, such as safflower, sunflower, corn, canola and olive are the best. Watch out for oils labeled "light," which is often a reference to color and flavor rather than fat or calories. The best margarines are those listing a liquid oil or water as the first ingredient.

Salad Dressings

The new nonfat and low-fat dressings on grocery store shelves will help remove fat from your diet. By reading labels, you can compare grams of fat and milligrams of sodium per tablespoon. Choose dressings that contain no more than 1 gram of fat per tablespoon. Flavored vinegars and lemon juice are alternatives when trying to add flavor to salads and marinades.

Snacks

Traditionally, snack foods have been high in fat and calories. New items such as "lite corn chips" are still 33 percent fat. But baked pretzels are a good choice because they usually contain little fat. Plain, air-popped popcorn is also a low-fat snack, but not all popcorn is. Butter flavored popcorn and cheese popcorn often are high in fat, containing more fat than potato or corn chips. Many of the microwave popping corns also are high in fat.

Canned Foods

Watch for salt in canned and processed foods. Low-sodium canned soups and vegetables have one-third less sodium than the regular products. Fruits canned in their own juices are lower in sugar and calories than those canned in heavy syrup.

Making Your Favorite Recipes Heart Smart®

The foods you love may be the very ones that hate your body. Flip through your recipe file, and you'll probably find desserts crammed with shortening and sugar, fat-filled casseroles and artery-clogging sauces.

So what's your option? Toss out all the recipes you've grown to love in the name of living the Heart Smart® lifestyle?

Definitely not.

You don't have to be a kitchen genius to give your longtime favorite recipes complete makeovers, turning them from heart-harmful to Heart Smart®, without sacrificing flavor. With today's emphasis on fresh ingredients and piquant herbs and spices, it's easier than it ever was.

Pare The Fat

In many recipes, you can easily substitute, eliminate or reduce the amount of ingredients high in saturated fat. Instead of butter or shortening, use vegetable oils, such as corn, safflower, soybean or olive oil, or use soft tub margarine. Canned, evaporated skim milk is better than cream or whole milk. Nonfat plain yogurt often can take the place of sour cream. And cocoa powder is a good stand-in for baking chocolate. To top salads, try one of the new nonfat, or low-fat dressings, salsa or a flavored vinegar. Two egg whites will do the work of one whole egg, without the fat that's contained in an egg yolk.

Side-step The Fat

Broiled or baked fish or chicken can be just as tasty as pan fried, yet much lower in fat and calories. Barbecuing meats with a low-fat sauce or marinade is another heart-healthy option. Try mixing nonfat Italian dressing with lemon or lime juice or use a red wine vinegar. The acid in the vinegar or lemon juice tenderizes the meat and gives it a great taste. Stir-frying with a bare minimum of vegetable oil is also an acceptable method, or you can use a small amount of water, broth, wine-flavored vinegar or lemon juice. Deep frying with animal fats is, of course, the least healthy choice of all.

No matter how you cook your meat, be sure to cut off all visible fat first. That prevents melted fat from seeping into the meat as it cooks.

Trim The Fat

When choosing a red meat, select the leanest cuts. Leaner meats are red, while meats with more fat marbled through the tissue appear pinkish. The most economical cuts of meat are often the leanest. When buying poultry, keep in mind that the white meat has much less fat than dark.

When cooking leaner cuts, keep the meat covered to capture its own moisture and use a lower temperature to heat it slowly. That way it'll be just as delicious and tender as a choicer cut.

Another way to add juicy flavor to your meat is to cook it in vegetable juices and low-fat, low-sodium broths.

Skim The Fat

It's easy to make stocks for soups, gravies or sauces better for your heart. First, chill the broth and allow all the fat to rise and solidify. Then, skim the fat off. If you don't have the time to chill it, use a spoon or paper towel to skim off the liquid fat. You can use these techniques with canned broth, too.

Modifications and Substitutions Worth Knowing

Instead of:	Use:
1 whole egg	2 egg whites or 1/4 cup egg substitute
Whole milk	Skim or 1/2-percent milk
Evaporated milk or cream	Skim evaporated milk
Whole milk yogurt	Low-fat or nonfat yogurt
Sour cream	Plain nonfat or low-fat yogurt
Whole milk cheese	Low-fat cheese made with part-skim milk
1 cup butter, shortening or lard	1 cup margarine (with liquid oil listed as the first ingredient on the label) or 2/3 cup oil
Peanut butter	Non-hydrogenated style (natural) peanut butter
Mayonnaise	Low-fat or nonfat mayonnaise
Chicken broth	Defatted, low-sodium chicken broth
Bouillon cube	Low-sodium bouillon cube
1 ounce baking chocolate	3 tablespoons cocoa powder plus 1 tablespoon oil
Sugar	Up to half the sugar called for
Garlic salt	Garlic powder

Heart Smart® Cookbook

Eating Out, Eating Heart Smart®

If you have an appetite for eating out, but you don't want your heart to pick up the tab, you need to be a little more discriminating about where you go and what you order.

Even at the most modest little eateries, the management is learning that health-conscious diners want more than food that just tastes good. A National Restaurant Association survey recently found, for example, that 39 percent of adults say that when eating out, they look for low-fat items and foods cooked without salt on the menu.

Although many restaurants have embraced this trend — going so far as to mark the heart-healthy items on their menus — many others have not. That's why you have to be more selective where you eat out. Be sensible about this. You know your chances of eating a healthy meal are much better at a restaurant known for excellent seafood than for wonderful ribs. Don't kid yourself by promising to get a salad at the rib house.

It's much easier to order wisely if you have the opportunity to look over the menu in advance, without the distraction of bustling waiters and tableside chitchat. One way to do this is to drop by the restaurant during an off-peak hour, such as after the lunch cleanup but before the dinner rush, to review the menu and inquire about special requests, such as foods cooked without added fat or salt. This will give you a chance to discuss your questions with the waiters under relatively calm, unhurried conditions.

If you don't have time to go to the restaurant in person, consider telephoning. Explain that you'd like to make a reservation, but have a few questions about the menu. Don't be shy. Any establishment that isn't willing to spend a few minutes talking with a potential customer isn't worth your business. Being prepared ahead of time enables you to order exactly what you want without holding up others at your table.

If you find yourself at a restaurant without having done this, forge ahead anyway.

This could take some patience. At some restaurants, waiters don't have a clue about how foods are prepared or what they're marinated in. But don't allow yourself to be brushed off. If your waiter doesn't know, simply explain that you are on a restricted diet and ask him or her to find out. Remember, you're the one paying the bill — and leaving the tip.

When you do find restaurants or waiters that make your special orders work, be sure to thank them appropriately. The kitchen staff will especially enjoy an acknowledgment, because they rarely have contact with customers.

When tailoring restaurant food to your needs, you might ask if the restaurant can or will:

• Serve margarine instead of butter?

• Serve skim instead of whole milk?

• Prepare a dish using vegetable oil such as safflower, sunflower, soy, corn, olive, or canola or margarine made with vegetable oil instead of butter, lard or shortening?

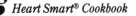

• Trim visible fat off meat or remove skin from poultry?

• Prepare an item by a low-fat cooking method such as broiling, baking, steaming, poaching or stir-frying rather than a high-fat method, such as deep fat frying?

• Limit portion size to 4 ounces to 6 ounces of cooked meat, fish or poultry?

• Serve gravy, dressings or sauces on the side?

• Serve fruit, fruit ice, sherbets or low-fat yogurt for dessert?

• Prepare a dish without added salt or monosodium glutamate (MSG)?

Learn to Read Menu-ese

When a menu says –

Au gratin	Hash
Bearnaise	Hollandaise
Braised	In its own gravy
Butter	Lemon butter
Casserole	Parmesan
Cheese sauce	Pesto
Cream	Pot pie
Escalloped	Prime
Fried	Sauteed

– it means HIGH IN FAT

When a menu says –

Broiled	Poached
Chargrilled	Roasted
Cooked in its own juice	Dry broiled
Cooked in wine	Steamed
Cooked in lemon water	Stir-fried

– it means LOW IN FAT

When a menu says –

Barbecued	Smoked
In broth	With soy sauce
In cocktail sauce	Teriyaki
Pickled	In tomato base or juice

– it means HIGH IN SODIUM

Tips for Restaurant Eating

• Eat raw vegetables or fruit as an appetizer to help fill you up.

• Be stingy with salad dressings, and be sure to order them on the side so you control the portion. Keep in mind that clear dressings are usually a better choice than creamy ones

• Beware of chef's salads. If they're made with high-fat cheese and lunch meats and regular salad dressing, they can contain more fat and calories than a deluxe hamburger.

• Eat whole wheat breads and use margarine — not butter — sparingly.

• Fish is almost always a good choice, and you can enjoy shellfish, such as lobster, clams and shrimp, if you use lemon juice instead of dipping them in butter.

• Choose more plant foods, which are low in fat and calories, such as fruits, vegetables and legumes.

• Trim all visible fat off meats and skip all thick, rich sauces and gravies.

• When ordering pizza, choose a thick crust, eliminate or limit the amount of meat and request that your pizza be made with low-fat cheese.

• For dessert, order fresh fruit, sorbet or sherbet. Frozen low-fat or nonfat yogurt and soft-serve ice cream are also good options instead of high-fat, high-cholesterol ice cream. They contain only a fraction of the calories found in premium ice cream and can be just as satisfying.

• Use skim milk in your coffee. Cream and half and half are loaded with fat.

• If you're having drinks, resist creamy, sweet drinks such as hummers, pina coladas and whiskey sours. Try a wine spritzer, seltzer or mineral water with a lime or lemon twist.

Balancing the Scales with Less Food and More Fitness

If you want to lose weight permanently, start by losing your diet books.

For most people, diets simply don't work.

It's an oft-quoted statistic, but it bears repeating: No matter what diet they use, more than 90 percent of dieters regain the weight. That's because most diet plans have one basic flaw: They're designed as a temporary change in eating habits, to be endured only until the desired weight is reached. After going off a diet, many dieters promptly resume their old eating habits. Not surprisingly, the weight returns.

The only way to control weight is to make permanent changes in the lifestyle habits that make you overweight. That means developing a healthy eating plan that you can maintain for the rest of your life. If you've been sedentary, it also means finding a form of exercise that you enjoy and can incorporate into your daily activities.

Excess body fat is one of the most common health problems facing many people today. Although a few extra pounds seems to pose no serious threat to long-term health, the same is not true for the severely overfat.

Not only does excess body fat have a negative impact on self-image and self-esteem, but it also has been linked to coronary artery disease, elevated blood cholesterol, high blood pressure, diabetes, arthritis, certain forms of cancer and gallbladder disease. Reducing body fat can improve or alleviate many of these medical conditions.

What Is Too Fat?

Overweight and overfat don't mean the same thing. Some people, such as athletes, are quite muscular and weigh more than average for their heights. They might be considered overweight on some height and weight charts. But their body composition — the amount of fat versus fat-free tissue — is excellent.

Others people might weigh an average amount, and look thin, yet carry too much fat in their muscles.

Still others might be both overweight and overfat.

Some body fat is necessary. The amount of essential fat varies. Women carry more essential fat — 12 percent — compared to men — 3 percent. Experts generally agree that a desirable percentage of body fat is about 18 percent to 25 percent for women and 10 percent to 18 percent for men. Women with more than 35 percent body fat and men with more than 25 percent are obese.

Guidelines for Adult Body Fat

	Men	Women
Lean	5-9%	12-17%
Desirable	10-18%	18-25%
Above Desirable	19-24%	26-34%
Obese	25% plus	35% plus

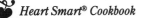

One way to determine the percentage of body fat is to measure skin fold thickness. A trained professional can administer the test and perform the calculations. Assessing body composition has advantages over using the standard height-weight tables because it can help you make the important distinction between being overweight and being overfat.

Balancing the Scales

Whether you lose weight, gain weight or maintain weight depends on a very simple equation. The amount you weigh is determined by how many calories you take in versus the number of calories you use up.

Learning how to balance your energy intake — calories in food — with your energy output — calories expended in activity — is the key to achieving and maintaining your desired weight. If you eat more calories than you use, the excess calories will be stored as fat. On the other hand, if you eat fewer calories than you use, you'll burn off fat. Each pound of fat the body stores is equal to about 3,500 calories.

A healthy weight reduction plan usually results in the loss of one to two pounds a week. If you lose weight faster, it might mean your body is drawing upon fat-free tissue — muscle — instead of its fat reserves.

The Heart Smart® approach to weight reduction is to combine smaller portions of food — about 200 to 300 fewer calories each day — and physical activity to burn 200 to 300 calories. For example, adding 30 minutes of brisk walking to your daily activities will use up 180 to 210 extra calories per day. If you maintain this schedule every day for a year, you'd burn an extra 1,260 to 1,470 calories per week, or about 19 to 22 pounds in one year. To lose an additional 21 to 31 pounds, try to cut back 200 to 300 calories in your diet each day. If you stick to it, this combination of exercise and diet modification will result in a total reduction of 40 to 53 pounds in one year.

This should show you how easy it is to trim a few hundred calories out of your daily eating plan:

FOOD	CALORIES
1 ounce of chips or crackers	150
1 can of sugared cola	150
1 can of beer	150
2 ounces of peanuts	300
4 to 6 cookies	300
1 cup ice cream	250-300

Exercising Your Right To Fitness

Aerobic exercise burns up the most calories. Aerobic activities:

• Use large muscle groups, such as arms and/or legs.

• Are rhythmic and continuous, building up to 30 minutes without stopping.

• Increase heart rate and respiration.

Some popular forms of aerobic exercise include jogging, brisk walking, swimming, biking, cross-country skiing and aerobic dancing. Not only will aerobic exercise burn calories, but regular exercise will also improve cardiovascular health, relieve tension and provide an outlet for fun and socializing.

Most experts recommend participating in some form of aerobic exercise at least three times per week for a minimum of 20 to 30 continuous minutes. If necessary, you can start off with a shorter time span and gradually build up to the minimum. Additional exercise beyond the minimum will burn even more calories.

Of course, before you begin any exercise program, you should first check with your physician regarding the type and intensity of exercise you should choose. Try to select an activity you really enjoy because you're more likely to stay with it. Also, set aside a regular time each day for your activity, whether it's early in the day, during your lunch hour or in the evening.

No matter when you exercise, always make

sure you take time to warm up and cool down. Stretching before and after exercise keeps muscles loose and helps prevent injuries.

Planning Your Meals

A well-balanced diet should be part of any weight control plan. A diet high in complex carbohydrates — whole grains, fruits, vegetables and legumes — moderate amounts of lean protein — skinless poultry, fish, egg whites, lean red meats and legumes — and low in fat is your best bet.

Foods high in complex carbohydrates are excellent because they generally are low in calories, low in fat, contain little cholesterol and can be low in sodium. These foods are also a good source of energy for the working muscles, rich in vitamins and minerals and a good source of fiber. Eating foods high in fiber often helps weight loss efforts by providing a feeling of fullness.

If you want to lose fat, it's this simple: Avoid fatty foods. Fats are a concentrated source of calories, providing more than twice the calories than a similar quantity of carbohydrates or protein. Margarine, vegetable oils, mayonnaise, salad dressings, gravies and frostings are loaded with fat.

Estimating the Calories You Need

To estimate your daily caloric requirements, multiply your current weight in pounds by 11 if you're a woman or 12 if you're a man. This number is the daily calories you need to maintain your weight, assuming you are sedentary or only moderately active. To lose one pound per week, you just need to subtract 250 calories from your daily caloric requirements and increase physical activity to burn an extra 250 calories each day.

Any successful weight control plan also should include enough calories to satisfy daily nutrient requirements. Experts

generally recommend that your daily intake not fall below 1,200 calories unless you are under a physician's supervision. A diet lower than 1,200 calories might not ensure adequate nutrition.

Food for Sport

For an athlete, a split-second of speed can mean the difference between winning and losing. It's no wonder, then, that so many athletes look for a magic food or dietary supplement that will improve their performance. Their quest probably is fruitless. A balanced diet is more important.

A balanced diet for an athlete is 60 to 70 percent calories coming from carbohydrates, 15 to 20 percent calories from protein, and the remaining calories from fat. Water is the most important fluid.

For most athletes, usually vitamin and mineral supplements are a waste. Athletes can get adequate vitamins and minerals from food; the excess from supplements is flushed down the toilet.

Carbohydrates

Carbohydrates provide the major fuel for working muscles. Your body stores carbohydrates in the muscles and the liver as glycogen, which is converted to energy when your muscles come calling. The best way to store glycogen is to eat a diet high in carbohydrates.

There are two types of carbohydrates:
- Complex carbohydrates, including potatoes, cereals and pasta. Complex carbohydrates are nutrient dense; they contain vitamins and minerals and often fiber. Another advantage is that you digest them slowly, so their energy is released in a sustained steady stream.
- Simple carbohydrates — or simple sugars — including granulated sugar, honey and fructose from fruit. Simple sugars can take your blood sugar on a roller coaster ride, sending you up, and, more importantly — down — too fast. That can leave you feeling weak.

Fat

Fats are the second stage of an athlete's energy rocket; they don't kick in until at least 8 to 10 minutes of exercise. That's partly why some people carry extra fat and endurance athletes usually don't. Unlike endurance athletes, most people don't exercise long enough to get to the second stage. When athletes get to that stage, they use fat as an energy source better than most people because training helps their bodies make more efficient use of fats.

Remember, fat is a concentrated source of calories that adds up fast, which can be a problem for athletes such as gymnasts who need lean bodies. So the current Heart Smart® recommendations for fat intake apply to both the general public and athletes. Plus, fat should be avoided in pre-game meals because it slows digestion and can prolong the feeling of fullness.

Protein

Bodies need energy during exercise, but athletes might be surprised to know that protein provides less than 20 percent of it. We already know that the two main fuel sources for

 Heart Smart® Cookbook

exercising bodies are carbohydrates and fats.

So what is protein's purpose? It helps heal injuries and repair tissues — a process the body is constantly undergoing.

Some athletes mistakenly believe they need more protein because muscles are composed of protein. But they're wrong; they can't force extra protein into muscles. The only way to increase muscle size and strength is to exercise and eat a balanced diet.

In fact, most people — athletes and non-athletes alike — already eat so much protein that they exceed the government's Recommended Daily Allowance. For example, 4 to 6 ounces of meat, fish or poultry a day as part of a well-balanced diet provides ample protein for most people.

That's why protein powders and supplements usually are a waste of money. Even vegetarians seldom need protein supplements, as long as they eat a balanced diet that includes non-meat protein foods such as legumes, tofu and whole grains.

Water/Fluids

Water is the most important fluid for athletes. Without sufficient water to cool their bodies during exercise, athletes' performance will suffer. The best way to know if you have enough fluids in your system is to weigh yourself before and after an event or working out. If more than 2 percent of your body weight is lost, your performance might suffer.

If you don't get enough water before, and don't drink during and after working out, you could face serious consequences such as heat exhaustion and heat stroke. Drinking during exercise is especially important; you can't overcompensate before and figure it will carry you through. Don't assume that because you don't feel thirsty, you don't need water. You'll need even more water in hotter temperatures. Cool water (45 to 55 degrees) is absorbed the fastest. Specialized sports drinks are fine, but they usually are not necessary unless you are exercising in extreme conditions or for more than an hour.

Figuring your water needs

Before exercise .... 1 to 1 1/2 cups
During exercise,
every 15 minutes .... 1 cup
After exercise for each
pound lost .... 2 cups

Part II

Recipes

Appetizers, Snacks

Asparagus with Raspberry Vinaigrette

In the spring, savor fresh asparagus with this tangy dressing. You can even use this recipe as a wonderful salad. Olive oil contains the same amount of fat as other oils. However, this fat is mostly monounsaturated. Monounsaturated fats have been known to help lower blood cholesterol levels.

1 tablespoon olive oil
1 tablespoon raspberry vinegar
1/2 teaspoon honey
1 pound fresh asparagus
1 to 2 cups boiling water, just to depth of
    1 inch in bottom of pan with steamer
    or asparagus rack
Ice water for cooling asparagus
4 leaves Bibb lettuce
Fresh parsley sprigs for garnish

In a small bowl, whisk oil, vinegar and honey until vinaigrette is well blended. Set aside. Snap off tough ends of asparagus and discard. Place spears in vegetable steamer basket or asparagus rack over boiling water in pan. Cover and cook until tender, about 6 to 8 minutes. Drain immediately and plunge into cool water. Chill. Arrange asparagus on 4 plates lined with lettuce leaves. Drizzle with vinaigrette. Garnish with parsley sprigs. Makes 4 servings.

Good: Potassium
Excellent: Vitamin A
Good: Vitamin C

Diabetic Exchanges: 1 vegetable, 1 fat

Nutrition Information Per Serving

Energy	62 calories
Fat	4 g
Saturated fat	1 g
Cholesterol	0
Sodium	6 mg
Carbohydrate	6 g
Protein	3 g

Bean and Cheese Nachos

Enjoy the same south-of-the-border taste you find at restaurants without the unnecessary fat and calories.

1 tablespoon vegetable oil
1 medium onion, chopped
1 clove garlic, minced
1 cup drained, cooked pinto beans, partially mashed
1 teaspoon ground cumin
6 corn tortillas, 6-inch rounds
Vegetable cooking spray
1 cup part skim-milk mozzarella cheese, grated
6 jalapeno peppers, thinly sliced

Preheat oven to 400 degrees. Heat oil in nonstick skillet over medium-high heat. Add onion and garlic and saute about 5 minutes. Add beans and cumin. Reduce heat and simmer, stirring constantly for 10 minutes. Remove from heat and keep warm.

Cut each tortilla into 4 triangles and arrange on baking sheet coated with vegetable cooking spray. Bake until crisp, 5 to 7 minutes.

Remove the triangles from the oven and spread with bean mixture, about 1 teaspoon per triangle. Sprinkle with cheese and top with jalapenos. Return to oven until cheese melts, about 2 to 3 minutes, then serve hot with Salsa (see recipe below). Makes 6 servings.

Diabetic Exchanges: 2 starch, 1/2 medium fat meat, 1/2 fat.

Good: Potassium
Good: Iron
Good: Vitamin A
Good: Vitamin C

Salsa

1 pound fresh tomatoes (3 medium), finely chopped, skin removed
1/2 cup scallions, finely chopped, including green tops
1 clove garlic, minced
1 to 2 tablespoons jalapeno or other hot pepper (if using fresh, it's best to remove stems and seeds), minced
1/4 cup fresh cilantro, minced
1/2 teaspoon fresh lime juice, or to taste

Combine all ingredients and puree in blender or food processor for a smoother consistency. Makes six 1/2-cup servings.

Diabetic Exchanges: 1 vegetable

Nutrition Information Per Serving		
	NACHOS	SALSA
Energy	213 calories	18 calories
Fat	7 g	0
Saturated fat	2 g	0
Cholesterol	11 mg	0
Sodium	153 mg	8 mg
Carbohydrate	29 g	4 g
Protein	11 g	1 g

Cajun Crabmeat Spread

This is a party favorite that goes well with toasted crusts of bread or whole-grain crackers.

1 package (8 ounces) light cream cheese, softened
1 tablespoon nonfat plain yogurt
3/4 cup 1-percent low fat cottage cheese
1/2 teaspoon paprika
3/4 teaspoon ground red pepper
1/4 teaspoon garlic powder
1/4 teaspoon ground thyme
1 can (6 ounces) crabmeat, drained
1/4 cup finely chopped green pepper
Chili peppers as garnish, if desired
Cocktail bread

In a large bowl, beat cream cheese, yogurt, cottage cheese, paprika, red pepper, garlic powder and thyme until well blended, about 1 minute. Stir in crabmeat and green pepper. Place in serving bowl, cover and chill. Before serving, garnish with chili peppers, if desired. Serve with cocktail bread. Makes 2 1/2 cups. Each serving is 1 slice of bread, 1 teaspoon spread.

Diabetic Exchanges: 1/3 starch

Nutrition Information Per Serving

Energy ....27 calories
Fat ....trace
Saturated fat ....trace
Cholesterol ....3 mg
Sodium ....67 mg
Carbohydrate ......4 g
Protein ....1 g

Garlic Bread Triangles

These taste great with soups and salads, and a mound of them in a festive basket really sparks up a buffet. Use garlic powder instead of garlic salt, which is very high in sodium.

3 slices (1 ounce each) whole wheat bread
2 tablespoons reduced-calorie margarine, melted
1/2 teaspoon Italian seasoning
1/4 teaspoon garlic powder
1/8 teaspoon paprika

Preheat oven to 400 degrees. Trim crust from bread. Combine margarine with Italian seasoning, garlic powder and paprika in a small bowl; stir well. Brush the mixture evenly over both sides of bread. Stack the bread slices. Cut stack diagonally into quarters, forming 12 small triangles. Place bread triangles in a single layer on a baking sheet. Bake 8 minutes or until crisp. Makes 6 servings of 2 triangles each.

Diabetic Exchanges: 1/2 starch, 1/2 fat

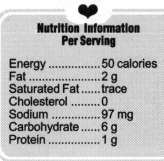

Nutrition Information Per Serving

Energy ....50 calories
Fat ....2 g
Saturated Fat ......trace
Cholesterol 0
Sodium ....97 mg
Carbohydrate ......6 g
Protein ....1 g

Marshmallow Fruit Dip

This is a more healthful version of a dip often found at festive parties; enjoy it without the guilt of the high-fat version. Kids love this recipe for dipping pieces of fruit.

1/4 cup light cream cheese, softened
1/4 cup low-fat vanilla yogurt
1/2 cup marshmallow creme

In a small bowl, whip cream cheese until smooth. Stir in yogurt and marshmallow creme. Makes 1 cup. Suggested serving, 1 tablespoon.

Diabetic Exchanges: Not appropriate for diabetics

Nutrition Information Per Serving

Energy .... 38 calories
Fat .... 1 g
Saturated fat .... trace
Cholesterol .... 4 mg
Sodium .... 16 mg
Carbohydrate ...... 6 g
Protein .... 1 g

 *Heart Smart® Cookbook*

Mushroom Almond Pate

Who says pate has to be high in fat and salt? This one has only 10 calories per serving. In comparison, 1 tablespoon of chicken liver pate contains 52 calories and 130 milligrams of cholesterol.

1/4 cup slivered almonds
1 teaspoon vegetable oil
1 small onion, chopped
1 clove garlic, minced
3/4 pound mushrooms, sliced
1/2 teaspoon salt
1/2 teaspoon dried thyme leaves

Preheat oven to 350 degrees. Spread almonds in a shallow pan and toast in oven about 8 minutes or until lightly browned. Set aside. Heat oil in a skillet over medium heat. Add onion, garlic, mushrooms, salt and thyme. Cook, stirring occasionally, until onion is soft and most of pan juices have evaporated.

In a food processor or blender, whirl almonds to form a paste. With motor running, add mushroom mixture and whirl until pate is smooth. Serve on crackers or with vegetable sticks Makes about 32 one-tablespoon servings.

Diabetic Exchanges: 1 tablespoon = free; 3 tablespoons = 1/2 vegetable, 1/2 fat

Nutrition Information Per Serving

Energy	10 calories
Fat	trace
Saturated fat	0
Cholesterol	0
Sodium	31 mg
Carbohydrate	1 g
Protein	trace

Pita Chips and Salsa

Pita chips are just as crunchy as fried tortilla chips, but they don't have all that fat. You can easily make your own salsa (there's a recipe for one on Page 34) to use in this recipe.

2 cups nonfat plain yogurt
1 cup salsa (any commercial variety)
4 six-inch pita bread pockets

Mix together nonfat plain yogurt and salsa in medium bowl. Cover and refrigerate.

Preheat oven to 325 degrees. Cut each pita bread into 4 pie-shaped wedges with kitchen shears or sharp knife. Split each section in half to yield 8 pie-shaped pieces from each pita. Bake 8 to 12 minutes or until crisp and light golden brown. Serve with yogurt-salsa sauce for dipping. Makes 32 triangles, each 1 serving.

Diabetic Exchanges: 1/4 starch

Nutrition Information Per Serving

Energy	20 calories
Fat	trace
Saturated fat	trace
Cholesterol	trace
Sodium	51 mg
Carbohydrate	4 g
Protein	1 g

Stuffed Mushrooms

**This is a delicious and easy appetizer sure to please any seafood lover.
You can make these stuffed mushrooms ahead, refrigerate them and pop them
in the oven right before your guests arrive. When asked to bring an appetizer, this
is a favorite one to bring.**

8 ounces whole mushrooms (1 to
  1 1/2 inches wide)
2 tablespoons soft tub margarine
4 tablespoons white onions, chopped
2 cups soft fine bread crumbs
4 ounces imitation crab legs, chopped fine
1/4 cup white wine

Clean the mushrooms, remove stems and
set the stems aside. In a large skillet over
medium heat, saute caps in the margarine
until nearly cooked. Remove from pan and
set aside to cool. Chop the stems finely and
add, with chopped onions, to the skillet. Cook
until onions are glazed.
In a mixing bowl, combine onion-mush-
room mixture, bread crumbs, crab and just
enough white wine to hold the mixture
together. Divide mixture into balls and fill
mushroom caps. Just before serving, bake at
350 degrees until hot and slightly browned.
Makes 16 servings.

Diabetic Exchanges: 1 vegetable, 1/2 fat

Nutrition Information
Per Serving

Energy ....42 calories
Fat ....2 g
Saturated fat ....trace
Cholesterol ....7 mg
Sodium ....84 mg
Carbohydrate ......4 g
Protein ....2 g

Vegetable Deviled Eggs

These deviled eggs have no cholesterol but lots of flavor. Try the filling as a low-fat vegetable dip. It's great to include with relish trays. Try this as a sandwich spread, too. By using only egg whites, there is only a trace of saturated fat and cholesterol in this recipe.

In most recipes, two egg whites can replace one whole egg. One egg white has just 16 calories instead of the 63 found in one egg yolk, no fat instead of 5.6 grams of fat — 1.7 grams of it saturated — and no cholesterol, compared to 214 milligrams.

1 tablespoon diced onion
1 medium raw carrot, peeled, cut in 1-inch
  pieces
1 medium celery stalk, trimmed
1 cup 1-percent low-fat cottage cheese,
  drained
2 tablespoons reduced-calorie mayonnaise
1/2 teaspoon sugar
1 teaspoon lemon juice
15 hard boiled egg whites, cut in half, yolks
  discarded
Parsley (optional) for garnish

Place onion, carrot and celery in food processor with metal blade inserted and chop fine. Add cottage cheese, mayonnaise, sugar and lemon juice to mix and blend in processor until smooth. Place approximately 1 tablespoon into each egg white half. Garnish with parsley, if desired. Makes 30 halves, or 15 servings.

Diabetic Exchanges: 1/2 low-fat meat

Nutrition Information Per Serving

Energy	17 calories
Fat	trace
Saturated fat	trace
Cholesterol	trace
Sodium	62 mg
Carbohydrate	1 g
Protein	3 g

Vegetable Dip

Many dips have 30 to 40 calories per tablespoon. When using these dips, vegetables with dip become a very high-fat, high-calorie appetizer. Do your heart a favor and pair those cut vegetables with this low-fat dip instead of a sour-cream-based, high-fat dip.

1 cup 1-percent low-fat cottage cheese
1/3 cup buttermilk
1 tablespoon lemon juice
3 tablespoons reduced-calorie mayonnaise
1 package (10 ounces) frozen spinach, thawed
  and drained
1/3 cup finely shredded carrot
1/2 cup finely chopped onion
2 teaspoons dill weed
1 tablespoon parsley
Celery seed to taste

Blend cottage cheese, buttermilk, lemon juice and mayonnaise until smooth. Add all other ingredients and blend well. Chill mixture and serve with fresh vegetables. Makes approximately 2 cups, 32 servings of 1 tablespoon each.

Diabetic Exchanges: 1 tablespoon = free

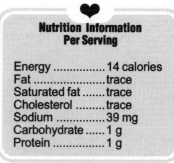

Nutrition Information
Per Serving

Energy .... 14 calories
Fat .... trace
Saturated fat .... trace
Cholesterol .... trace
Sodium .... 39 mg
Carbohydrate ...... 1 g
Protein .... 1 g

Lasagna Noodle Chips

Not only are these crisp snacks low in fat and salt, but they also offer quite a change from the usual crunchy snack fare. Corn chips contain 75 calories and 5 grams of fat per half-ounce serving, compared to these Lasagna Noodle Chips at 15 calories and a trace of fat per half-ounce.

1 package (16 ounces) lasagna noodles
2 tablespoons vegetable oil
1/4 cup water
Vegetable cooking spray
1/4 cup fine dry bread crumbs (unseasoned)
1/3 cup grated Parmesan cheese
1 1/2 teaspoons dried whole basil, crushed
1 1/2 teaspoons dried parsley flakes, crushed
1 1/2 teaspoons dried whole oregano, crushed
1 teaspoon garlic powder
1 1/2 teaspoons paprika
No-salt seasoning to taste (optional)

Preheat oven to 400 degrees. Cook noodles according to package directions, omitting salt. Drain well and separate noodles carefully. Pat noodles with towels to absorb excess moisture.

Combine oil and 1/4 cup water in a small bowl; stir well, and brush both sides of noodles with oil mixture. Cut each noodle crosswise into 2- inch pieces and arrange in a single layer on baking sheets coated with vegetable cooking spray. You will have to work in batches. Set aside.

Combine bread crumbs, Parmesan cheese, basil, parsley, oregano, garlic powder, paprika and no-salt seasoning, if desired, in a bowl. Mix well. Using 1/8 teaspoon, sprinkle mixture over each chip. Save any leftover spices for another use. Bake for 16 minutes or until crisp and lightly golden. Watch closely. Cool and store in an airtight container. Makes 12 dozen. A serving is 5 chips.

Diabetic Exchanges: 1 starch

Nutrition Information Per Serving

Energy	15 calories
Fat	trace
Saturated Fat	trace
Cholesterol	trace
Sodium	6 mg
Carbohydrate	3 g
Protein	1 g

Breads,
Muffins

Zucchini Bread

This recipe uses less sugar than conventional recipes, so it's a heart-healthy way to use up those abundant supplies of zucchini.

3 cups all-purpose flour, sifted, plus
    2 teaspoons for dusting pans
1 teaspoon baking powder
1 teaspoon baking soda
1/4 teaspoon salt
2 teaspoons cinnamon
1 teaspoon nutmeg
1/4 teaspoon allspice
6 egg whites or 3/4 cup egg substitute
1 1/2 cups sugar
3/4 cup vegetable oil
1 1/2 teaspoons vanilla
2 cups lightly packed, coarsely grated
    zucchini, washed, ends removed,
    not peeled
1 cup raisins
Vegetable cooking spray

Preheat oven to 350 degrees.
  Sift 3 cups flour, baking powder, baking soda, salt, cinnamon, nutmeg and allspice together into a medium-sized bowl.
  In a separate bowl, beat the egg whites or egg substitute with the sugar, oil and vanilla. Stir zucchini and raisins into egg mixture. By hand, stir in the flour mixture just until flour is blended.
  Spray two 8-by-4-inch loaf pans with vegetable cooking spray and dust with flour. Divide batter between the 2 pans. Bake 50 to 60 minutes. Makes 2 loaves or 32 one-slice servings.

  Diabetic Exchanges: 1 starch, 1 fat (occasional use)

Nutrition Information Per Serving

Energy	138 calories
Fat	5 g
Saturated fat	1 g
Cholesterol	0
Sodium	62 mg
Carbohydrate	22 g
Protein	2 g

Cranberry Bread

Freeze an extra bag of cranberries around Thanksgiving and enjoy this quick bread anytime of the year.

2 cups all-purpose flour
1 cup sugar
2 teaspoons baking powder
1/2 teaspoon baking soda
1 cup halved raw cranberries, washed, stems
    removed
1/4 cup chopped pecans or walnuts
1/2 cup wheat germ
3 tablespoons grated orange rind
2 egg whites
1/2 cup orange juice
1/4 cup warm water
2 tablespoons vegetable oil
Vegetable cooking spray

Preheat oven to 350 degrees. Sift together flour, sugar, baking powder and baking soda. Stir in cranberries, pecans or walnuts, wheat germ and orange rind. In a separate bowl, combine egg whites, orange juice, water and oil. Add to flour mixture, stirring just enough to moisten ingredients.

Coat a 9-by-5-by-3-inch loaf pan with vegetable cooking spray, and spoon mixture into it. Bake for 50 to 60 minutes or until done. Cool in pan 5 minutes before removing and cooling on rack. Makes 16 thin one-slice servings.

Diabetic Exchanges: 1 starch, 3/4 fruit, 1/2 fat (occasional use)

Nutrition Information Per Serving	
Energy	146 calories
Fat	3 g
Saturated fat	trace
Cholesterol	0
Sodium	75 mg
Carbohydrate	27 g
Protein	3 g

Heart Smart® Cookbook

Pumpkin Pecan Harvest Bread

To make this a heart-healthy recipe, four egg whites replace two whole eggs.

1 3/4 cups fresh, cooked pumpkin
    (or canned pumpkin)
4 egg whites
1/4 cup vegetable oil
2 cups all-purpose flour
2 teaspoons baking powder
1 teaspoon baking soda
1 teaspoon cinnamon
1/2 teaspoon nutmeg
1 cup brown sugar
1/4 cup chopped pecans
Vegetable cooking spray
1 tablespoon confectioners' sugar for dusting

Excellent: Vitamin A

Diabetic Exchanges: 1 1/2 starch, 1 fat (occasional use)

Preheat oven to 350 degrees. In a large bowl mix together pumpkin, egg whites and oil. In another bowl, sift together flour, baking powder, baking soda, cinnamon and nutmeg. Add brown sugar and mix well. Add the flour mixture to the pumpkin mixture in two or three stages and combine well. Beat with whisk or electric mixer at medium speed for about 2 minutes. Stir in chopped pecans.

Coat a 9-by-5-inch bread pan with vegetable cooking spray. Pour the batter into the pan and bake for 50 minutes. Bread is done when knife inserted in center comes out clean. Remove from oven, let sit for about 5 minutes, then turn loaf out of pan to cool on rack. Dust with confectioners' sugar, if desired. Makes 1 loaf with 16 one-slice servings.

Nutrition Information Per Serving

Energy .... 160 calories
Fat .... 5 g
Saturated fat .... trace
Cholesterol 0
Sodium .... 112 mg
Carbohydrate ...... 27 g
Protein .... 3 g

Apple Raisin Bread

Foods high in complex carbohydrates provide a good source of energy for exercise. A slice of this raisin bread served with a glass of milk is a great pre-exercise snack.

Vegetable cooking spray
1 cup all-purpose flour
1 teaspoon baking soda
1 teaspoon baking powder
1/2 cup sugar
3/4 cup whole wheat flour
3/4 cup toasted wheat germ
1 teaspoon cinnamon
1/2 teaspoon allspice
2 egg whites
1/2 cup water
1 can (12 ounces) frozen unsweetened
    apple juice concentrate, defrosted
1 1/2 cups apple, peeled, seeded, cored
    and chopped
1/2 cup raisins, plumped in 1 cup water for
    5 minutes, then drained

Preheat oven to 350 degrees. Spray an 8-by-5-by-3-inch loaf pan with vegetable cooking spray.

In a large bowl sift together all-purpose flour, baking soda, baking powder and sugar. Add whole wheat flour, wheat germ, cinnamon and allspice and set aside.

In a separate bowl mix egg whites, water and apple juice concentrate. Mix in flour mixture and combine well. Add apple and raisins. Pour mixture into pan, which will be very full. Bake 50 to 60 minutes or until a wooden pick inserted in the middle comes out clean. Makes 12 one-slice servings.

Good: Potassium

Diabetic Exchanges: 2 starch, 1/2 fruit (occasional use)

Nutrition Information Per Serving

Energy .... 193 calories
Fat .... 1 g
Saturated fat .... trace
Cholesterol 0
Sodium .... 113 mg
Carbohydrate ...... 43 g
Protein .... 5 g

Heart Smart® Cookbook

Cinnamon Swirl Loaf

This is a bread so rich and sweet there is no need for margarine or jam.

1 package (1/4 ounce) active dry yeast
   or 1 cake compressed yeast
1/4 cup warm or lukewarm water
1/2 cup sugar
2 cups skim milk, scalded
1/2 cup vegetable oil
1 teaspoon salt
7 1/2 to 8 cups all-purpose flour, divided
4 egg whites
Vegetable cooking spray

Filling and topping
3/4 cup sugar
1 1/2 tablespoons cinnamon
4 teaspoons water
Vegetable cooking spray
2 tablespoons vegetable oil

Soften active dry yeast in warm water (100 to 115 degrees) or compressed yeast in lukewarm water (85 degrees).

Place sugar in a large mixing bowl; pour scalded milk over sugar, and add oil and salt; stir to dissolve sugar. Cool to lukewarm. Add 3 cups of flour; mix well. Stir in softened yeast and egg whites; beat well. Add about 4 1/2 cups flour, or enough to make a soft dough.

Use remaining 1/2 cup flour to coat work surface. Turn out dough on lightly floured surface. Cover with clean dish towel and let rest 10 minutes. Knead until smooth and elastic, about 8 to 10 minutes. Spray a large bowl with vegetable cooking spray. Place dough in bowl, turning dough ball once to grease top. Cover and let rise in warm place until size doubles, about 1 to 2 hours. Punch down and let rise again until almost double, about 1 hour. Punch down and divide dough in half. Cover and let rest 10 minutes.

FOR ASSEMBLY, FILLING AND TOPPING: Roll each half of the dough into a 15-by-7-inch rectangle, about 1/2-inch thick.

In a small bowl, mix sugar and cinnamon. Reserve 2 tablespoons of mixture; sprinkle remainder over rectangles of dough. Brush each dough rectangle with 2 teaspoons of water; smooth with spatula. Roll each as for jelly roll, beginning with narrow side. Seal long edge. Spray two 9 1/2-by-5-by-3-inch loaf pans with vegetable cooking spray. Place sealed edge down in loaf pans. Cover and let rise until almost double, 45 to 60 minutes.

Preheat oven to 375 degrees. Just before baking, brush loaves with vegetable oil and sprinkle with remaining 2 tablespoons of cinnamon-sugar mixture. Bake 35 to 40 minutes or until a hollow sound is produced when loaf is tapped. If crust browns too fast, cover with aluminum foil for the last 5 to 10 minutes. Remove from oven and let sit in pans 10 minutes. Invert onto cooling racks. Makes 2 loaves, or 32 one-slice servings.

Diabetic Exchanges: 2 starch, 1/2 fat (occasional use)

Nutrition Information Per Serving	
Energy	180 calories
Fat	4 g
Saturated fat	trace
Cholesterol	trace
Sodium	76 mg
Carbohydrate	31 g
Protein	4 g

Pumpernickel Raisin Bread

Pumpernickel is a type of rye bread. This recipe uses rye and whole wheat flours and is low in fat and high in nutrition.

1/2 cup dark molasses
1 1/2 cups warm water (105 to 115 degrees)
1 package (1/4 ounce) active dry yeast
1 tablespoon instant coffee crystals
2 tablespoons unsweetened cocoa powder
1 teaspoon salt
2 cups rye flour
2 cups whole wheat flour
2 cups bread flour, divided
1 tablespoon vegetable oil
1 tablespoon cold water
1 1/2 cups raisins
4 tablespoons cornmeal
1 to 2 egg whites beaten

Combine molasses and warm water in large mixing bowl. Add yeast and mix. Let stand for about 10 minutes, allowing it to turn slightly foamy. Sprinkle in instant coffee, cocoa and salt. Add rye flour and mix well. Add whole wheat flour and 1 cup of bread flour to make a sticky dough. Turn bread onto a surface floured with 1/4 cup of remaining bread flour. Gently knead dough, adding 1/2 cup bread flour gradually, Dough will be slightly sticky. Coat large bowl with oil. Place dough in bowl, turning to coat lightly with oil. Cover bowl with clean towel moistened with 1 tablespoon cold water. Set in warm place, allowing dough to rise until doubled or tripled in size, approximately 3 to 4 hours.

Turn dough onto surface floured with remaining 1/4 cup of bread flour; flatten to a rectangular shape and sprinkle with raisins. Roll up dough and knead for 14 to 5 minutes. Return to oiled bowl, cover and let rise to double in size, about 1 hour.

Sprinkle cornmeal on baking sheets. Turn dough out, cut into thirds and shape into 3 round loaves. Cover and let rise, 45 to 60 minutes, allowing enough space for each loaf to rise to twice its size.

Preheat oven to 400 degrees. Brush loaves lightly with beaten egg whites. Bake 35 to 45 minutes until dark brown. Bread should sound hollow when tapped. Cool on racks. Makes 3 loaves, 15 one-slice servings per loaf.

Diabetic Exchanges: 1 starch (occasional use)

Nutrition Information Per Serving

Energy	81 calories
Fat	trace
Saturated fat	trace
Cholesterol	0
Sodium	77 mg
Carbohydrate	18 g
Protein	2 g

Heart Smart® Cookbook

Whole Grain Raisin Bread

Molasses gives a unique flavor and a rich color to this moist, chewy bread, without making it too sweet. Molasses is a thick, brown syrup separated from sugar during processing. It contains about the same amount of calories as sugar, and it adds a little iron, calcium and potassium.

1 cake compressed yeast or 1 tablespoon active
    dry yeast (less than two 1/4-ounce packages)
1 to 3 tablespoons blackstrap molasses
3/4 cup warm (110 to 115 degrees) water
4 cups whole grain flour (wheat), plus
    1/2 cup for kneading
1 teaspoon salt
4 tablespoons vegetable oil
3/4 cup raisins or currants
3/4 cup warm skim milk (110 to
    115 degrees)
Vegetable cooking spray

If using compressed yeast, cream it with 1 tablespoon molasses and the water; do not leave it more than 5 minutes. If using active dry yeast, dissolve 3 tablespoons molasses in the water and sprinkle the yeast on top. Leave the yeast in a warm place to froth for about 10 minutes.

Put the 4 cups flour and salt in a large bowl and mix in the vegetable oil. Toss in the raisins or currants and make a well in the center. Put the yeast-molasses mixture and milk into a saucepan and warm them gently until the molasses has melted. Do not heat to more than 115 degrees. Pour the yeast-molasses-milk mixture into the flour and mix everything together to make a moist dough. Turn it out onto a work surface dusted with remaining flour and knead it until smooth. Return the dough to the bowl and cover the bowl

with a clean cloth or plastic wrap. Place bowl in a warm place for 1 hour, or until dough doubles in size.

Preheat oven to 375 degrees. Spray a 9-by-5-inch loaf pan with vegetable cooking spray. Knead the dough again and put it into the greased pan. Put it on top of the oven, cover with a clean cloth and leave for 15 minutes, or until it has risen 1/2 inch over the edge of the pan. Bake the loaf for 40 to 50 minutes, then turn it onto a wire rack to cool thoroughly. Makes 1 loaf or 16 one-slice servings.

Good: Potassium

Diabetic Exchanges: 1 starch, 1 fruit, 1/2 fat

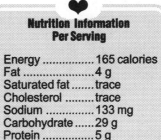

**Nutrition Information
Per Serving**

Energy .... 165 calories
Fat .... 4 g
Saturated fat .... trace
Cholesterol .... trace
Sodium .... 133 mg
Carbohydrate ...... 29 g
Protein .... 5 g

Whole Wheat Baguettes

A baguette is a long, narrow French bread typically low in fat.

1 package (1/4 ounce) active dry yeast
2 cups warm water (105 to 115 degrees),
    divided
1 tablespoon sugar
1 teaspoon salt
3 cups whole wheat flour
3 cups white flour, plus 1/4 cup or more for
    kneading the dough, divided
1 teaspoon vegetable oil, divided
1 tablespoon cornmeal (if using baking sheet)
1 egg white mixed with 1 tablespoon
    cold water

In a large bowl, dissolve yeast in 1/4 cup of warm water. Add sugar, salt and the remaining 1 3/4 cups of water. Gradually add 3 cups of each type of flour and mix well with wooden spoon until a dough forms. Then begin kneading with both hands on a board dusted with the remaining flour. Knead until no longer sticky, about 10 minutes. Add more flour to board if needed to prevent sticking. Place dough in a large bowl oiled with 1/2 teaspoon of vegetable oil. Cover with plastic wrap and let rise in a warm place until doubled in size, about 1 hour.

Punch dough down. Transfer to floured board and divide into three equal pieces. Roll and shape each piece into a smooth log about 10 to 12 inches long. Make a depression crosswise in the center of each roll, then fold dough in half along depression. Seal along edge. Roll each loaf back and forth, keeping loaf even in width as it lengthens to 15 to 16 inches. Use the remaining

1/2 teaspoon of oil to coat baguette pans. Place the loaves into pans. (Or rub the oil on a baking sheet, sprinkle with cornmeal and place all three loaves on the sheet.) Slash the top of each loaf diagonally in 3 or 4 places. Cover lightly with plastic wrap. Let rise until puffy but not doubled, about 30 to 45 minutes.

Preheat oven to 350 degrees. Brush loaves with egg white and water mixture. Bake until loaves are golden brown and sound hollow when tapped, about 25 minutes. To serve, cut each loaf into eight slices. Makes 24 one-slice servings.

Diabetic Exchanges: 1 1/2 starch

Nutrition Information Per Serving

Energy .... 112 calories
Fat .... 1 g
Saturated fat .... trace
Cholesterol 0
Sodium .... 84 mg
Carbohydrate ...... 23 g
Protein .... 4 g

Heart Smart® Cookbook

Whole Wheat Bread

If you must top your bread, ration the amount of margarine you use carefully. One tablespoon adds more than 100 calories to a slice of bread.

2 3/4 cups warm water (105 to 115 degrees), divided
1 package (1/4 ounce) active dry yeast
1/2 cup brown sugar
1/4 cup vegetable oil
3 cups whole wheat flour
5 cups sifted all-purpose flour, divided
Vegetable cooking spray

Into a small bowl containing 1/4 cup warm water, sprinkle yeast and stir to dissolve. Set aside.
In a medium bowl, combine remaining warm water, brown sugar and vegetable oil. Stir in whole wheat flour and 1 cup all purpose flour; beat well. Stir in dissolved yeast. Add 3 more cups of all purpose flour to make a moderately stiff dough. Turn out on surface floured with remaining cup of all purpose flour and knead 10 to 12 minutes by hand until smooth and satiny. Or if using mixer fitted with kneading blade, place remaining cup of flour in bowl and knead on medium speed six minutes until smooth and satiny. Shape dough into a ball; place in bowl sprayed with vegetable cooking spray, turning once to oil all surfaces. Cover; let rise in warm place until doubled in size, about 90 minutes.
Punch down. Cut into 2 portions; shape each into a smooth ball. Cover and let rest 10 minutes. Shape in loaves; place in 8 1/2-by-4 1/2-by-2 1/2-inch loaf pans sprayed with

vegetable cooking spray. Let them rise until they double in size, about 75 minutes.
Preheat oven to 375 degrees. Bake loaves 45 minutes. If bread darkens too fast, cover with foil while baking finishes. Makes 2 loaves, or 32 one-slice servings.

Diabetic Exchanges: 1 1/2 starch

Nutrition Information Per Serving

Energy .... 126 calories
Fat .... 2 g
Saturated fat .... trace
Cholesterol 0
Sodium .... trace
Carbohydrate ...... 22 g
Protein .... 3 g

Apple Cinnamon Oat Bran Muffins

Fruit juice can be used for sweetness. In this recipe, the apple juice concentrate replaces half the usual amount of sugar.

Vegetable cooking spray or 12 paper
 baking cups
2 1/4 cups oat bran
1/4 cup brown sugar
1 1/4 teaspoons cinnamon
1 tablespoon baking powder
1/2 cup raisins
1/2 cup evaporated skim milk
3/4 cup frozen apple juice concentrate,
 defrosted
2 egg whites
3 tablespoons vegetable oil
1 medium apple, peeled, cored
 and chopped

Preheat oven to 425 degrees. Spray muffin pan with vegetable cooking spray or line with paper baking cups.

Mix oat bran, brown sugar, cinnamon, baking powder and raisins in a large bowl. In another bowl, mix skim milk, apple juice concentrate, egg whites and oil. Add to the dry mixture and mix. Gently stir in the chopped apple. Fill pan or paper baking cups with batter. Bake for 17 minutes. After cooling, store in a large plastic bag to retain moisture and softness. Makes 12 muffins, each 1 serving.

Diabetic Exchanges: 1 1/2 starch, 1/2 fruit, 1/2 fat

Nutrition Information Per Serving

Energy .... 154 calories
Fat .... 5 g
Saturated fat .... trace
Cholesterol .... trace
Sodium .... 114 mg
Carbohydrate ...... 23 g
Protein .... 5 g

Banana Oatmeal Muffins

The fresh bananas provide the same flavor found in high-fat versions of this recipe so you won't even notice a difference.

1 cup rolled oats, uncooked
1/3 cup brown sugar, firmly packed
1/3 cup vegetable oil
1 teaspoon vanilla
2 bananas, mashed
1 cup skim or 1/2-percent low-fat milk
3 egg whites
1 1/2 cups all-purpose flour (or 3/4 cup all-purpose flour and 3/4 cup whole wheat flour)
2 teaspoons baking powder
1/8 teaspoon salt
1 teaspoon cinnamon
1/4 teaspoon allspice
16 paper baking cups

Preheat oven to 400 degrees.

Combine oats, brown sugar, oil, vanilla, mashed bananas and milk in bowl. Mix well and set aside. In separate bowl, whip egg whites until fluffy; fold into oat mixture. In separate bowl, combine flour, baking powder, salt, cinnamon and allspice; gradually add dry ingredients to batter. Line muffin pans with 16 paper baking cups, and pour batter into cups, filling each about two-thirds full. Bake 18 to 20 minutes or until golden brown. Makes 16 muffins, each 1 serving.

Diabetic Exchanges: 1 starch, 1/2 fruit, 1/2 fat

♥ Nutrition Information Per Serving

Energy .... 134 calories
Fat .... 5 g
Saturated fat .... 1 g
Cholesterol .... trace
Sodium .... 76 mg
Carbohydrate ...... 20 g
Protein .... 3 g

Bran-Blueberry Muffins

This recipe provides fiber for your diet, and you can still enjoy blueberry muffins as good as those from the bakery.

1 cup mini-biscuits shredded wheat cereal
    (or about 1 1/2 large biscuits, crumbled)
1 cup 100% Bran cereal
1 1/3 cups skim milk
3 egg whites, slightly beaten
1 teaspoon vanilla
1/2 cup sugar
1/3 cup vegetable oil
1 1/4 cup all-purpose flour
1/4 teaspoon salt
1/2 teaspoon baking soda
1 tablespoon baking powder
1 cup blueberries
14 paper baking cups

Preheat oven to 400 degrees. Mix both cereals and milk in a bowl; let cereal moisten. Add slightly beaten egg whites, vanilla, sugar and oil. In another bowl, combine flour, salt, baking soda and baking powder; gradually add to the cereal mixture. When all is mixed, add blueberries and stir gently. Line muffin pans with paper baking cups. Pour batter into paper baking cups, filling them three-fourths full. Bake for 20 minutes. Remove and cool on rack. Makes 14 muffins, each 1 serving.

Diabetic Exchanges: 1 starch, 1/2 fruit, 1 fat (occasional use)

Nutrition Information Per Serving

Energy	145 calories
Fat	5 g
Saturated fat	trace
Cholesterol	trace
Sodium	193 mg
Carbohydrate	23 g
Protein	4 g

Corn Muffins

Brown sugar, used in this recipe, has a stronger flavor than granulated white sugar because it contains more molasses, but remember that all sugars are equal when it comes to calories.

12 paper baking cups or vegetable cooking spray
2 cups all-purpose flour
1 cup yellow cornmeal
1 tablespoon baking powder
4 egg whites (large eggs) or 1/2 cup egg substitute
1/4 cup light brown sugar
1/4 cup granulated white sugar
1 cup buttermilk
4 tablespoons oil

Preheat oven to 350 degrees. Place 12 paper baking cups in muffin pan or spray pan lightly with vegetable cooking spray.

Thoroughly sift flour, cornmeal and baking powder together in a large bowl and set aside. In another bowl, whisk together egg whites or egg substitute, brown sugar, white sugar and buttermilk until well mixed. Pour over dry ingredients and add oil. Fold in with a rubber spatula just until dry ingredients are moistened. Scoop batter into pan or 12 paper baking cups, dividing batter evenly and filling each about two-thirds full. Bake 25 to 30 minutes, or until golden brown and firm in the center. Let cool in pan 5 minutes. Makes 12 muffins, each 1 serving.

Diabetic Exchanges: 2 starch, 1 fat (occasional use)

Nutrition Information Per Serving	
Energy	199 calories
Fat	5 g
Saturated fat	trace
Cholesterol	9 mg
Sodium	125 mg
Carbohydrate	33 g
Protein	5 g

Lemon-Ginger Muffins

Nonfat yogurt makes this muffin moist without adding fat. Most muffins contain twice the fat of this tasty moist muffin.

Vegetable cooking spray or paper baking
   cups
1/3 cup stick margarine at room temperature
1 cup sugar
4 egg whites or 1/2 cup egg substitute
2 tablespoons fresh ginger root,
   finely chopped
2 tablespoons lemon peel, finely grated
1 teaspoon baking soda
1 cup plain nonfat yogurt
2 cups all-purpose flour

Preheat oven to 375 degrees. Spray muffin panwith vegetable cooking spray or line with 12 paper baking cups.

In a large bowl, beat margarine and sugar until fluffy. Beat in egg whites, one at a time, or egg substitute. Add ginger root and lemon peel. In separate bowl, add baking soda to yogurt and stir; mixture will bubble. Fold flour into margarine mixture one-third at a time, alternating with yogurt. Blend well. Divide batter evenly in muffin pan or baking cups. Bake 18 to 20 minutes, until golden brown. Makes 12 muffins, each 1 serving.

Diabetic Exchanges: not appropriate for diabetics

Nutrition Information
Per Serving

Energy .... 188 calories
Fat .... 5 g
Saturated fat .... 1 g
Cholesterol .... 1 mg
Sodium .... 152 mg
Carbohydrate ...... 32 g
Protein .... 4 g

Banana French Toast

This French toast is so tasty and sweet we don't even add syrup.

1 whole egg, slightly beaten
2 egg whites
1 tablespoon honey
1/4 teaspoon cinnamon
1/4 cup skim milk
1 mashed, overripe banana
Vegetable cooking spray
10 slices whole wheat bread

Heat griddle or skillet to medium heat. In a shallow bowl or pie pan, mix egg, egg whites, honey, cinnamon, milk and banana. Spray vegetable cooking spray onto the griddle. Dip bread in the egg mixture, turning to coat both sides. Cook on griddle, about 4 minutes on each side or until golden brown. Makes 5 two-slice servings.

Good: Potassium

Diabetic Exchanges: 2 starch, 1/2 fat

Nutrition Information Per Serving

Energy	187 calories
Fat	4 g
Saturated fat	trace
Cholesterol	55 mg
Sodium	359 mg
Carbohydrate	33 g
Protein	8 g

Buttermilk Pancakes

The fresh blueberries in the topping make these better than any of their high-fat restaurant cousins.

1 cup all-purpose flour
1 teaspoon sugar (optional)
3/4 teaspoon baking powder
1/4 teaspoon salt
2 egg whites
1 cup buttermilk (made from skim milk)
1 tablespoon vegetable oil
Vegetable cooking spray

Sift together flour, sugar, if desired baking powder and salt in a medium bowl and set aside.

In another bowl, beat egg whites slightly by hand; add buttermilk and oil, and mix well. Add wet ingredients to the dry mixture, stirring just enough to combine.

Coat a skillet with vegetable cooking spray; heat over medium heat. Pour batter into skillet, making pancakes approximately 3 to 4 inches in diameter. Cook until bottoms are golden brown and bubbles on the top begin to break. Flip over and cook until golden brown. Makes 4 servings, 3 pancakes each.

Diabetic Exchanges:
2 starch, 1/2 fat

Nutrition Information Per Serving

Energy	176 calories
Fat	5 g
Saturated fat	1 g
Cholesterol	2 mg
Sodium	275 mg
Carbohydrate	26 g
Protein	7 g

Blueberry Topping

1 pint blueberries, fresh or frozen and defrosted
2 tablespoons sugar (optional, or reduce amount)
1 tablespoon cornstarch
1/2 teaspoon cinnamon
1 teaspoon vanilla

Rinse and drain berries and place them in a medium saucepan. Add sugar, cornstarch, cinnamon and vanilla. Cook over medium to low heat 5 to 8 minutes, stirring to prevent scorching. Serve hot or warm over buttermilk pancakes. Makes about 1 1/4 cups topping, about 4 servings.

Diabetic Exchanges: 1 fruit

Nutrition Information Per Serving

Energy	70 calories
Fat	trace
Saturated fat	0
Cholesterol	0
Sodium	trace
Carbohydrate	17 g
Protein	trace

Cinnamon Apple Oat Bran Cereal

This is a wonderful way to spice up morning oatmeal, and it's easy besides.

4 cups water
1 1/3 cups uncooked oat bran cereal
1 teaspoon cinnamon
1 teaspoon vanilla
2 tablespoons raisins
1/4 cup unsweetened applesauce
2 cups skim milk
2 tablespoons brown sugar

In a heavy saucepan, bring water to a boil over high heat. Stir in oat bran cereal very slowly, to avoid lumping. Stir constantly. Return to boil; reduce heat. Add cinnamon, vanilla, raisins and applesauce. Cook 1 to 2 minutes, or until desired consistency is reached, stirring constantly. Top each serving with skim milk and brown sugar. Makes 4 servings.

Excellent: Potassium
Good: Fiber

Diabetic Exchanges: 2 starch, 1/2 milk (occasional use)

Nutrition Information Per Serving

Energy .... 198 calories
Fat .... 2 g
Saturated fat .... trace
Cholesterol .... 2 mg
Sodium .... 66 mg
Carbohydrate ...... 35 g
Protein .... 10 g

Gingerbread Waffles

This is a gingerbread treat kids will love for breakfast. Gingerbread has been a favorite of children ever since it was first prepared by a baker in Greece about 2400 B.C.

1 package (1/4 ounce) active dry yeast
2 tablespoons sugar
1 cup warm water (105 to 115 degrees)
1 cup all-purpose flour
1 cup whole-wheat flour
1/3 cup instant nonfat dry milk
2 teaspoons ground ginger
1 teaspoon ground cinnamon
2 teaspoons light molasses
1/4 teaspoon ground cloves
3 tablespoons vegetable oil
1 whole egg
4 egg whites
Vegetable cooking spray

Combine yeast, sugar and water in a large mixing bowl; let stand 5 minutes. Add both flours, dry milk, ginger, cinnamon, light molasses, cloves, oil, egg and egg whites. Beat at medium speed with an electric mixer until blended. Cover and chill 8 hours.

Coat an 8-inch square waffle iron with vegetable cooking spray; allow to preheat as directed by the manufacturer. Stir batter; spoon 1/4 cup batter per waffle onto hot waffle iron. Bake about 5 minutes or until steaming stops. Repeat procedure using remaining batter. Makes 12 one-waffle servings.

Diabetic Exchanges: 1 1/4 starch, 1/2 fat

Nutrition Information Per Serving

Energy .... 133 calories
Fat .... 4 g
Saturated fat .... trace
Cholesterol .... 18 mg
Sodium .... 33 mg
Carbohydrate ...... 19 g
Protein .... 5 g

HeartSmart® Cookbook

Granola

Try this low-fat granola for a great snack, even for kids. Traditional granola and granola bars may derive 40 to 50 percent of their calories from fat. In this version, just 24 percent of calories are from fat.

2 1/2 cups rolled oats
1/2 cup slivered almonds
1/2 cup toasted wheat germ
1/4 cup honey
1/3 cup frozen apple juice concentrate
Vegetable cooking spray
1/4 cup raisins
1/2 cup dried fruit, chopped
    (apples, apricots or any other
    dried fruit)

Preheat oven to 300 degrees. In a large mixing bowl combine the oats, almonds and wheat germ; set aside. Stir together honey and apple juice concentrate.

Pour over oat mixture, stirring until coated. Spread mixture evenly in a 9-by-13-inch baking pan sprayed with vegetable cooking spray. Bake uncovered for 45 to 50 minutes or until brown. Stir every 15 minutes and several times during the last 15 minutes. Remove from oven. Stir in raisins and dried fruit. Transfer to another pan and cool. Store in an airtight container. Makes ten 1/2-cup servings.

Good: Potassium

Diabetic Exchanges: 2 starch, 1 fat (occasional use)

Nutrition Information Per Serving

Energy	185 calories
Fat	5 g
Saturated fat	1 g
Cholesterol	0
Sodium	34 mg
Carbohydrate	32 g
Protein	7 g

Homemade Egg Substitute

This egg substitute can be refrigerated for a week if the eggs were fresh. After that, it can be frozen.

6 egg whites
2 tablespoons nonfat dry milk
2 teaspoons vegetable oil

Beat egg whites lightly. Add dry milk and oil, and beat until well blended. Makes approximately 4 quarter-cup servings.

Diabetic Exchanges: 1 lean meat

Nutrition Information Per Serving

Energy ....52 calories
Fat ....2 g
Saturated fat ....trace
Cholesterol ....trace
Sodium ....87 mg
Carbohydrate ......2 g
Protein ....6 g

Muesli with Yogurt Topping

Muesli is a cereal mixture first developed by a Swiss nutritionist more than a half-century ago.

1/2 cup rolled oats
1/4 cup wheat germ
1/8 cup unsalted sunflower seeds
1/4 cup raw oat bran, available at some
    supermarkets and at most health food
    stores and bulk food counters
1/2 cup currants or raisins
1/2 cup dried apricots, chopped
1/8 cup slivered almonds
1/8 cup grated apple
Yogurt Topping (recipe follows)

Preheat oven to 350 degrees. Combine oats, wheat germ, sunflower seeds and bran; spread on a cookie sheet. Bake for 10 minutes, stirring occasionally. Remove from oven and let cool completely.

Combine oat mixture with currants or raisins, dried apricots, almonds and grated apple. Divide among 5 bowls. Top each with 1/4 cup Yogurt Topping. Makes 5 servings.

Good: Fiber
Excellent: Potassium

Yogurt Topping
1 1/4 cups plain low-fat yogurt
1 1/4 tablespoons brown sugar
3/4 teaspoon ground cinnamon

Mix yogurt, brown sugar and cinnamon in a bowl until well blended. Refrigerate until use. Makes 1 1/4 cups, 5 servings.

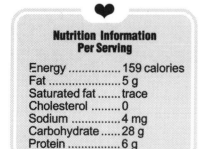

Nutrition Information
Per Serving

Energy .... 159 calories
Fat .... 5 g
Saturated fat .... trace
Cholesterol 0
Sodium .... 4 mg
Carbohydrate ...... 28 g
Protein .... 6 g

Nutrition Information
Per Serving

Energy .... 50 calories
Fat .... trace
Saturated fat .... trace
Cholesterol .... 4 mg
Sodium .... 41 mg
Carbohydrate ...... 8 g
Protein .... 3 g

Diabetic Exchanges: 2 starch, 1/4 milk, 1 fat

Oven-Baked Vegetable Omelet

This omelet can be in the oven baking while you finish getting ready in the morning.

Vegetable cooking spray
2 eggs
8 egg whites
1 package (10 ounces) frozen chopped
    broccoli, thawed and drained
1/3 cup onion, finely chopped
1/2 cup mushroom, cleaned, chopped
1/4 cup Parmesan cheese, grated
2 tablespoons skim milk
1/2 teaspoon dried basil
1/4 teaspoon garlic powder
1 medium tomato, washed, cored, seeded,
    cut into six slices

Preheat oven to 325 degrees. Spray an 11-by-7-inch rectangular baking pan with vegetable cooking spray.

In a 2 1/2-quart bowl, beat eggs and egg whites until light and fluffy. Stir in broccoli, onion, mushrooms, Parmesan cheese, milk, basil and garlic powder. Pour mixture into pan. Arrange tomato slices on top. Bake uncovered until set, 25 to 30 minutes. Remove from oven and serve. Makes 6 servings.

Good: Potassium
Good: Vitamin A
Good: Vitamin C

Diabetic Exchanges: 1 lean meat, 1 vegetable

Nutrition Information Per Serving

Energy .... 90 calories
Fat .... 3 g
Saturated fat .... 1 g
Cholesterol .... 71 mg
Sodium .... 183 mg
Carbohydrate ...... 6 g
Protein .... 10 g

Spiced Apple Spread

Using a spicy spread that has only a trace of fat is a great way to start your day.

3/4 cup 1-percent low-fat cottage cheese
6 tablespoons unsweetened applesauce
1/4 teaspoon cinnamon

In a food processor or blender, mix together cottage cheese, applesauce and cinnamon until smooth. Makes 16 servings, 1 tablespoon each.

Diabetic Exchanges: 1 tablespoon = free

Nutrition Information Per Serving

Energy .... 10 calories
Fat .... trace
Saturated fat .... trace
Cholesterol .... trace
Sodium .... 43 mg
Carbohydrate ...... 1 g
Protein .... 1 g

Turkey Breakfast Sausage

If you love the flavor of sausage, this is a wonderful low-fat alternative to traditional pork sausages.

1 1/2 pounds ground turkey, uncooked
1 egg white
1/4 teaspoon sage
1/4 teaspoon marjoram
1/4 teaspoon thyme
1/8 teaspoon summer savory
1/4 teaspoon black pepper
Vegetable cooking spray

Combine turkey, egg white, sage, marjoram, thyme, summer savory and pepper in a bowl; stir well. Shape mixture into 12 patties and chill at least 1 hour. If not to be used immediately, the patties should be wrapped, labeled and stored in the freezer.

Coat a skillet with vegetable cooking spray. Place skillet over medium-high heat until hot. Place patties in skillet; cook 5 minutes on each side or until done. Makes 12 servings, 1 patty per serving.

Diabetic Exchanges: 1 1/2 lean meat

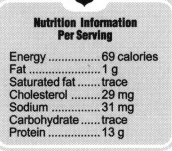

**Nutrition Information
Per Serving**

Energy .... 69 calories
Fat .... 1 g
Saturated fat .... trace
Cholesterol .... 29 mg
Sodium .... 31 mg
Carbohydrate ..... trace
Protein .... 13 g

Heart Smart® Cookbook

Eggless Tofu Sandwich Spread

This will satisfy your appetite for a home-style egg salad sandwich, but without all the cholesterol.

1 pound tofu
1/4 cup reduced-calorie mayonnaise
1/4 teaspoon salt
2 teaspoons Dijon mustard
1/4 teaspoon garlic powder
White pepper to taste
1/8 teaspoon turmeric
1 green pepper, seeded and minced
1 stalk celery, minced
3 green onions, with tops, minced
3 tablespoons fresh chopped parsley or
        1 teaspoon dried

Press tofu to remove liquid, drain and discard liquid. Mash tofu with fork to crumbly consistency. Add rest of ingredients. Mix well. Makes approximately 2 1/2 cups spread, or 5 half-cup servings.

Good: Vitamin C

Diabetic Exchanges: 1/2 medium-fat meat, 1 vegetable, 1/2 fat

♥ Nutrition Information Per Serving

Energy	90 calories
Fat	6 g
Saturated fat	trace
Cholesterol	1 mg
Sodium	169 mg
Carbohydrate	5 g
Protein	7 g

Chicken-in-a-Pocket Sandwich

Neufchatel cheese contains 74 calories per ounce, compared with cream cheese, which contains 98 calories per ounce.

2 ounces Neufchatel cheese, cut into chunks
1 green pepper, seeded and diced
4 to 5 green onions, diced, including green tops
2 to 3 stalks celery, diced
1/8 teaspoon garlic powder (optional)
12 ounces cooked, skinless, boneless chicken breast, diced
2 tablespoons reduced-calorie ranch dressing
2 rounds of pita bread, cut in halves crosswise to form 4 pocket sandwiches
1 cup shredded lettuce or spinach leaves
1/2 cup alfalfa sprouts
1 to 2 carrots, finely shredded
1 ounce cheddar cheese, shredded

In a 1-quart microwave-safe dish, combine Neufchatel cheese, green pepper, green onions, celery and garlic powder. Microwave on low just until cheese softens, about 1 minute. (If you don't have a microwave, heat in the top of a gently simmering double boiler until cheese softens.) Stir cooked chicken and ranch dressing into microwave dish or double boiler. In microwave, cook on low 1 more minute. In double boiler, stir and cook until heated through, about 3 to 4 minutes. Keep warm.

Line each pita half with 1/4 of the shredded lettuce or spinach and sprouts. Add 1/4 of the chicken mixture to each. Sprinkle each

sandwich with 1/4 of the shredded carrots and cheddar cheese. Microwave on low about 15 seconds, just long enough to melt cheese. If you use a conventional oven, run under the broiler about 30 seconds. Makes 4 sandwiches, each 1 serving.

Excellent: Potassium
Excellent: Vitamin A
Excellent: Vitamin C

Diabetic Exchanges: 4 lean meat, 1 starch

Nutrition Information Per Serving

Energy	295 calories
Fat	10 g
Saturated fat	4 g
Cholesterol	92 mg
Sodium	327 mg
Carbohydrate	17 g
Protein	33 g

Heart Smart® Cookbook

Falafel Pita Sandwich with Cucumber Yogurt Sauce

Falafel is a chick-pea patty that can be a low-fat bargain when it's baked instead of deep-fried. The pita bread is great for other sandwiches, too. One pocket contains 106 calories and 1/2 gram of fat.

1 medium potato, cooked and peeled
3 tablespoons vegetable oil
2 small onions, peeled and finely chopped
1 hot green pepper, seeded and minced
2 cloves garlic, peeled and minced
1 large bunch parsley, leaves minced
3 cups cooked, ground garbanzo beans, or
    2 cans (19 ounces each), drained
1 tablespoon plain low-fat yogurt
1 teaspoon paprika
Juice of 1 lemon, or 2 to 3 tablespoons
    reconstituted
Vegetable cooking spray
6 whole-wheat standard size (about 7 ' inches) pita bread pockets
2 cups lettuce, shredded
12 slices tomato
Cucumber Yogurt Sauce (recipe follows)

Preheat oven to 350 degrees. Mash potato. Set aside.

Heat oil in skillet over medium heat and saute onions, green pepper and garlic until soft, about 3 minutes. Stir in parsley and cook about 1 minute. In a large bowl, combine the garbanzo beans with the onion mixture; mix well. Add yogurt, paprika and lemon juice; mix well.

Form into 24 patties using 2 tablespoons of mixture for each. (You may find it easier to spoon 2 tablespoons of mixture onto a baking sheet rather than to form into balls.)

Place on baking sheet sprayed with vegetable cooking spray and bake for 10 minutes on each side.

Cut pita bread in half and open pockets. Enclose 2 patties in each pocket. Top each with an equal portion of shredded lettuce and 1 tomato slice. Serve with Cucumber Yogurt Sauce (recipe follows). Makes 6 servings, 2 pita halves per serving.

Excellent: Potassium
Excellent: Iron
Good: Vitamin A
Excellent: Vitamin C

Diabetic Exchanges: 4 starch, 1 fat, 1/2 lean meat

Nutrition Information Per Serving

Energy	394 calories
Fat	11 g
Saturated fat	trace
Cholesterol	trace
Sodium	945 mg
Carbohydrate	62 g
Protein	14 g

Cucumber Yogurt Sauce
1/2 cup vinegar
2 tablespoons fresh dill weed, or
    1 1/2 teaspoon dried
2 thin (1/4-inch or thinner) slices of
    medium-size onions, in rings
1/4 teaspoon white pepper
4 cucumbers, peeled, seeded and thinly sliced
2 cups low-fat yogurt

Mix vinegar, dill, onions and white pepper in covered bowl. Add cucumber slices and marinate, preferably overnight, covered in the refrigerator.

Drain cucumbers, discard marinade. Remove onion and discard (if desired, you may leave it in). Stir cucumbers and onion, if desired, into yogurt. Makes about 4 cups sauce, more than enough for 6 sandwiches.

Diabetic Exchanges: 1 vegetable, 1/2 milk

Nutrition Information Per Serving	
Energy	79 calories
Fat	1 g
Saturated fat	trace
Cholesterol	4 mg
Sodium	58 mg
Carbohydrate	13 g
Protein	5 g

Peanut Butter

This homemade peanut butter is low in salt, and it isn't hydrogenated like commercially made peanut butter.

1 1/3 cups unsalted dry-roasted peanuts
1/4 teaspoon salt
3/4 teaspoon ground cinnamon (optional)

Place peanuts and salt in a blender or food processor with metal blade inserted. Cover and blend or process until spreadable, 6 to 7 minutes. Stop and scrape sides of blender or food processor as necessary. Store in a covered container in refrigerator. It should be good for several months in refrigerator. Makes approximately 3/4 cup. A serving is 1 tablespoon.

Variation: Prepare as directed except add 3/4 teaspoon ground cinnamon to the peanuts and salt before blending.

Diabetic Exchanges: 1/2 high-fat meat, 1 fat

Nutrition Information Per Serving

Energy .... 86 calories
Fat .... 7 g
Saturated fat .... 1 g
Cholesterol 0
Sodium .... 40 mg
Carbohydrate ...... 3 g
Protein .... 4 g

Submarine Sandwich

We bet our low-fat version of this classic is as good as any you've tasted

1 loaf (16-ounce) unsliced French bread,
      16 to 20 inches long
2 tablespoons prepared mustard
4 ounces part-skim milk mozzarella cheese,
      thinly sliced
4 ounces turkey, thinly sliced
2 ounces lean ham, thinly sliced
2 cups lettuce, shredded
2 medium tomatoes, washed, cored,
      thinly sliced
1 medium onion, peeled, ends removed,
      thinly sliced
1 medium green pepper, washed,
      seeded, cored, thinly sliced
1/4 cup nonfat Italian dressing
6 long wooden picks or small skewers

Cut bread horizontally into halves. Spread
bottom half with mustard. Layer cheese,
turkey, ham, lettuce, tomatoes, onion and green
pepper on bottom half. Drizzle with Italian
dressing. Top with remaining bread half.
Secure loaf with picks or skewers or cut.
Makes 6 servings.

Good: Potassium
Good: Vitamin E
Good: Iron

Diabetic Exchanges: 2 1/2 starch,
1 1/2 lean meat, 1 vegetable, 1/2 fat

Nutrition Information
Per Serving

Energy	351 calories
Fat	9 g
Saturated fat	3 g
Cholesterol	35 mg
Sodium	895 mg
Carbohydrate	44 g
Protein	22 g

Black Bean Soup

To modify this classic, we substituted a dollop of yogurt in place of sour cream. All beans take a little extra time to prepare, but they are well worth the effort. One cup of the black beans used in this soup provides 15 grams of protein, .9 grams of fat and lots of fiber, vitamins and minerals.

1 cup black beans
7 cups water, divided
4 cups low-sodium chicken broth
1 tablespoon olive oil or vegetable oil
1 onion, minced (1 cup)
1 clove garlic, peeled and minced or pressed
1/4 cup chopped green pepper
1/4 cup finely diced carrots
1/4 teaspoon dried oregano
1/4 teaspoon ground cumin
1/4 teaspoon freshly ground black pepper
4 tablespoons low-fat yogurt
Chopped fresh parsley for garnish

If you have time to soak the beans overnight, wash and place in a 2-quart saucepan with 4 cups of water and leave at room temperature. Otherwise, put the beans and 4 cups of water in a large saucepan, bring to a boil, reduce heat slightly and let boil for 2 minutes. Remove from heat and let stand for 1 hour. Drain and discard the water.

Add 3 cups of fresh water and the broth. Bring to a boil, reduce heat to low and simmer, covered, for 2 to 3 hours or until tender.

In a skillet, heat the oil on medium-high heat. Add onion and garlic, stirring until translucent and soft, about 3 minutes. Do not let them brown. Add green pepper and carrots and saute until soft. Add vegetable mixture to the cooked beans and liquid. Add oregano, cumin and black pepper and simmer for another 30 minutes. If you like a smooth-textured soup, let soup cool slightly, then puree in blender or food processor. Serve hot garnished with a dollop of yogurt and parsley. Makes 4 servings.

Good: Fiber
Excellent: Potassium
Excellent: Vitamin A
Good: Vitamin C

Diabetic Exchanges: 1 starch, 1 lean meat, 1/2 fat

Nutrition Information Per Serving

Energy .... 160 calories
Fat .... 5 g
Saturated fat .... 1 g
Cholesterol .... 2 mg
Sodium .... 235 mg
Carbohydrate ...... 18 g
Protein .... 10 g

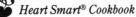

Butternut Squash Soup

Butternut squash is a winter squash with a sweet taste. It makes a soup with a most distinctive flavor.

1 tablespoon soft tub margarine
2 tablespoons water
2 cups finely chopped yellow onions
4 to 5 teaspoons curry powder
2 medium butternut squash, about
    3 pounds total
3 cups chicken stock or canned
    low-sodium chicken broth
2 apples, peeled, cored, chopped
1 cup apple juice
Freshly ground black pepper, to taste
1 shredded unpeeled Granny Smith apple,
    for garnish

Melt margarine in water in small soup pot or Dutch oven over low heat. Add onions and curry powder; cook covered, over low heat, until onions are tender, about 25 minutes.

Meanwhile, peel squash, scrape out seeds, chop squash in cubes and set aside. When onions are tender, pour in stock or broth. Add squash and apples; bring to a boil over medium heat. Reduce heat to low and simmer, partially covered, until squash and apples are very tender, about 25 minutes. Pour soup through a strainer, reserving liquid, and transfer solids to the bowl of a food processor fitted with steel blade, or use a food mill fitted with medium disc. A blender can also be used (cool mixture before pureeing.) Add 1 cup of the cooking stock and process until smooth.

Return pureed soup to pot and add apple juice and additional cooking liquid, about 2 cups, until soup is of desired consistency. Season to taste with pepper, simmer briefly to heat through and serve immediately, garnished with shredded apple. Makes four 1-cup servings.

Good: Fiber
Excellent: Potassium
Excellent: Vitamin A
Excellent: Vitamin C

Diabetic Exchanges: 2 starch

Nutrition Information Per Serving

Energy	146 calories
Fat	2 g
Saturated fat	trace
Cholesterol	0
Sodium	44 mg
Carbohydrate	30 g
Protein	3 g

Heart Smart® Cookbook

Cold Cherry Soup

If wonderful Michigan cherries aren't in season, frozen cherries that have been defrosted and drained will do just fine.

1 1/2 cups water
1/2 cup red wine
2 tablespoons sugar
2 tablespoons cornstarch
1 cup pitted fresh sweet cherries (about 1/3 pound), or 1 cup frozen, defrosted and drained well
1 cup fresh raspberries (about 1/2 pint) or 1 cup frozen, defrosted and drained well
1/4 teaspoon grated orange rind
1 carton (8 ounces) vanilla low-fat yogurt

Combine water, wine, sugar and cornstarch in a medium saucepan over medium heat. Stir well. Add cherries and raspberries. Cook, uncovered, stirring often, until fruit is soft, about 8 minutes. Remove from heat; let cool.

Position steel cutting blade in food processor bowl. Add fruit mixture and orange rind. Process until smooth, scraping sides of bowl with a rubber spatula between pulses. Strain puree through cheesecloth and discard seeds. Cover and chill at least 1 hour.

Combine 1/2 cup of the cherry puree with the yogurt in a small bowl and mix well. Spoon about 1/3 cup cherry-yogurt mixture into each of four small serving bowls. Set aside the remaining cherry-yogurt mixture – you should have about 2 tablespoons. Now take the remaining pure cherry puree – you should have about 1/2 cup – and divide it evenly among the four serving bowls, spooning it over the cherry-yogurt mixture in each bowl. Do not stir. Divide remaining 2 tablespoons cherry-yogurt mixture evenly among the 4 bowls by placing dollops on top of the cherry puree in each bowl. Pull a wooden toothpick through dollops to make a pattern. Chill for about an hour. Makes 4 servings.

Good: Potassium

Diabetic Exchanges: 1 starch, 1/2 fruit, 1/4 milk (occasional use)

Nutrition Information Per Serving

Energy .... 136 calories
Fat .... 1 g
Saturated fat .... trace
Cholesterol .... 4 mg
Sodium .... 42 mg
Carbohydrate ...... 24 g
Protein .... 4 g

Cream of Broccoli Soup

Served with a whole grain bread, this creamy soup could be a complete meal.

1 1/2 cups onion, chopped
1 tablespoon soft tub margarine
1 bay leaf
1 green pepper, chopped
4 cups broccoli, chopped
2 1/2 cups water (optional: defatted
    unsalted chicken broth)
1 teaspoon salt
2 cups evaporated skim milk
Pinch allspice
1/2 teaspoon pepper (or to taste)
1/2 teaspoon thyme
1/2 teaspoon basil
1 cup broccoli florets
3 to 5 green onions, chopped
1/2 cup non-fat plain yogurt

In large skillet or small soup pot, saute onion in margarine with bay leaf until translucent. Add chopped green pepper, broccoli, water (or broth) and salt. Cook covered over medium heat about 10 minutes, until broccoli is tender but still bright green. Remove from heat.

If using a blender, allow to cool at least 20 minutes. If using a food processor, you can go directly to the next step. Working gradually and in small batches, puree in a blender or food processor with evaporated skim milk until smooth. Add seasonings. Add broccoli florets and green onions and heat over medium heat until tender, about 4 minutes. Whisk in yogurt and stir gently over medium heat for 3 to 4 minutes. Serve immediately. Makes 8 servings.

Good: Fiber
Excellent: Potassium
Excellent: Vitamin A
Excellent: Vitamin C
Excellent: Calcium

Diabetic Exchanges: 2 vegetable, 1/2 milk

Nutrition Information Per Serving

Energy .... 100 calories
Fat .... 2 g
Saturated fat .... trace
Cholesterol .... 3 mg
Sodium .... 361 mg
Carbohydrate ...... 14 g
Protein .... 8 g

84

Cream of Chicken Soup

If cream-based soups are your weakness, try preparing this Heart Smart® Cream of Chicken Soup. Comparable cream soups can have as much as 60 percent of their calories from fat.

4 chicken breasts (about 2 pounds total), skinned
1 1/2 quarts stock (from boiled chicken), defatted
2 teaspoons chicken bouillon granules
1 cup grated raw potato
1 clove garlic, chopped
1 onion, chopped
1 cup celery, chopped
2 medium zucchinis, sliced
1 cup sliced raw carrots
2 tablespoons chopped fresh parsley
1/2 teaspoon thyme
1/2 teaspoon basil
1/8 teaspoon pepper
1 cup fresh sliced mushrooms
2 cups skim milk
2 tablespoons cornstarch mixed with
  3 tablespoons cold water

In a large pot, boil 4 chicken breasts, without skin, until cooked thoroughly. Debone chicken and cut it into bite-size pieces and set aside. Save chicken broth (add water to bring to 1 1/2 quarts, if necessary.) Add chicken bouillon granules and simmer until granules dissolve.

In a separate, smaller pot, mix 2 cups of the chicken stock with grated raw potato. Simmer 15 minutes, stirring frequently, until potato is tender and stock is thickened. Pour into blender and puree. Add pureed mixture back to original soup stock. Stir in garlic, onion, celery, zucchini, carrots, parsley, thyme, basil, pepper and mushrooms. Cover and simmer about 15 minutes or until vegetables are tender. Stir in milk and cook covered. Do not let mixture boil. Stir cornstarch mixture; add to hot soup. Add cooked chicken pieces. Cook, stirring until soup bubbles and thickens slightly (about 5 minutes.) Makes approximately 10 one-cup servings.

Excellent: Potassium
Excellent: Vitamin A

Diabetic Exchanges: 2 lean meat, 1 starch

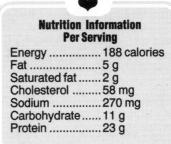

Nutrition Information Per Serving
Energy .... 188 calories
Fat .... 5 g
Saturated fat .... 2 g
Cholesterol .... 58 mg
Sodium .... 270 mg
Carbohydrate ...... 11 g
Protein .... 23 g

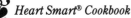

Gazpacho

We can think of no better way to take advantage of garden tomatoes, cucumbers and onions in the summer. Sweet peppers are very high in Vitamin C. Ounce for ounce, raw green peppers have 2 1/2 times as much Vitamin C as oranges, and red peppers have nearly 4 times as much.

4 large peeled tomatoes, or 1 can (28-ounces) tomatoes, cored, coarsely chopped
1/2 cup chopped onion
1 cup peeled, chopped, seeded cucumbers
1/2 cup cored, seeded, chopped sweet red pepper
1/2 cup cored, seeded, chopped green pepper
1 tablespoon lemon juice
1 teaspoon vegetable oil
1 small fresh hot green chili, seeded and finely chopped, or 1/8 teaspoon dried chili pepper
1 clove garlic, minced
1 teaspoon fresh cilantro
1 teaspoon ground oregano
Hot sauce and freshly ground pepper, to taste
Cilantro for garnish

In a blender or a food processor fitted with a steel blade, puree the vegetables. Blend after adding each vegetable. Add lemon juice, oil and seasonings; blend again. Add hot sauce and black pepper to taste. Cover and chill for at least 4 hours.

To serve, stir, taste and correct seasonings. Ladle into chilled soup bowls or mugs. Garnish with cilantro. Makes six 1-cup servings.

Good: Potassium
Good: Vitamin A
Excellent: Vitamin C

Diabetic Exchanges: 1 vegetable

Nutrition Information Per Serving

Energy	36 calories
Fat	1 g
Saturated fat	trace
Cholesterol	0
Sodium	9 mg
Carbohydrate	7 g
Protein	1 g

Hearty Potato Leek Soup

This soup can also be made with low-sodium bouillon, reducing the sodium to 53 milligrams per serving.

3 tablespoons vegetable oil
8 medium potatoes, peeled and cubed
3 leeks, washed and finely chopped
2 medium onions, peeled, ends removed, finely chopped
3 cloves garlic, peeled and minced
6 cups chicken broth
1 cup skim milk
1 1/4 teaspoon white pepper
1/2 teaspoon paprika
Green onions or parsley for garnish (optional)

In a large stock pot, heat the vegetable oil. Add potatoes, leeks, onions and garlic. Saute the vegetables over medium-high heat until they are translucent, about 5 to 6 minutes. Add chicken broth to the pot. Bring mixture to a boil and then allow to simmer, uncovered, for about 15 to 20 minutes or until the vegetables are tender. Remove from heat.

Using a potato masher, mash the cubes of potatoes, leaving some pieces whole. The consistency of the soup at this point should be relatively creamy. Return the soup to heat and add milk, white pepper and paprika. Stir and simmer over low heat, uncovered, an additional 10 minutes. Add garnish of green onions or parsley to each serving, if desired. Makes 12 servings.

Excellent: Potassium
Good: Vitamin C

Diabetic Exchanges: 2 starch

Nutrition Information Per Serving

Energy .... 165 calories
Fat .... 4 g
Saturated fat .... trace
Cholesterol .... trace
Sodium .... 473 mg
Carbohydrate ...... 27 g
Protein .... 6 g

Homemade Chicken Broth

"Bouquet garni" is a French term for any small bunch of herbs and seasonings tied together, often in cheesecloth. In this broth, the herbs give a great taste that makes the use of salt unnecessary.

1 cooked chicken or turkey carcass
    (skin and excess fat removed, or use
    skinless poultry parts)
4 quarts cold water
2 ribs of celery with tender leaves
1 large onion, peeled, ends removed, sliced
2 medium carrots, peeled, ends removed,
    sliced

Bouquet Garni
4 sprigs fresh parsley, or 1/2 teaspoon dried
1 teaspoon thyme
8 peppercorns
1 bay leaf
6 whole cloves
Cheesecloth and kitchen twine

Bring carcass and cold water slowly to a boil in 6-quart or larger soup pot and reduce heat at once. Simmer uncovered about 1/2 hour. Remove residue that rises to the top. Add celery, onion, carrots. Continue to simmer, partly covered, 1 to 1 1/2 hours. During last half-hour, add bouquet garni. (To prepare bouquet garni, bunch the seasonings together into 4-inch square of double-layer cheesecloth tied with cotton kitchen twine.)

Strain broth, discarding vegetables and bouquet garni. Remove any chicken meat from carcass. Add meat back to broth, if desired. Refrigerate broth overnight. The next day, skim and discard fat that floats to the top. Place in 2-cup containers; freeze for up to 3 months. Keeps in refrigerator for 3 to 4 days. Makes about 4 quarts or 16 one-cup servings.

Diabetic Exchanges: 1/2 lean meat, 1/2 vegetable

Nutrition Information Per Serving

Energy .... 44 calories
Fat .... 1 g
Saturated fat .... trace
Cholesterol .... 1 mg
Sodium .... 118 mg
Carbohydrate ...... 3 g
Protein .... 5 g

88

Minestrone Soup

Serve this with a crust of Italian bread for a hearty meal that will leave the whole family satisfied.

1 onion, chopped
1 clove garlic, chopped
4 celery stalks, chopped
2 tablespoons vegetable oil
9 cups water (may have to add a
    little more water as you go along,
    depending on desired thickness)
1/4 cup lentils
1/4 cup split peas
1/4 cup barley
1 can (8 ounces) tomato sauce
1 package (20-ounces) frozen mixed
    vegetables
2 teaspoons basil
1 teaspoon oregano
2 teaspoons beef- or chicken-flavored
    bouillon granules
1/2 cup small shell macaroni
1/2 head coarsely shredded cabbage

Cook chopped onion, garlic and celery in oil until tender. Do not brown. Set aside.

Heat 9 cups of water to boiling. Add lentils, split peas and barley. Cook for 15 minutes. Then add cooked onion-garlic-celery mixture, tomato sauce, mixed vegetables, basil, oregano and bouillon, and cook for another 15 minutes. Then add small shell macaroni and shredded cabbage and cook until tender. Makes 14 one-cup servings.

Excellent: Vitamin A
Good: Vitamin C
Good: Potassium
Good: Fiber

Diabetic Exchanges: 1 starch, 1 vegetable, 1/2 fat

Nutrition Information Per Serving

Energy .... 116 calories
Fat .... 3 g
Saturated fat .... trace
Cholesterol .... trace
Sodium .... 412 mg
Carbohydrate ...... 20 g
Protein .... 4 g

Sweet Pea Soup

Many creamy soups derive too many calories from fat. Try thickening your soup with pureed vegetables and yogurt.

1 tablespoon soft tub margarine
1 package (10 ounces) frozen peas, thawed
1 head Boston lettuce, washed, drained,
    patted dry, chopped
4 green onions, washed, ends removed,
    chopped
5 cups canned low-sodium chicken broth
Coarse or cracked ground pepper, to taste
6 teaspoons plain, low-fat yogurt

In a heavy, large saucepan over low heat, melt margarine. Add peas, lettuce and onions. Cook until onions are just soft, stirring occasionally, about 5 minutes. Add broth. Increase heat and bring to a boil. Reduce heat and simmer until peas are tender, 8 minutes. Cool.

Puree soup (in batches, if necessary) in blender. Season with pepper. Reheat in saucepan until warmed through. Ladle soup into bowls. Garnish each with 1 teaspoon of yogurt. Makes 6 servings.

Good: Fiber
Excellent: Potassium

Diabetic Exchanges: 1 lean meat, 1/2 starch

**Nutrition Information
Quantity/Serving**

Energy	108 calories
Fat	3 g
Saturated fat	trace
Cholesterol	2 mg
Sodium	134 mg
Carbohydrate	11 g
Protein	8 g

Vegetable Barley Soup

When using canned broth, chill the can before opening it and skim off fat as soon as you open the can.

1/2 cup barley, long- or quick-cooking
2 quarts meat stock or canned
    low-sodium broth
1/2 cup carrots, diced
1/2 cup celery, diced
1/2 cup onion, diced
1 can (1 pound) low-sodium whole
    tomatoes, drained; or
    3 to 4 medium tomatoes
1/2 teaspoon thyme leaves, crushed
1 bay leaf
1/2 pound fresh sliced mushrooms
1 small zucchini, diced

IF USING LONG-COOKING BARLEY:
Rinse barley in colander and remove any foreign objects. In small soup pot, combine barley with meat stock or broth. Cook over medium heat about 1 hour. Add carrots, celery, onion, tomatoes, thyme and bay leaf. Continue cooking for 20 minutes. Then add mushrooms and zucchini. Cook over low heat another 15 minutes.

IF USING QUICK-COOKING BARLEY:
Combine broth with carrots, celery, onion, tomatoes, thyme and bay leaf and cook for 20 minutes. Then add mushrooms, zucchini and barley. Cook over low heat another 15 minutes. Makes 8 one-cup servings.

Excellent: Potassium
Excellent: Vitamin A
Good: Vitamin C

Diabetic Exchanges: 1 starch

**Nutrition Information
Per Serving**

Energy .... 90 calories
Fat .... 1 g
Saturated fat .... trace
Cholesterol .... trace
Sodium .... trace
Carbohydrate ...... 16 g
Protein .... 5 g

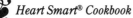

Salads, Dressings and Sauces

Blue Cheese Dip, Dressing or Topping

This is great on a salad, but it makes a wonderful vegetable dip, too. Fill a scooped-out red pepper with it and serve with cut vegetables. Typical blue cheese dressings have about 77 calories, 167 milligrams of sodium, 8 grams of fat, 1.5 grams of saturated fat and 9 milligrams of cholesterol per tablespoon.

2 cups 1-percent low-fat cottage cheese
3 ounces crumbled blue cheese
2 tablespoons chopped green onion
1/4 teaspoon garlic powder
1 teaspoon Worcestershire sauce
1 tablespoon lemon juice
1 cup plain nonfat yogurt
1 tablespoon dried parsley, or
    2 tablespoons fresh chopped

Mix cottage and blue cheeses using the highest speed of your blender or mixer until smooth. Beat in onion, garlic powder, Worcestershire sauce and lemon juice. Fold in yogurt. Stir in parsley. Cover and chill before serving. Serve with vegetable sticks or crackers, or use as a dressing for salads or a topping on baked potatoes. Makes 4 cups. A serving is 1 tablespoon.

Diabetic Exchanges: 1 tablespoon = free

**Nutrition Information
Per Serving**

Energy .... 12 calories
Fat .... 1 g
Saturated fat .... trace
Cholesterol .... 1 mg
Sodium .... 51 mg
Carbohydrate ...... trace
Protein .... 1 g

 Heart Smart® Cookbook

Creamy Garlic Dressing

Compared with other creamy dressings, this dressing is low in calories and sodium.

1/2 cup reduced-calorie mayonnaise
1/2 cup plain nonfat yogurt
1 tablespoon chopped green onion
1 teaspoon chopped fresh parsley, or 1/2
    teaspoon dried
1 small clove garlic, peeled and minced
1/8 teaspoon freshly ground black pepper
4 1/2 teaspoons tarragon-flavored vinegar
1 tablespoon lemon juice

In a small bowl, mix together mayonnaise and yogurt until smooth. Add green onion, parsley, garlic and black pepper; mix until well combined. Whisk in vinegar and lemon juice. Makes approximately 1 cup. A serving is 1 tablespoon.

Diabetic Exchanges: 1 tablespoon = free

Nutrition Information Per Serving

Energy .... 15 calories
Fat .... 1 g
Saturated fat .... trace
Cholesterol .... 1 mg
Sodium .... 28 mg
Carbohydrate ...... 2 g
Protein .... trace

Italian Dressing

By making your own dressings like this one, you control the amount of fat and save a lot of money.

1 cup olive oil
1 cup red wine vinegar
1 cup water
2 cloves garlic, peeled, ends removed, minced
1/2 teaspoon dried oregano
1/2 teaspoon black pepper
1 teaspoon dried basil
1/4 teaspoon dried thyme
2 tablespoons lemon juice

Mix olive oil, vinegar, water, garlic, oregano, pepper, basil, thyme and lemon juice in a 4-cup or larger jar. Chill. Shake well before using. Makes 3 cups. A serving is 1 tablespoon.

Diabetic Exchanges:
1 fat

Nutrition Information Per Serving

Energy .... 40 calories
Fat .... 4 g
Saturated fat .... 1 g
Cholesterol 0
Sodium .... trace
Carbohydrate ...... 1 g
Protein 0

 Heart Smart® *Cookbook*

Ranch Dressing

You can pare the fat from this recipe even further by using the new nonfat mayonnaise.

5 teaspoons powdered ranch dressing mix
1/3 cup reduced-calorie mayonnaise
1 cup plain nonfat yogurt
1 tablespoon fresh dill, snipped; or
    1 1/2 teaspoons dried
1 tablespoon fresh parsley, snipped, or
    1 1/2 teaspoons dried

   Combine ingredients in a bottle with a tight-fitting cover. Shake vigorously. Chill. Makes about 1 1/2 cups. A serving is 1 tablespoon.

   Diabetic Exchanges: 1 tablespoon = free

Nutrition Information Per Serving

Energy .... 12 calories
Fat .... 1 g
Saturated fat .... trace
Cholesterol .... 1 mg
Sodium .... 59 mg
Carbohydrate ...... 1 g
Protein .... 1 g

Heart Smart® Cookbook

Fruit Salad

This salad is quick and gets its extra zing from chopped walnuts. Try a variety of your favorite fruits.

2 apples
2 pears
1 small cantaloupe or honeydew melon
1 banana
1/2 cup orange juice
1/4 cup raisins
1 tablespoon chopped walnuts
1/2 teaspoon cinnamon

Wash apples and pears in cool water. Core apples, pears and melon. Cut all fruit into bite-size pieces. Add orange juice and toss. In a separate bowl mix raisins, nuts and cinnamon. Spoon fruit salad into 10 small bowls and sprinkle one teaspoon raisin-nut mixture over each serving. Makes approximately ten 1-cup servings.

Good: Potassium
Good: Vitamin A
Good: Vitamin C

Diabetic Exchanges: 1 1/2 fruit

Nutrition Information Per Serving

Energy	85 calories
Fat	trace
Saturated fat	0
Cholesterol	0
Sodium	5 mg
Carbohydrate	21 g
Protein	1 g

Herbed Chicken Salad

Adding lots of chopped vegetables to this recipe gives color and extra Vitamins A and C.

2 cups cooked chicken, cut into bite-size pieces
1/4 cup plain nonfat yogurt
1/4 cup reduced-calorie mayonnaise
2 green onions with tops, thinly sliced
1 small carrot, grated
2 radishes, grated
3 tablespoons chopped celery
2 tablespoons chopped green pepper
2 tablespoons chopped fresh parsley
1 teaspoon Worcestershire sauce
1 teaspoon herb seasoning (no-salt herb blend)
1/4 teaspoon freshly ground black pepper,
    or to taste
1 1/2 tablespoons tarragon vinegar
4 leaves of lettuce, rinsed and dried
1 can (8-ounce) mandarin oranges packed
    in fruit juice, drained; or
3 small tomatoes, sliced

Combine all ingredients except lettuce, oranges and tomatoes. Mix well, cover and refrigerate at least 1 hour. To serve, place a scoop of salad on a lettuce leaf and garnish with orange segments or tomato slices. Makes four 1/2-cup servings.

Excellent: Potassium
Excellent: Vitamin A
Excellent: Vitamin C

Diabetic Exchanges: 3 lean meat, 1 vegetable, 1/2 fruit

Nutrition Information Per Serving	
Energy	199 calories
Fat	7 g
Saturated fat	1 g
Cholesterol	63 mg
Sodium	86 mg
Carbohydrate	12 g
Protein	23 g

Cinnamon-Spiced Applesauce

This is a great way to use apples that are beginning to get soft.

6 medium McIntosh apples, peeled, cored and
   sliced, about 6 cups (if you substitute
   another variety of apple, you may have to
   adjust cooking time)
3/4 teaspoon ground cinnamon
1/4 cup granulated sugar

In a 2-quart microwave-safe casserole dish,
combine apples and cinnamon. Cover tightly.
Microwave on high, 8 to 9 minutes or until
apples are tender, stirring several times during
cooking. If using a conventional oven, preheat
oven to 350 degrees. Combine apples and
cinnamon in a 1 1/2-quart casserole. Bake about
25 minutes, or until apples are soft and can be
pierced easily with a knife.
   Mash apples to desired consistency with fork
or potato masher, or put in a food processor or
grinder. Stir in sugar. Makes four 1/2-cup
servings.

Diabetic Exchanges: 2 1/2 fruit

Nutrition Information
Per Serving

Energy .... 142 calories
Fat .... trace
Saturated fat .... trace
Cholesterol 0
Sodium .... trace
Carbohydrate ...... 37 g
Protein .... trace

Cranberry-Orange Chutney

This is a wonderful accompaniment for Sole Fillets with Curry Sauce. See page 182.

1 medium thin-skin orange, unpeeled, seeded and cut in eighths
1 medium red apple, unpeeled, cored, seeded, cut in eighths
1 1/2 cups cranberries, washed, stems removed
1 peeled small onion, quartered
1 cup orange juice, divided
2 to 4 tablespoons sugar
1 teaspoon grated or finely chopped ginger root, or 1/2 teaspoon ground ginger
1/4 teaspoon ground nutmeg
1 teaspoon curry powder
1/4 cup raisins

With steel cutting blade in food processor bowl, process orange, apple, cranberries and onion with 1/2 cup of the orange juice until finely chopped (or put in a blender or grinder or chop by hand, using a sharp knife. If you chop by hand, don't add the orange juice at this point). Set aside.

In large saucepan over high heat, bring to a boil the remaining one-half cup orange juice (or 1 cup if you didn't add the 1/2 cup earlier), sugar, ginger root or ginger, nutmeg and curry powder.

Nutrition Information Per Serving

Energy	24 calories
Fat	trace
Saturated fat	trace
Cholesterol	0
Sodium	trace
Carbohydrate	6 g
Protein	trace

Reduce heat, add chopped ingredients and raisins and simmer, covered, 15 minutes. Remove from heat and allow to cool. Store in airtight container in refrigerator. Makes about 4 cups. This can be kept up to 3 months in the freezer, 1 month in the refrigerator. A serving is 3 tablespoons

Diabetic Exchanges: 1/2 fruit

Low–Sugar Tangy Cranberry Sauce

Use this with your holiday meals instead of canned cranberry sauce, which contains 209 calories per 1/2-cup serving. You'll also want to try our way of preparing turkey, on Page 144.

1 cup frozen apple juice concentrate
4 cups fresh cranberries, washed, stems
    removed
1 tablespoon grated orange peel or
    1 tablespoon orange marmalade

Bring apple juice concentrate to a boil in a saucepan. Add cranberries. Reduce heat, cover and simmer, stirring frequently, 7 to 10 minutes or until thickened. Stir in grated orange peel or marmalade and remove from heat. Let cool at room temperature; cover and refrigerate. Makes 8 servings, about 1/2 cup each.

Diabetic Exchanges: 1 1/4 fruit

**Nutrition Information
Per Serving**

Energy .... 78 calories
Fat .... trace
Saturated fat .... trace
Cholesterol 0
Sodium .... 9 mg
Carbohydrate ...... 20 g
Protein .... trace

Ambrosia Fruit Salad

All yogurts are not alike; compare labels to ensure you're getting a nonfat kind.

3 medium peeled oranges, broken into
    sections
1 large apple, seeded and diced, with
    peel left on
1 large pear, seeded and diced, with
    skin left on
1 cup seedless grapes
1 cup nonfat peach yogurt

Combine fruit pieces in a bowl. Gently toss with yogurt to coat. Cover and chill several hours. Makes 6 servings, each 1 cup.

Good: Potassium
Excellent: Vitamin C

Diabetic Exchanges: 1 1/2 fruit, 1/2 milk

Nutrition Information
Per Serving

Energy .... 107 calories
Fat .... trace
Saturated fat .... trace
Cholesterol .... trace
Sodium .... 30 mg
Carbohydrate ...... 22 g
Protein .... 3 g

Apple, Zucchini and Bell Pepper Salad

Prepared salads take on a whole new personality when you combine colorful fruits and vegetables, as we did here.

1/2 cup low-calorie Italian dressing
1 teaspoon dried basil
Freshly ground pepper, to taste
3 medium-sized red or Golden Delicious
    apples, unpeeled
1 medium-sized red onion, peeled and thinly
    sliced lengthwise
1 red or green bell pepper, seeded and cut
    into matchstick pieces
1 pound zucchini, thinly sliced or grated

In a large salad bowl, combine Italian dressing, basil and ground pepper. Core and dice unpeeled apples and add to dressing. Add onion, bell pepper and zucchini; stir lightly. Cover and chill at least 4 hours. Just before serving, mix salad again until well combined. Makes 8 servings.

Good: Potassium
Good: Vitamin C

Diabetic Exchanges: 1 vegetable, 1/2 fruit

Nutrition Information Per Serving

Energy .... 65 calories
Fat .... 2 g
Saturated fat .... trace
Cholesterol .... 1 mg
Sodium .... 120 mg
Carbohydrate ...... 12 g
Protein .... 1 g

Fruit Salad with Poppy Seed Dressing

Try this dressing in place of commercial toppings on any combination of fruits. If fresh fruit is not in season, use fruits canned in their own juices.

6 cups fresh fruit
  (One nice combination is 1 cup each of sliced strawberries, cantaloupe balls, honeydew balls, seedless red or green grapes, blueberries, and sliced peaches or nectarines.)

Wash and prepare fruits, and mix them in a large bowl. Divide into 6 dessert dishes and chill at least 1 hour before serving. Serve with Poppy Seed Dressing (recipe follows) on side. makes 6 servings.

Good: Fiber
Excellent: Potassium
Good: Vitamin A
Excellent: Vitamin C

Diabetic Exchanges: 1 1/2 fruit, 1/4 milk (occasional use)

Poppy Seed Dressing
4 tablespoons sugar
4 teaspoons freshly grated orange peel
  (or 1 tablespoon dried)
3/4 cup low-fat yogurt
1 tablespoon lemon juice
2 tablespoons frozen orange juice concentrate
1 teaspoon poppy seeds

Combine sugar and orange peel in blender or food processor with steel blade in place and process until peel is finely minced. Add yogurt, lemon juice, orange juice concentrate and poppy seeds. Blend or process about 5 seconds. Makes about 1 cup, enough for 6 servings.

Nutrition Information Per Serving

Energy	121 calories
Fat	1 g
Saturated fat	trace
Cholesterol	2 mg
Sodium	29 mg
Carbohydrate	28 g
Protein	3 g

 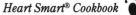

Nutty Flavored Fruit Salad

Nuts are a good source of protein, but they are high in calories and fat. This recipe uses just a hint of nuts for added flavor for a heart-healthy salad.

1 can (8 ounces) crushed pineapple, packed in natural juice
3/4 cup carrot, shredded
3/4 cup celery, chopped
1 cup pears, chopped, unpeeled
1/4 cup raisins
1/3 cup plain low-fat yogurt
2 tablespoons peanut butter
1/4 teaspoon ginger

Drain pineapple and reserve 1 tablespoon of juice. In a large mixing bowl combine pineapple, carrot, celery, pears and raisins. In a small bowl combine the yogurt, peanut butter, ginger and reserved pineapple juice. Stir yogurt dressing into the fruit mixture to coat totally. Cover and chill. Makes 6 servings.

Good: Potassium
Excellent: Vitamin A

Diabetic Exchanges: 1 fruit, 1 vegetable, 1/2 fat

Nutrition Information Per Serving

Energy	105 calories
Fat	3 g
Saturated fat	trace
Cholesterol	trace
Sodium	53 mg
Carbohydrate	19 g
Protein	3 g

 Heart Smart® Cookbook

Chinese Chicken Slaw

Water chestnuts give this recipe crunchiness without adding the fat found in nuts. Use the Italian Dressing recipe on Page 97.

1/2 cup Italian Dressing
2 teaspoons reduced-sodium soy sauce
1 cup shredded green cabbage
1 cup cooked and cubed chicken breast
4 ounces fresh water chestnuts, sliced and drained; or 1 can (4 ounces) sliced water chestnuts, drained and rinsed
4 ounces fresh bamboo shoots, drained; or 1 can (4 ounces) bamboo shoots, drained and rinsed
1 cup frozen pea pods, thawed; or 1 cup fresh pea pods, cleaned
1/4 cup red bell pepper, washed, seeded, cored, julienne sliced
1/4 cup sliced green onions, washed

In a small bowl, whisk together dressing and soy sauce; set aside and bring to room temperature.

In a large bowl, toss cabbage, chicken, water chestnuts, bamboo shoots, pea pods, pepper and green onions. Pour dressing over salad and toss to coat well. Chill. Makes about six 1-cup servings.

Good: Potassium
Excellent: Vitamin C

Diabetic Exchanges: 1 lean meat, 1 vegetable, 1 fat

Nutrition Information Per Serving

Energy	130 calories
Fat	7 g
Saturated fat	1 g
Cholesterol	24 mg
Sodium	130 mg
Carbohydrate	7 g
Protein	10 g

 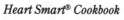

Hawaiian Tossed Chicken Salad

This salad is a great way to use grilled chicken left over from summer backyard barbecues. Use cashews sparingly, because they are very high in fat.

1/2 pound skinless chicken breast, grilled, chilled and chopped
1 small head iceberg lettuce (about 6 cups), shredded
1 medium tomato, chopped
1/2 cucumber, sliced
1 can (8 ounces) pineapple chunks, packed in natural juice, drained
1/4 cup dry-roasted cashews
4 tablespoons low-fat salad dressing

Toss chicken, lettuce, tomato, cucumber and pineapple in a serving bowl. Sprinkle with cashews. Serve with your favorite low-fat dressing, 1 tablespoon per serving. Makes 4 servings.

Good: Fiber
Excellent: Potassium
Good: Vitamin C

Diabetic Exchanges: 2 lean meat, 1 vegetable, 1/2 fruit, 1/2 fat

Nutrition Information Per Serving

Energy .... 195 calories
Fat .... 5 g
Saturated fat .... 1 g
Cholesterol .... 37 mg
Sodium .... 162 mg
Carbohydrate ...... 37 g
Protein .... 16 g

Mandarin Orange Chicken Salad

This salad gets its rich favor from marinating the chicken in a classic marinade.

1 1/2 cups white vinegar
1 tablespoon lemon juice, freshly squeezed if
    possible
2 tablespoons Dijon mustard
1/2 teaspoon garlic powder; or 1 clove of
    garlic, peeled and minced
1/4 teaspoon freshly ground pepper
1 tablespoon crushed dried tarragon or 2
    tablespoons fresh tarragon
2/3 cup vegetable oil
4 chicken breasts, (4 ounces each),
    boneless and skinless
8 large leaves of fresh spinach
16 unsweetened mandarin orange sections
Vegetable cooking spray
4 green onions, tops included, chopped finely

In a medium bowl, mix vinegar, lemon juice, mustard, garlic powder or garlic, pepper, tarragon and oil. Whisk to blend. Reserve 1/2 cup of the dressing in the refrigerator for the finished salad; use the rest to marinate the chicken.

Wash chicken well under running water and pat dry. Slice into strips about 2 inches long, 1/2 inch wide and 1/4 inch thick. (Chicken that has been frozen and slightly thawed is easier to slice.) Using the

dressing set aside for a marinade, marinate the chicken strips at least 1 hour in a shallow dish in the refrigerator.

Meanwhile, rinse and drain spinach leaves. For each serving, line a glass plate with 2 spinach leaves torn into pieces. Chill until ready to serve. Drain mandarin orange sections and refrigerate separately.

Spray a medium skillet with vegetable cooking spray. Discard marinade and saute chicken over medium heat 7 to 10 minutes, or until chicken is cooked through, turning once to cook evenly. Divide chicken strips into 4 portions and lay them across the spinach. Top each plate with 4 mandarin orange sections and 1/4 of the diced green onions. Divide reserved 1/2 cup of salad dressing into 4 portions and drizzle each over a plate of salad. Serve immediately. Makes 4 servings.

Nutrition Information Per Serving

Energy .... 271 calories
Fat .... 8 g
Saturated fat .... 1 g
Cholesterol .... 72 mg
Sodium .... 289 mg
Carbohydrate ...... 22 g
Protein .... 33 g

Good: Fiber
Excellent: Potassium
Excellent: Iron
Excellent: Vitamin A
Excellent: Vitamin C
Good: Calcium

Diabetic Exchanges:
3 lean meat, 1 fruit,
1 vegetable

Heart Smart® Cookbook

Sea Salad with Pasta

When shopping for ingredients for this recipe, read labels carefully. Imitation crab can be high in sodium.

2 cups uncooked sea shell pasta, in various colors
8 ounces cooked crabmeat, real or imitation
1 pint cherry tomatoes, cut in halves or quarters, depending on size
1 red bell pepper, seeded and diced
2 zucchini, sliced julienne style
3 to 4 green onions with tops, diced
2 cups broccoli florets
1 1/3 cups reduced-calorie ranch dressing
6 large lettuce leaves

Cook pasta al dente or until slightly firm, stirring occasionally. Rinse in cold water and drain. Set aside to cool.

Add chilled crab, tomatoes, red bell pepper, zucchini, green onions and broccoli florets to cooled pasta in a large serving bowl. Add dressing and toss gently. Chill at least 1 hour. Recommended storage in refrigerator is up to about 24 hours, assuming salad was constantly chilled. Serve on lettuce. Makes 6 servings.

Good: Fiber
Excellent: Potassium
Excellent: Vitamin A
Excellent: Vitamin C

Diabetic Exchanges: 2 vegetable, 1 starch, 1 lean meat

Nutrition Information Per Serving

Energy	163 calories
Fat	2 g
Saturated fat	trace
Cholesterol	38 mg
Sodium	221 mg
Carbohydrate	26 g
Protein	13 g

Tuna Nicoise Salad

This is a low-fat interpretation of the classic French salad. Three ounces of tuna canned in oil has 255 calories, 19 grams of fat. Three ounces of tuna canned in water has just 105 calories, just 7.5 grams of fat.

Dressing
1 tablespoon olive oil
1/3 cup white or red wine vinegar
1 tablespoon (or to taste) lemon juice, freshly squeezed if possible
1 clove garlic, peeled
1/2 teaspoon fresh dill, snipped; or a dash of dried to taste
1/2 teaspoon fresh chives, snipped; or a dash of dried, to taste; optional

Salad
1 can (6 1/2 ounces) tuna, water-packed, drained (use low-sodium to cut down on sodium)
1 1/2 cup fresh or frozen green beans
3 cups loosely packed torn lettuce (romaine or leaf)
1/4 cup chopped red cabbage
1/4 cup green onions, diagonally sliced
1 can (8 ounces) sliced water chestnuts, drained
1 tomato, cut in wedges

FOR DRESSING: Mix olive oil, vinegar and lemon juice to taste. Peel garlic clove and marinate about 1 hour with dill and chives in oil mixture in a small stainless steel or porcelain bowl.

FOR SALAD: Rinse tuna in a strainer under cold water to remove excess salt; drain well. Add tuna to oil-and-vinegar mixture; toss and marinate at least 1 hour. Remove garlic before serving.

If you use fresh green beans, wash them and cook them, covered, for about 30 seconds in boiling water. Remove and plunge into ice water to stop the cooking. When cool, slice them into desired lengths. If you use frozen, defrost and drain. Do not cook.

Rinse and pat dry torn lettuce leaves. For each serving, arrange 1/2 of the lettuce with 1/2 the red cabbage on serving plate. Add 1/2 the green beans, green onions, water chestnuts and tomato wedges to each. Cover each plate with 1/2 the marinated tuna.

Makes 2 servings.

Good: Fiber
Excellent: Potassium
Excellent: Vitamin A
Excellent: Vitamin C

Diabetic Exchanges: 3 vegetable, 2 lean meat, 1 starch, 1/2 fat

Nutrition Information Per Serving

Energy	309 calories
Fat	10 g
Saturated fat	1 g
Cholesterol	32 mg
Sodium	64 mg
Carbohydrate	32 g
Protein	30 g

Heart Smart® Cookbook

Armenian Bean Salad

The sodium level in this recipe is based on information for unrinsed beans. Rinsing canned beans will reduce the sodium content as much as 40 percent.

1 can (15 ounces) kidney beans, rinsed
1 can (15 ounces) white northern beans, rinsed
1 large tomato, cut into small pieces
1 small onion, cut into small pieces
1 cup fresh parsley, finely chopped
1 whole lemon
2 tablespoons olive oil

In a large serving bowl, toss together kidney beans, northern beans, tomato, onion and parsley. Squeeze the juice of 1 lemon over the mixture. Add the olive oil and gently toss. Makes 6 servings.

Good: Fiber
Excellent: Potassium
Excellent: Iron
Good: Vitamin C

Diabetic Exchanges: 2 starch, 1/2 lean meat, 1/2 fat

Nutrition Information Per Serving

Energy .... 207 calories
Fat .... 5 g
Saturated Fat ...... 1 g
Cholesterol 0
Sodium .... 471 mg
Carbohydrate ...... 31 g
Protein .... 9 g

Barley Salad

This salad is a great take-along for picnics because it doesn't contain milk or eggs that can spoil. It also keeps well in the refrigerator for several days.

1 1/2 cups water
1/2 cup barley, long- or quick-cooking
1 cup sliced fresh mushrooms
1/3 cup thinly sliced carrots
1/3 cup thinly sliced zucchini
3 tablespoons sliced green onion
3 tablespoons finely chopped parsley
3 tablespoons lemon juice
1 tablespoon vegetable oil
1/4 teaspoon garlic powder
1/2 teaspoon dried basil or 1 1/2 teaspoon fresh
6 lettuce leaves (optional garnish)
6 tomato wedges (optional garnish)

Boil water in small saucepan over high heat. Stir in barley. Cover, reduce heat to low and cook until tender, about 1 hour for long-cooking barley, 10 to 12 minutes for quick-cooking barley. Drain and chill at least 1 hour.

In a medium bowl, combine mushrooms, carrots, zucchini, green onion, parsley and chilled barley. Whisk together lemon juice, oil, garlic powder and basil in a small bowl. Add dressing to salad. Toss lightly to coat ingredients. Chill at least 3 hours or overnight.

Serve on lettuce and garnish with tomato wedges, if desired. Makes 6 servings (4 cups).

Good: Fiber
Excellent: Potassium
Excellent: Vitamin A

Diabetic Exchanges: 1 starch, 1/2 fat

Nutrition Information Per Serving

Energy .... 111 calories
Fat .... 3 g
Saturated fat .... trace
Cholesterol 0
Sodium .... 20 mg
Carbohydrate ...... 19 g
Protein .... 3 g

Bulgur Tomato Salad

Bulgur is the Turkish word for cracked wheat. In the Middle East, it is served as a side dish.

1 cup bulgur (cracked wheat)
2 cups cold water
2 medium tomatoes, washed, stems removed, chopped (about 1/2 cup)
1/2 cup onion, peeled, ends removed, finely chopped
1/2 cup finely snipped parsley
1/4 cup green pepper, washed, stems and seeds removed, finely chopped
2 tablespoons finely snipped mint, plus 8 to 16 leaves for garnish (optional)
2 tablespoons vegetable oil
3 tablespoons lemon juice
1/8 teaspoon pepper
8 to 16 lettuce leaves

Cover bulgur with cold water. Let stand until tender (about 1 hour); drain.

Mix bulgur, tomatoes, onion, parsley, green pepper and mint. Sprinkle with oil, lemon juice and pepper. Stir until evenly coated. Cover and refrigerate at least 2 hours.

Spoon bulgur onto lettuce leaves. Garnish with mint leaves, if desired. Makes 8 servings.

Good: Fiber
Excellent: Potassium
Good: Vitamin A
Good: Vitamin C

Diabetic Exchanges: 1 starch, 1/2 fat

Nutrition Information Per Serving

Energy .... 107 calories
Fat .... 4 g
Saturated fat .... trace
Cholesterol 0
Sodium .... 131 mg
Carbohydrate ...... 15 g
Protein .... 4 g

 *Heart Smart® Cookbook*

Rotini with Broccoli, Peppers and Onions

This salad is a wonderfully easy and colorful combination of shapes. It is also a good choice for an outdoor buffet because it will not easily spoil.

1 package (1 pound) rotini pasta (multicolored)
Boiling water for cooking pasta according to package directions, plus 1/4 cup boiling water for cooking broccoli (if not using microwave), divided
1 package (8 ounces) fresh mushrooms
1 cup broccoli florets
3 cups ice water for cooling broccoli
1 green pepper, seeded and diced
1 sweet red bell pepper, seeded and diced
2 green onions, including green tops, diced, or 1/2 small Bermuda onion, peeled and chopped fine
1/2 cup olive oil
1/4 cup red wine vinegar
3/4 teaspoon salt
1/4 teaspoon pepper
1/4 cup chopped fresh parsley
1 teaspoon dried tarragon or dried oregano or 1 tablespoon of either herb, fresh
16 cherry tomatoes, halved

Cook pasta al dente according to package directions, but eliminate any salt called for in the directions.

While pasta is cooking, clean and slice mushrooms. Place in a nonstick skillet over medium heat and saute until mushrooms are tender and give up their liquid, about 5 minutes. Drain well and set aside.

Place broccoli on a rack in a small saucepan with 1/4 cup boiling water and steam, covered, over medium heat for 4 minutes. Remove from heat and cool in ice water. Do not overcook. Broccoli should remain firm and bright green. Drain broccoli and set aside.

Drain pasta and let cool about 5 minutes. Mix pasta, mushrooms, broccoli, green and red peppers and onions, or onion in a large serving bowl. Set aside in the refrigerator.

In a covered jar, combine oil, vinegar, salt, pepper, parsley, and tarragon or oregano; shake well. Pour dressing over pasta-vegetable mixture and toss well. Chill about 3 hours before serving; add tomatoes just before serving. Makes approximately 11 or 12 cups, or 6 generous servings.

Good: Vitamin C

Diabetic Exchanges: 2 starch, 1 fat

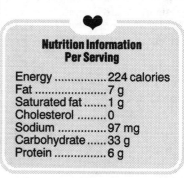

**Nutrition Information
Per Serving**

Energy	224 calories
Fat	7 g
Saturated fat	1 g
Cholesterol	0
Sodium	97 mg
Carbohydrate	33 g
Protein	6 g

Potato Salad

Traditional potato salad provides 260 calories and 15 grams of fat. This recipe contains just 106 calories and 3 grams of fat per serving. You could use nonfat mayonnaise to lower calories and fat further.

1 pound medium round white potatoes
3 cups water
1/4 cup green onions, finely chopped, including green tops
1/4 cup red bell pepper, seeded and finely chopped
1/2 cup celery, chopped
1/3 cup light or reduced-calorie mayonnaise
2 tablespoons plain low-fat yogurt
1 teaspoon prepared mustard
1 teaspoon horseradish
1/8 teaspoon white pepper
Dash of paprika for garnish
1/4 cup carrots, shredded

Combine whole, unpeeled potatoes and 3 cups water in a large saucepan; bring to a boil. Cover, reduce heat and simmer until tender, about 35 minutes. Drain potatoes and allow to cool to the touch. Peel potatoes. Cut into cubes and set aside. Combine green onions, red bell pepper, celery and diced potatoes. Chill for at least 2 hours.

Mix mayonnaise, yogurt, mustard, horseradish and white pepper and pour over chilled vegetable mixture, tossing gently. Sprinkle paprika on top and garnish with shredded carrots. Makes 6 small servings.

Good: Potassium
Good: Vitamin A
Good: Vitamin C

Diabetic Exchanges: 1 starch, 1/2 fat

Nutrition Information Per Serving

Energy .... 106 calories
Fat .... 3 g
Saturated fat .... trace
Cholesterol .... 4 mg
Sodium .... 37 mg
Carbohydrates .... 17 g
Protein .... 2 g

Tabbouleh

Parsley is so often used as a garnish that many people don't realize its nutritional value. One-half cup has only 10 calories yet contains half of both the Vitamin C and Vitamin A recommended daily.

1/2 cup fine bulgur or cracked wheat
2 to 3 green onions, finely chopped
1 cup finely chopped mint (optional), or to taste
3 large tomatoes, chopped or cut in wedges
4 cups parsley, chopped, stems removed (about 3 to 4 bunches, depending on size)
1 large cucumber, peeled, seeded and chopped
2 tablespoons olive oil
Juice of 3 lemons
1/2 teaspoon pepper
6 large lettuce leaves

Wash bulgur. Drain and place in large bowl with enough water to cover, and soak 1 hour. Drain well again. Place wet bulgur in towel and squeeze out excess water.

Meanwhile, in a large bowl, mix green onions, mint, if desired, tomatoes, parsley and cucumber. Add oil, lemon juice and pepper. Stir in bulgur. Refrigerate at least 1 hour. Serve on lettuce leaves. Makes 6 servings.

Excellent: Fiber
Excellent: Potassium
Excellent: Vitamin A
Excellent: Vitamin C

Diabetic Exchanges: 2 vegetable, 1 starch, 1 fat, 1/2 fruit

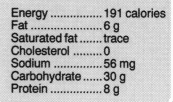

Nutrition Information Per Serving

Energy .... 191 calories
Fat .... 6 g
Saturated fat .... trace
Cholesterol 0
Sodium .... 56 mg
Carbohydrate ...... 30 g
Protein .... 8 g

Caesar Salad

Our Heart Smart® version of this classic will satisfy your taste buds with a fraction of the cholesterol in the traditional recipe.

1 clove garlic
3 anchovies (optional)
1/2 teaspoon Dijon mustard
1/4 cup low-calorie Italian dressing
1/4 cup freshly chopped parsley
2 small or 1 large bunch romaine lettuce
1/4 cup croutons
1 tablespoon grated Parmesan cheese

Crush garlic in a large salad bowl; add the anchovies, if desired, and mash with a fork. With a wire whisk, beat in mustard, Italian dressing and parsley. Add lettuce and toss until leaves are lightly coated with dressing. Add croutons and Parmesan cheese, toss lightly and serve. Makes 4 servings.

Good: Vitamin A
Good: Vitamin C

Diabetic Exchanges: 1 vegetable, 1/2 fat

❤ Nutrition Information Per Serving

Energy .... 40 calories
Fat .... 2 g
Saturated fat .... trace
Cholesterol .... 2 mg
Sodium .... 185 mg
Carbohydrate ...... 4 g
Protein .... 2 g

Spinach Salad

Vinegars made from fruit juice or wine add a great taste to salads even without oils. Try raspberry vinegar on this salad for variety.

1 pound fresh spinach, stems removed,
   washed, drained, torn into bite-size pieces
1/2 pound mushrooms, sliced
6 red onion rings
18 cherry tomatoes, stems removed
3/4 cup alfalfa sprouts
2 teaspoons vegetable oil
1/4 cup red wine vinegar
1/4 teaspoon freshly ground pepper
1 garlic clove, peeled and crushed
1 tablespoon low-sodium soy sauce

In a large salad bowl combine spinach, mushrooms, onion rings, tomatoes and alfalfa sprouts. Set aside. In a tightly covered container combine oil, vinegar, pepper, garlic and soy sauce and shake well. Pour dressing over salad and toss. Serve immediately. Makes 6 servings.

Excellent: Potassium
Excellent: Vitamin A

Diabetic Exchanges:
2 vegetable, 1/2 fat

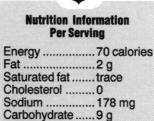

Nutrition Information
Per Serving

Energy .... 70 calories
Fat .... 2 g
Saturated fat .... trace
Cholesterol 0
Sodium .... 178 mg
Carbohydrate ...... 9 g
Protein .... 4 g

 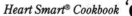

Vegetable Layer Salad

This potluck classic is updated so you can bring it when you're dining with your most Heart Smart® friends.

1 head lettuce, torn into bite-size pieces
1/2 cup chopped red onion
1 cup nonfat plain yogurt
1 tablespoon mayonnaise-type dressing
1/2 cup chopped celery
1/2 cup chopped red or green pepper
1 1/2 cups frozen peas, thawed and drained
1 tablespoon sugar
1 1/2 cups (6 ounces) shredded part-skim
   milk mozzarella cheese or your choice
   of low-fat cheese (6 grams of fat
   or less per ounce)
1/2 cup diced extra-lean ham
1 can (8 ounces or about 2/3 cup) water
   chestnuts, drained and sliced

In a large, clear bowl or 13-by-9-inch baking dish, layer lettuce and onion. Combine yogurt and mayonnaise-type dressing in a small bowl. Spoon 1/2 of the yogurt dressing evenly over top of lettuce and onion. Layer celery, red or green pepper and peas on top. Spread remaining yogurt dressing over top. Sprinkle sugar, cheese and ham over top. Cover and refrigerate at least 8 hours. Top with water chestnuts. Makes 12 servings.

Good: Potassium

Diabetic Exchanges: 2 vegetable,
1/2 medium-fat meat

Nutrition Information
Per Serving

Energy .... 92 calories
Fat .... 3 g
Saturated fat .... 1 g
Cholesterol .... 11 mg
Sodium .... 174 mg
Carbohydrate ...... 9 g
Protein .... 7 g

Winter Salad Platter

The red cabbage adds color and contains more Vitamin C than green cabbage.

1/2 package (10 ounces) frozen baby lima beans
1/4 teaspoon dried thyme leaves
1 cup canned garbanzo beans, rinsed, drained
1 tablespoon sliced pimiento
Pepper to taste
1/2 cup red cabbage, shredded
2 cups spinach, cleaned, stems removed, torn into pieces
2 cups iceberg lettuce, cleaned, torn into pieces
1 small green pepper, seeded, chopped
1/2 small red onion, peeled, finely chopped
1 cup canned diced beets, rinsed, drained
Lemon juice or nonfat dressing, if desired (use is not included in nutritional analysis)

Cook lima beans according to package directions, omitting any added salt or butter, and drain well. Add thyme to the cooked lima beans and set aside.

Combine garbanzos and pimiento in a small mixing bowl; add pepper to taste.

Combine the red cabbage, spinach, iceberg lettuce, green pepper and onion in a large mixing bowl.

Arrange the tossed greens on a large platter. Mound the beets in the center of the platter. Arrange the garbanzo mixture around the beets; arrange the lima beans around the garbanzos. Serve with lemon juice or your favorite nonfat dressing. Makes 6 servings.

Excellent: Potassium
Good: Iron
Good: Vitamin A
Excellent: Vitamin C

Diabetic Exchanges: 1 starch

Nutrition Information Per Serving

Energy .... 82 calories
Fat .... 1 g
Saturated fat .... 1 g
Cholesterol 0
Sodium .... 243 mg
Carbohydrate ...... 15 g
Protein .... 4 g

Meatless Meals

Spicy Tofu with Red Pepper and Pea Pods

Tofu is a good source of vegetable protein and although it is not low-fat, the fat in it is mostly unsaturated.

1 medium onion, quartered, separated
    into pieces
2 cloves garlic, minced
1 teaspoon minced ginger root
1 teaspoon ground cumin
1 teaspoon ground coriander
1/4 teaspoon sugar
1/8 teaspoon ground red pepper
1 sweet red pepper, thinly sliced
3/4 cup green pea pods, stems trimmed
1/4 head cabbage (about 8 ounces),
    chopped
1 1/2 cups mushrooms, quartered
1 teaspoon cornstarch
1/2 cup chicken broth
2 tablespoons vegetable oil
8 ounces firm tofu, drained and cut into
    1/2-inch cubes
1 tablespoon white vinegar
3 cups hot cooked brown rice

In a large bowl, add onion, garlic, ginger root, cumin, coriander, sugar and ground red pepper. In a second medium bowl, add sweet red pepper and pea pods. Set aside. In a third medium bowl, add cabbage and mushrooms. Set aside. In a small bowl, sprinkle cornstarch over chicken broth. Set aside.

In a wok or large skillet, heat the vegetable oil over high heat. Add tofu and stir-fry until lightly browned. Remove with a slotted spoon and set aside. Add the onion mixture, stirring constantly for 30 seconds. Add sweet red pepper-pea pod mixture, stirring for 2 minutes. Add cabbage-mushroom mixture, stirring for 2 minutes. Gradually add cornstarch-broth mixture and stir until slightly thickened. Stir tofu back in, add vinegar, toss and heat through. Serve over rice. Makes 6 servings.

Good: Fiber
Good: Potassium
Good: Iron
Excellent: Vitamin C

Diabetic Exchanges:
1 1/2 starch, 1 medium-fat meat, 1 vegetable

Nutrition Information Per Serving

Energy .... 221 calories
Fat .... 7 g
Saturated fat .... 1 g
Cholesterol 0
Sodium .... 17 mg
Carbohydrate ...... 33 g
Protein .... 7 g

Vegetarian Chili

With just 13 percent of its calories coming from fat, this chili makes a low-fat meal. Serve it with cornmeal muffins.

1 tablespoon olive or vegetable oil
1 cup chopped onion
3 cloves garlic, minced (1 tablespoon)
1 green pepper, seeded and chopped
1 can (28 ounces) low-sodium tomatoes, drained and chopped
1 can (15 ounces) tomato puree
1/2 teaspoon ground coriander
Pinch of ground cloves
Pinch of ground allspice
2 teaspoons oregano
2 tablespoons brown sugar
3 to 4 teaspoons mild chili powder
Dash of Tabasco sauce, or to taste
1 teaspoon ground cumin
2 cups cooked kidney or pinto beans
    (use rinsed and drained
    canned beans, or prepare and cook
    dried beans)
1 cup frozen corn, defrosted

Good: Fiber
Excellent: Potassium
Excellent: Iron
Excellent: Vitamin A
Excellent: Vitamin C

Diabetic Exchanges: 3 starch, 2 vegetable, 1 lean meat

In a large heavy saucepan, heat oil and saute onion, garlic and green pepper until soft, about 7 to 10 minutes. Add tomatoes and tomato puree, coriander, cloves, allspice, oregano, brown sugar, chili powder, Tabasco sauce, cumin and beans. Stirring constantly, bring the chili to a boil. Reduce heat, cover and simmer 15 minutes. Add corn, cover and simmer 15 minutes more. Makes 4 servings.

Nutrition Information Per Serving

Energy .... 295 calories
Fat .... 5 g
Saturated fat .... trace
Cholesterol 0
Sodium .... 508 mg
Carbohydrate ...... 50 g
Protein .... 13 g

Macaroni and Cheese

Use fresh-grated Parmesan cheese; you can use small amounts for the same flavor with less fat.

2 cups uncooked macaroni
2 egg whites, slightly beaten
1 cup skim milk
3 cups 1-percent low-fat cottage cheese,
    pureed in blender or food processor
1 cup (4 ounces) shredded extra-sharp
    Cheddar cheese
1/8 teaspoon salt
1/2 teaspoon white pepper
1 tablespoon chopped fresh parsley
Vegetable cooking spray
2 tablespoons bread crumbs
2 teaspoons grated Parmesan cheese
1/2 teaspoon paprika

Preheat oven to 350 degrees.

Cook macaroni according to package directions, omitting salt and leaving slightly undercooked; drain.

Combine egg whites, skim milk, cottage cheese, Cheddar cheese, salt, white pepper and parsley and blend well. Mix sauce with macaroni and spoon into 1-quart baking dish sprayed with vegetable cooking spray. In a small bowl, combine bread crumbs, Parmesan cheese and paprika. Sprinkle on top of macaroni mixture. Bake in oven for 1 hour. Makes 8 servings.

Good: Potassium

Diabetic Exchanges: 2 lean meat, 2 starch

Nutrition Information Per Serving

Energy .... 281 calories
Fat .... 7 g
Saturated fat .... 4 g
Cholesterol .... 19 mg
Sodium .... 504 mg
Carbohydrate ...... 34 g
Protein .... 21 g

Frittata with Broccoli and Potatoes

A frittata is an Italian omelet. In this recipe, prepared in the oven, the egg whites puff up as nicely as a souffle.

3 medium-large potatoes, peeled, finely diced
1 tablespoon vegetable oil
10 ounces chopped broccoli (fresh, or frozen and defrosted; or you may substitute any vegetable)
1/2 cup coarsely chopped mushrooms
1/4 cup chopped onion, peeled
8 egg whites, slightly beaten
2 whole eggs, slightly beaten
1/4 cup grated Parmesan cheese
1 teaspoon dried parsley flakes
1/4 teaspoon dried basil
1/4 teaspoon oregano
1/4 teaspoon black pepper
1/2 teaspoon paprika

Preheat oven to 350 degrees.

In a large cast-iron or other oven-type broiler-proof skillet, cook potatoes in oil over medium heat, stirring once or twice, for about 10 minutes, or until tender and slightly browned. Add the broccoli (or substitute vegetable), mushrooms and onion, and cook an additional 5 minutes, stirring occasionally.

In a separate bowl, beat egg whites and whole eggs with Parmesan cheese, parsley, basil, oregano and black pepper. Pour egg mixture gently and evenly over mixture in skillet. Place skillet in preheated oven for 10 minutes or until eggs are almost set on top.

(Watch closely.) Then broil 6 inches from heat for 3 minutes or until lightly browned and set. Sprinkle with paprika. Makes 6 servings.

Excellent: Potassium
Good: Vitamin A
Excellent: Vitamin C

Diabetic Exchanges: 2 vegetable, 1 medium-fat meat, 1/2 starch

Nutrition Information Per Serving

Energy .... 163 calories
Fat .... 5 g
Saturated fat .... 2 g
Cholesterol .... 74 mg
Sodium .... 182 mg
Carbohydrate ...... 18 g
Protein .... 11 g

Pizza with Sauce Classico

Sometimes nothing satisfies like a piping hot pizza. You can enjoy this one without worrying.

Dough
1 package active dry yeast
1 cup warm water (105- to -116 degrees)
3 1/2 cups unbleached flour, plus 1/4 cup
    for the work surface
1/4 teaspoon salt
1 tablespoon olive oil

Dissolve yeast in water, stir well and set aside.

FOOD PROCESSOR METHOD: Combine 3 1/2 cups of flour and salt in food processor mixing bowl. Add the yeast mixture and olive oil and process until mixed and dough cleans the sides of the bowl. Remove from food processor and continue as below.

HAND MIXING METHOD: Combine 3 1/2 cups of flour and salt in a 3- to 4-quart mixing bowl. Make a well in the center of the flour and add the water-yeast mixture and olive oil. Stir and mix well until a mass of dough is formed and dough cleans the sides of the bowl. Turn dough onto a work surface floured with the remaining 1/4 cup of flour. Knead for 6-8 minutes. Move some of the flour from the work surface to a mixing bowl and place dough in bowl. Cover with plastic wrap and a kitchen towel. Set the bowl in a warm place for the dough to rise until doubled in bulk, about 90 minutes. Divide the dough in half. Roll each piece into a 13- to 14-inch circle about 1/8 inch thick. Transfer dough to a pizza screen or pan. Roll the edge of the dough to form a thick border all around. Makes 2 pizza crusts. (See baking directions in accompanying recipe next page.)

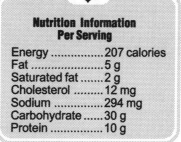

**Nutrition Information
Per Serving**

Energy .... 207 calories
Fat .... 5 g
Saturated fat .... 2 g
Cholesterol .... 12 mg
Sodium .... 294 mg
Carbohydrate ...... 30 g
Protein .... 10 g

Meatless Meals

Sauce Classico

Vegetable cooking spray
1 large onion, chopped or finely diced
3 cloves garlic, minced or pressed
12 ounces fresh mushrooms, thinly sliced
2 large (28 ounces each) cans Italian plum
   tomatoes, drained, then chopped
1/2 cup dry red wine
1 1/2 teaspoons dried oregano
1/2 teaspoon dried basil
1/2 teaspoon fennel seeds, crushed
  or whole
1 green pepper, seeded and thinly sliced
3/4 pound part-skim milk mozzarella
  cheese, grated

Spray the bottom of a large, heavy-bottomed pan with vegetable cooking spray. Slowly cook onion until translucent, about 3 minutes. Add garlic and cook 1 to 2 minutes more. Add mushrooms and cook until they release their liquid, about 6 minutes. Add tomatoes, red wine, oregano, basil and fennel. Cover and simmer over low heat for 30 minutes.

BAKING DIRECTIONS

Preheat oven to 450 degrees.

Spoon 1/2 the sauce onto each unbaked pizza shell. Distribute green pepper evenly on both pizzas. Sprinkle each with mozzarella cheese. Bake the pizzas 20 to 25 minutes until crust is crisp and brown. Makes enough topping for 2 pizzas, or 16 one-slice servings.

Good: Vitamin C
Good: Potassium

Diabetic Exchanges: 2 vegetable,
1 medium-fat meat, 1 starch

Spinach Calzone

A calzone is an Italian pocket made of bread dough and filled with vegetables, cheeses and meats. This one uses low-fat cheeses.

Vegetable cooking spray
2/3 cup skim milk ricotta cheese
1 cup frozen chopped spinach, thawed
    and drained
2/3 cup shredded part-skim milk mozzarella
    cheese
1 tablespoon grated Parmesan cheese
1/2 teaspoon dried basil or 1 teaspoon
    chopped fresh
1/4 teaspoon dried oregano
1/8 teaspoon pepper
1 loaf (1 pound) frozen bread dough, thawed
5 teaspoons all-purpose flour
1 egg white
Quick Tomato Sauce (recipe at right)

Preheat oven to 375 degrees. Spray a baking sheet with vegetable cooking spray and set aside.

In a large bowl, combine ricotta, spinach, mozzarella, Parmesan cheese, basil, oregano and pepper. Divide the bread dough into 5 equal-sized pieces. Using 1 teaspoon of flour for each piece of dough, roll each piece into a 5- to 6-inch circle. Place 1/5 of the spinach filling over half of each circle. Fold the dough over the filling and firmly pinch the edges together and seal. Brush the tops with the egg white. Bake until golden and puffed, 20 to 25 minutes. Serve with Quick Tomato Sauce (recipe follows). Makes 5 servings.

Quick Tomato Sauce
2 pounds ripe plum tomatoes
1 quart boiling water
1 quart ice water
1 small onion, chopped
1 garlic clove, minced
1 tablespoon olive oil
1 bay leaf
1 1/2 teaspoons dried basil or
    1 tablespoon chopped
Pepper to taste

Using tongs, place tomatoes into the boiling water for 20 seconds. Place in ice water. Peel, cut in half, seed and chop tomatoes.

In a medium saucepan, over medium heat, saute onion and garlic in olive oil for about 7 minutes, until soft. Add tomatoes, bay leaf, basil and pepper. Cook 20-30 minutes, stirring occasionally, until the tomatoes are soft and sauce is thickened. Discard bay leaf. Serve or cover and store in the refrigerator up to 2 days. Makes about 1 1/2 cups, 5 servings.

Excellent: Vitamin A
Good: Calcium

Diabetic Exchanges: 2 starch, 2 medium-fat meat, 1 vegetable

Nutrition Information
Quantity/Serving

Energy	336 calories
Fat	8 g
Saturated fat	3 g
Cholesterol	19 mg
Sodium	568 mg
Carbohydrate	47 g
Protein	16 g

Enchilada Bake

This is an unusual cross between lasagna and enchiladas. It can be made ahead and refrigerated.

1/2 cup onion, chopped
1 clove garlic, minced
1 cup fresh mushrooms, sliced
1 green pepper, chopped
Vegetable cooking spray
1/2 cup dry beans, cooked; or 2 cups canned beans, rinsed in hot water for 1 minute
1 1/2 cups stewed tomatoes
1 tablespoon chili powder
8 corn tortillas
4 ounces part-skim milk mozzarella cheese, grated
4 ounces low-fat Cheddar cheese, grated

Preheat oven to 350 degrees.
Saute onion, garlic, mushrooms, and pepper in large skillet sprayed with vegetable cooking spray. Add the beans, tomatoes and chili powder. Simmer gently for about 30 minutes.

Spray a 1 1/2-quart casserole with vegetable cooking spray. Layer the tortillas, cheeses and sauce until all ingredients are used, ending with a layer of sauce. Bake for 15 to 18 minutes. Makes 6 servings.

Good: Fiber
Excellent: Potassium
Good: Iron
Good: Vitamin A
Excellent: Vitamin C
Good: Calcium

Diabetic Exchanges: 2 starch,
1 1/2 medium-fat meat, 1 vegetable

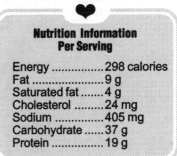

Nutrition Information
Per Serving

Energy .... 298 calories
Fat .... 9 g
Saturated fat .... 4 g
Cholesterol .... 24 mg
Sodium .... 405 mg
Carbohydrate ...... 37 g
Protein .... 19 g

Heart Smart® Cookbook

Vegetable Burrito

Refried beans are usually very high in fat, and the fat is highly saturated. Read labels to find refried beans with no added fat.

1 tablespoon vegetable oil
1/3 cup onion, chopped
1 large carrot, thinly sliced
1 small clove garlic, minced or pressed
1 teaspoon chili powder
1/4 teaspoon ground cumin
1/4 teaspoon dry oregano leaves
1 small zucchini, diced
1/2 cup frozen corn, thawed
6 flour tortillas (7- to 9-inch diameter)
1 can (16 ounces) low-fat vegetarian
    refried beans
3 ounces low-fat Cheddar cheese
6 tablespoons plain nonfat yogurt

Heat oil in a frying pan over medium high heat. When oil is hot, add onion, carrot, garlic, chili powder, cumin and oregano. Cook, stirring, until onion is soft (about 10 minutes). Stir in zucchini and corn. Cook until zucchini is tender-crisp (7 to 8 minutes more).

Wrap tortillas in foil and heat for 15 minutes in a 350-degree oven; or wrap in plastic and microwave on high for 30 to 45 seconds. Spread bean mixture in center of each tortilla. Spoon onion-carrot filling into tortillas. Top with cheese. Wrap ends of tortilla over filling and fold sides to center, or simply roll up. Garnish each tortilla with 1 tablespoon plain nonfat yogurt. Makes 6 servings.

Good: Fiber
Good: Potassium
Good: Iron
Excellent: Vitamin A

Diabetic Exchanges: 2 starch, 1 vegetable, 1 fat

**Nutrition Information
Per Serving**

Energy .... 231 calories
Fat .... 7 g
Saturated fat .... 2 g
Cholesterol .... 9 mg
Sodium .... 480 mg
Carbohydrate ...... 34 g
Protein 12g

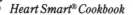

Poultry

Barbecue Chicken

This barbecue sauce contains only 30 milligrams of sodium per ounce. Traditional sauce contains 254 milligrams of sodium per ounce.

4 skinless chicken breast (each 4 ounces,
1 pound total), washed well in several
changes of water
1/2 cup Heart Smart® Barbecue Sauce
(recipe follows)

Prepare charcoal grill or preheat broiler. Baste chicken breasts with HeartSmart® Barbecue Sauce and grill with the cover closed until meat turns opaque, about 3 to 5 minutes on each side. (Cut into the meat to check – chicken breasts with bones may take a little longer than boneless ones.) Baste after turning the chicken. Serve with sauce on the side if desired. Makes 4 servings.

Good: Potassium

Diabetic Exchanges: 3 lean meat, 3/4 fruit

**Nutrition Information
Per Serving**

Energy	188 calories
Fat	4 g
Saturated fat	1 g
Cholesterol	72 mg
Sodium	92 mg
Carbohydrate	10 g
Protein	27 g

Poultry

Heart Smart® Barbecue Sauce

1 tablespoon soft tub margarine
1 can (15 ounces) low-sodium tomato sauce
2 tablespoons Worcestershire sauce
1/4 cup honey
6 tablespoons brown sugar
1/2 teaspoon dry mustard
1/2 teaspoon chili powder
1 teaspoon paprika
1/8 teaspoon black pepper
1/8 teaspoon hot-pepper sauce
1/2 teaspoon garlic powder
1/4 teaspoon nutmeg
1/3 cup onion, grated
1 1/2 tablespoons cornstarch
3 tablespoons cold water
1 tablespoon cider vinegar
1 tablespoon lemon juice
1 teaspoon grated lemon rind

Combine margarine, tomato sauce, Worcestershire sauce, honey, brown sugar, dry mustard, chili powder, paprika, black pepper, hot-pepper sauce, garlic powder, nutmeg and grated onion in a heavy saucepan over medium-high heat and bring to a boil. Reduce heat and simmer, covered, 15 minutes.

In a small bowl, blend cornstarch with cold water until lumps have disappeared. Add to sauce mixture, stirring with wire whisk until thickened. Add cider vinegar, lemon juice and lemon rind. Simmer, stirring constantly, 5 minutes longer.

Makes 2 1/2 cups, enough for basting 5 pounds of chicken breasts. A serving is 2 tablespoons.

Diabetic Exchanges: 3/4 fruit

Nutrition Information Per Serving

Energy .... 48 calories
Fat .... trace
Saturated fat .... trace
Cholesterol 0
Sodium .... 30 mg
Carbohydrate ...... 10 g
Protein .... trace

Chicken and Broccoli with Wild Rice

Wild rice actually is a seed of tall, slender grass that grows from the water looking much like rice from a paddy. It has a nutty flavor and is great in salads, stuffing and side dishes.

1 package (6 ounces) long-grain and wild rice
2 tablespoons cornstarch
1 cup skim milk
3/4 cup water
1/2 teaspoon chicken flavored bouillon granules
Vegetable cooking spray
1/2 cup fresh mushrooms, cleaned, sliced
1/3 cup green onions, ends removed, sliced
2 packages (10 ounces each) frozen broccoli in spears or chopped, defrosted, drained
4 cups cooked chicken breasts, coarsely chopped and skinless
1/4 cup bread crumbs
1/4 cup plus 2 tablespoons Parmesan cheese
2 tablespoons parsley

Cook rice according to package directions, omitting fat; set aside. This will take about 25 minutes.

Preheat oven to 350 degrees.

Mix cornstarch with skim milk, stirring until smooth in small saucepan. Cook over medium heat, stirring constantly until thickened and bubbly. Add water and bouillon granules, stirring until dissolved.

Coat a small skillet with vegetable cooking spray; place over medium heat until hot. Add mushrooms and onions and saute 2 to 3 minutes or until tender. Stir rice, mushrooms and onions into cornstarch-milk mixture in saucepan. Coat a 9- by 13-inch baking dish lightly with cooking spray. Arrange broccoli spears or chopped broccoli on bottom. Top with chicken and pour rice-mushroom-onion sauce over chicken. Sprinkle with bread crumbs, Parmesan cheese and parsley. Bake uncovered for 30 minutes or until top is golden brown. Makes 8 servings.

Excellent: Potassium
Good: Vitamin A
Excellent: Vitamin C

Diabetic Exchanges: 2 lean meat, 2 vegetable, 1 1/2 starch

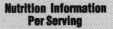

Nutrition Information Per Serving

Energy	272 calories
Fat	7 g
Saturated fat	2 g
Cholesterol	52 mg
Sodium	183 mg
Carbohydrate	29 g
Protein	24 g

Chicken Couscous

Couscous is a fine-grain pasta made from flour and water, usually available in specialty aisles of the grocery store.

1 tablespoon vegetable oil
1 large onion, cut in half, thinly sliced
2 cloves garlic, peeled and minced
2 red or green bell peppers, seeded and sliced in julienne strips
1/2 pound small, skinless, boned chicken breasts, washed well and patted dry
1 tomato, peeled and diced
2 small sweet potatoes, peeled and cubed
1 medium carrot, cut in 1/2-inch slices
1 stalk celery, cut in 1/2-inch slices
1/2 teaspoon saffron threads (optional)
1 teaspoon ground coriander
1/2 teaspoon ground cinnamon
2 cups water
1 cup cooked garbanzo beans; or 1 can (10-ounces), rinsed and drained
1 medium zucchini, cut in 1/2-inch slices
2 cups hot, cooked couscous (prepared according to package directions, but omitting salt, butter or margarine)

In a Dutch oven, heat oil and saute onion and garlic over medium heat for 3 minutes. Add bell peppers and cook 1 to 2 minutes. Add chicken, tomato, sweet potatoes, carrot, celery, saffron, if desired, coriander, cinnamon and water. Bring to a boil, cover, reduce heat and simmer 30 minutes. Add garbanzo beans and zucchini. Cover and cook another 10 minutes.

To serve, spread prepared couscous around edge of a deep serving platter and arrange chicken-vegetable mixture in center. Or place couscous in the bottom of each serving bowl and top with chicken mixture. Pass Harissa (Hot Pepper Sauce, see recipe below). Makes 4 servings, with generous helpings of vegetables.

Good: Fiber
Excellent: Potassium
Good: Iron
Excellent: Vitamin A
Excellent: Vitamin C

Diabetic Exchanges: 3 starch, 2 lean meat, 2 vegetable

Harissa (Hot Pepper Sauce)

2 1/2 teaspoons ground cayenne pepper
1 tablespoon chili powder
1 to 2 tablespoons water

In a small bowl mix cayenne pepper and chili powder. Add enough water to make a sauce of the desired consistency. Makes enough for 4 servings of Chicken Couscous.

**Nutrition Information
Per Serving**

Energy .... 388 calories
Fat 7g
Saturated fat .... 1 g
Cholesterol .... 36 mg
Sodium .... 348 mg
Carbohydrate ...... 59 g
Protein .... 20 g

Heart Smart® Cookbook

Chicken Piccante with Artichokes

Artichokes canned in water are low in fat and calories. One-half cup of artichoke hearts contains only 37 calories and a trace of fat. Those canned in oil are a different story altogether.

2 cups chicken broth
6 boneless, skinless breasts of chicken
   (4 ounces each), washed and patted dry
1 whole lemon, cut into 8 wedges
1/4 cup green onions, washed, ends
   removed, chopped
30 baby mushroom caps, cleaned well
6 artichoke hearts, canned in natural water,
   drained
3 cloves garlic, peeled and minced
Pinch of white pepper
2 tablespoons cornstarch
1/2 cup dry white wine
3 cups rice cooked

Preheat oven to 350 degrees.
  Bring chicken broth to a boil in a large skillet, reduce heat and simmer. Place chicken breasts in broth and poach, covered, for 10 minutes. Remove chicken from broth and set aside in a 9-by-13-inch baking dish. Squeeze lemon into broth and place lemon wedges in the broth. Add onions, mushrooms, artichokes, garlic and white pepper; simmer 5 minutes.
   In a small bowl, mix cornstarch in wine, stirring until it is a smooth liquid; add to broth a little at a time until broth is thick and smooth. Remove lemon wedges and discard.

Pour sauce and vegetable mixture over chicken breasts and heat in oven for 15 minutes. Serve over rice. Makes 6 servings

  Excellent: Potassium
Good: Vitamin C

  Diabetic Exchanges: 3 lean meat, 1 vegetable, 1 starch

Nutrition Information Per Serving

Energy .... 211 calories
Fat .... 4 g
Saturated fat .... 1 g
Cholesterol .... 66 mg
Sodium .... 396 mg
Carbohydrate ...... 14 g
Protein .... 30 g

Poultry

Chicken Veronique

Green grapes give this chicken dish a unique flavor, but you can use other fruits, too.

4 skinless, boned chicken breasts
　　(each 4 ounces after boning), evenly
　　flattened to 1/4-inch to 1/2-inch thickness
1/2 teaspoon white pepper
1 teaspoon tarragon, or less, to taste
Vegetable cooking spray
1/2 cup skim milk
1/2 cup low-sodium chicken broth, defatted
1 large garlic clove, peeled and slit halfway
　　through
1 tablespoon cornstarch diluted in
　　2 tablespoons skim milk
1/2 cup seedless green grapes, washed

Wash chicken thoroughly. Season flattened chicken breasts with pepper and tarragon. Coat a nonstick skillet with vegetable cooking spray and set it over medium heat for about 1 minute. Saute chicken in heated skillet about 6 minutes on each side. Add milk, broth and garlic; simmer uncovered about 15 minutes. Add cornstarch mixture to sauce; heat and stir until shiny, about 4 to 5 minutes. Just before serving, stir in green grapes. Remove garlic clove. Serve chicken with grapes and sauce ladled on each breast. Makes 4 servings.

　Good: Potassium

　Diabetic Exchanges: 4 lean meat,
1/2 fruit

Nutrition Information Per Serving

Energy	174 calories
Fat	3 g
Saturated fat	1 g
Cholesterol	73 mg
Sodium	86 mg
Carbohydrate	6 g
Protein	28 g

Heart Smart® Cookbook

Lemon Chicken

The use of pears in this dish gives the chicken a distinctive flavor.

4 skinless, boned chicken breasts
   (4 ounces each)
1/4 cup all-purpose flour
1/2 teaspoon ground ginger
1/4 teaspoon pepper
1 tablespoon vegetable oil
1/2 cup water
1 teaspoon grated lemon rind
3 tablespoons lemon juice
1 teaspoon cornstarch
2 teaspoons water
1 pear, unpeeled, cored and finely chopped
4 teaspoons slivered almonds
1 to 2 tablespoons minced fresh parsley

Place chicken between 2 sheets of wax paper; flatten to 1/4 inch using a meat mallet or rolling pin. Combine flour, ginger and pepper; stir well. Dredge chicken in flour mixture. Add oil to large nonstick skillet and place over medium-high heat until hot. Add chicken; cook 3 minutes on each side or until browned. Remove from skillet. Transfer chicken to a serving platter and keep warm. Wipe pan drippings from skillet with a paper towel. Add 1/2 cup water, lemon rind and lemon juice to skillet; stir well. Dissolve cornstarch in 2 teaspoons water; add to skillet, stirring well. Stir in pear; cook over medium-high heat, stirring constantly, until slightly thickened. Remove from heat and spoon over chicken. Sprinkle with almonds and parsley. Serve immediately. Makes 4 servings.

Good: Potassium

Diabetic Exchanges: 3 lean meat, 1/2 starch, 1/2 fruit

Nutrition Information Per Serving

Energy	243 calories
Fat	8 g
Saturated fat	2 g
Cholesterol	72 mg
Sodium	64 mg
Carbohydrate	15 g
Protein	29 g

Heart Smart® Roast Turkey

Here's how to turn your holiday into a Heart Smart® holiday. White turkey meat contains 3.6 grams of fat per 4-ounce serving; dark meat contains 8 grams of fat per 4-ounce serving. Gravy that is made from defatted broth is not high in fat. If you do not have time to chill fat, use a skimmer. If you use the corn bread dressing, the corn bread can be prepared one day in advance. After it cools, wrap in aluminum foil and store in refrigerator for use as dressing.

1/4 cup white wine
3/4 cup defatted chicken broth
1 turkey (10- to 12-pound), washed
   and patted dry
Bread stuffing

Preheat oven to 325 degrees.
In a small bowl, combine wine and broth. Fill neck and body cavity of turkey with your favorite low-fat bread stuffing. Truss the turkey. Place turkey, breast side up, on a rack in a roasting pan. Insert a meat thermometer into the thickest part of the thigh meat without touching bone. Brush turkey with a small amount of wine mixture. Roast in oven, basting often, for 4 to 4 1/2 hours, or until meat thermometer reaches 185 degrees. Serve with Turkey Gravy (recipe at right). Makes 12 four-ounce servings.

Good: Potassium

Diabetic Exchanges:
4 lean meat

Nutrition Information Per Serving

Energy .... 193 calories
Fat .... 6 g
Saturated fat .... 2 g
Cholesterol .... 87 mg
Sodium .... 80 mg
Carbohydrate 0
Protein .... 33 g

Turkey Gravy

1 clove garlic, peeled and split (optional)
2 tablespoons vegetable oil
1 medium onion, peeled and chopped
   finely
1 carrot, grated, chopped or shredded
1 stalk celery with leaves, chopped finely
1 cup dry white wine
1 can (14 1/2 ounces) low-sodium
   chicken broth
Water as needed
1 bay leaf
1/2 teaspoon ground thyme
1/4 teaspoon ground sage
Defatted juice from cooked turkey
   (approximately 1/3 cup)
3 tablespoons cornstarch or all-purpose
   flour blended with 1/4 cup sherry or
   red wine
Fresh ground pepper to taste

If you are roasting a turkey, you might want to make the stock for the gravy before you prepare the turkey. Here's how to make the stock: Rub a 3-quart saucepan with the split clove of garlic, if desired, and discard garlic. Heat oil in saucepan over medium heat and stir in onion, carrot and celery.

Heart Smart® Cookbook

**Nutrition Information
Per Serving**

Energy .... 36 calories
Fat .... 1 g
Saturated fat ...... trace
Cholesterol .... trace
Sodium .... 9 mg
Carbohydrate ...... 7 g
Protein .... 1 g

Cover, reduce heat and cook slowly 5 to 8 minutes or until tender. Uncover, increase heat and saute lightly for about 5 minutes, stirring often. Add wine, broth and water as needed to cover ingredients by 1 inch. Add bay leaf, thyme and sage and simmer, partially covered, 30 to 40 minutes. Remove from heat. If you prefer a smooth gravy, strain stock, pushing down on contents to extract all liquid. There should be 2 to 3 cups stock. Cover and refrigerate until turkey is done, reserving the saucepan for later when you finish the gravy.

To finish the gravy, defat the juice from the turkey using a gravy separator, suction bulb or paper towels. Discard fat. Combine defatted juice (you should have at least 1/3 cup if you cooked a 10- to 12-pound turkey) and the 2 to 3 cups of prepared stock in the saucepan. Bring to a boil and reduce heat slightly. Meanwhile, in a separate bowl, mix together the cornstarch or flour with the sherry or red wine until smooth. Gradually

whisk into saucepan. Slowly bring gravy to a boil again, stirring constantly. Reduce heat to low and simmer, stirring constantly, about 5 minutes. Remove bay leaf. Add pepper to taste and serve hot with turkey. Makes about 2 cups gravy. A serving is 1/4 cup.

Diabetic Exchanges: 1/2 starch

Apple Raisin Stuffing

1/2 cup raisins
1/3 cup heated rum (or 1/2 teaspoon rum extract mixed with 1/3 cup boiling water)
1 loaf (1 1/2 pounds) whole wheat, pumpernickel or bran bread, or any combination, dried (see directions)
1 1/2 cups (12-ounce can) low-sodium chicken broth, chilled and defatted (see directions)
Fresh ground pepper, to taste
1 teaspoon thyme
1 1/2 teaspoons sage
1/2 teaspoon savory
1/4 cup chopped parsley
3 medium apples, unpeeled, seeded, chopped
2 large onions, peeled, ends removed, chopped (about 2 cups)
4 stalks celery, diced (about 1 1/2 cups)
3 tablespoons soft tub margarine, melted
3 egg whites, lightly beaten

Place raisins in a small bowl and cover with heated rum or rum extract and boiling water mixture; marinate at least 1 hour to allow raisins to absorb the liquid. If bread needs to be dried, spread slices on a rack for a half day or

place in a 300-degree oven until dried, about 15 minutes. Cut bread into cubes or break into crumb size with spoon or food processor. Chill low-sodium chicken broth overnight in the refrigerator or 1 hour in the freezer to enable you to skim off fat. Set aside. Combine bread cubes or crumbs with pepper, thyme, sage, savory and parsley; mix well. Add apples, onions, celery and margarine and mix well. Add defatted broth and beaten egg whites; mix well. Stir in plumped raisins, draining off the unabsorbed liquid if desired.

This recipe makes enough to stuff a 10- to 14-pound turkey. Spoon stuffing into a cleaned turkey. Don't pack too tightly; allow some space for expansion upon heating. After cooking, remove stuffing to a separate bowl before carving the turkey. Keep stuffing warm in a 200-degree oven until ready to serve. Makes about 12 servings.

COOKS' NOTE: As an alternative, if you aren't cooking a whole turkey, spray a 5-quart ovenproof baking dish with vegetable cooking spray. Bake the stuffing, alone or topped with turkey cut into 1/4-inch strips, in a pre-heated, 350-degree oven 20 minutes uncovered and 35-40 minutes more covered.

Good: Fiber
Good: Potassium

Diabetic Exchanges: 2 starch, 1 fruit, 1 fat

Nutrition Information Per /Serving

Energy	247 calories
Fat	5 g
Saturated fat	trace
Cholesterol	0
Sodium	316 mg
Carbohydrate	42 g
Protein	7 g

Corn Bread Dressing

Corn Bread for Dressing, coarsely crumbled (about 12 cups, recipe follows)
4 medium onions, peeled, finely chopped
3 celery ribs, washed, finely chopped (including tender leaves)
1/2 cup chicken broth, fat removed
1 3/4 teaspoons thyme
1 teaspoon sage
1/2 teaspoon baking powder
1/4 cup chopped fresh parsley, or 2 tablespoons dried
1/2 teaspoon salt
Dash cayenne pepper
Freshly ground black pepper to taste
3 egg whites, lightly beaten

Crumble corn bread in a large bowl. In a skillet, combine the onions and celery. Add chicken broth. Bring to a boil over high heat

Nutrition Information Per Serving

Energy	186 calories
Fat	6 g
Saturated fat	1 g
Cholesterol	trace
Sodium	237 mg
Carbohydrate	27 g
Protein	6 g

about 3 minutes until vegetables are tender but still crisp. Drain and add vegetables to the corn bread. Sprinkle thyme, sage, baking powder, parsley, salt, cayenne and black pepper over the dressing. Add the egg whites and mix the dressing to moisten evenly without packing the dressing. A 10- to 12-pound turkey will hold 7 to 9 cups of corn bread dressing in the large cavity. Stuff dressing loosely. Place extra stuffing in a covered baking dish and bake during last 30 minutes while turkey is roasting and resting. Makes 14 1 cup servings.

Diabetic Exchanges: 1 1/2 starch, 1 vegetable, 1 fat

Corn Bread for Dressing

Vegetable cooking spray
6 egg whites
1 1/2 cups skim milk
1 1/2 cups cornmeal (not stone-ground)
1 1/2 cups all-purpose flour (not self-rising)
1/3 cup vegetable oil
1 tablespoon baking powder
1/2 teaspoon salt
1 1/2 teaspoons sugar

Preheat oven to 450 degrees. Lightly spray two 9-inch cake pans with vegetable cooking spray.
In a large mixing bowl, combine the egg whites and milk. Whisk lightly to blend. In

another bowl, sift together the cornmeal and flour. Add the egg whites and milk; blend well. Add the vegetable oil, baking powder, salt and sugar. Mix well. Pour the batter into the prepared pans. Bake for 20 minutes or until a knife inserted in the center comes out clean. Invert the corn bread onto a rack to cool. Cool completely, at least 20 minutes, before making dressing.

 Heart Smart® Cookbook

Turkey Burgers

Your best bet when purchasing ground turkey is to look for turkey breast, because it's the leanest choice.

1 pound ground turkey
1/2 cup dried bread crumbs, preferably
    whole wheat
3 tablespoons Spanish onion, peeled,
    ends removed, finely chopped
2 tablespoons catsup
1 tablespoon lemon juice
1 teaspoon Worcestershire sauce
1 teaspoon low-sodium soy sauce
1/2 teaspoon paprika
1/4 teaspoon hot pepper sauce
Freshly ground black pepper, to taste
1/4 cup celery, washed, ends removed,
    finely chopped
6 whole wheat burger buns

Preheat grill or broiler.
Combine ground turkey, bread crumbs, onion, catsup, lemon juice, Worcestershire sauce, soy sauce, paprika, hot pepper sauce, black pepper and celery in a large bowl. Mix and shape into 6 patties. Broil or grill. Cook 5 minutes on each side or until reaching desired doneness. Serve on whole wheat buns. Makes 6 servings.

Good: Potassium

Diabetic Exchanges: 3 lean meat, 2 starch

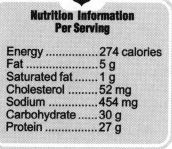

**Nutrition Information
Per Serving**

Energy ....274 calories
Fat ....5 g
Saturated fat ....1 g
Cholesterol ....52 mg
Sodium ....454 mg
Carbohydrate ......30 g
Protein ....27 g

Turkey Tacos

To speed things up, you can also wrap the tortillas in paper towels, place them in the microwave and heat for 20 to 30 seconds on high power.

2 teaspoons vegetable oil
1 hot red chili pepper, minced (or to taste)
1 medium onion, peeled, ends removed, diced
2 garlic cloves, peeled and minced
1 pound cooked turkey, shredded
1/2 teaspoon ground cumin
1/2 teaspoon dried oregano
1/4 teaspoon dried cilantro or
   3/4 teaspoon fresh, minced
3 tablespoons low-sodium tomato paste
3/4 cup water
2 tablespoons lime juice
8 six-inch flour tortillas
4 ounces part-skim milk mozzarella cheese, shredded
1 1/2 cups lettuce, shredded
1 large tomato, chopped

Good: Vitamin A
Good: Vitamin C
Good: Calcium

Diabetic Exchanges: 3 lean meat, 1 starch

In a nonstick skillet heat oil and saute hot chili pepper, onion and garlic until tender. Add turkey to pan. Season with cumin, oregano and cilantro; mix well. Add tomato paste, water and lime juice. Mix well. Bring mixture to a boil. Cover and simmer 5 minutes or until liquid is absorbed.

Warm tortillas in a nonstick or well-seasoned, unoiled skillet for about 15 seconds on each side until warm. Top each tortilla with equal amounts of turkey mixture, cheese, lettuce and tomato. Fold each tortilla in half to form tacos. Makes 8 one-taco servings.

**Nutrition Information
Per Serving**

Energy .... 246 calories
Fat .... 7 g
Saturated fat .... 2 g
Cholesterol .... 47 mg
Sodium .... 110 mg
Carbohydrate ...... 21 g
Protein .... 23 g

Turkey Vegetable Stir-Fry

This is a great way to use leftover turkey meat from the holidays; your family won't even recognize it.

1 tablespoon cornstarch
1/2 teaspoon grated fresh ginger
1 can (10 1/2 ounces) low-sodium chicken broth, defatted
2 tablespoons reduced-sodium soy sauce
1 tablespoon dry sherry
1/2 teaspoon red chili powder, or 1/8 teaspoon cayenne pepper
2 cups cooked white meat turkey, cubed
1 tablespoon vegetable oil
2 cups sliced fresh mushrooms
1 package (6 ounces) frozen snow peas or pea pods, defrosted; or fresh pea pods
1 red bell pepper, seeded and sliced into julienne strips
4 green onions, with green tops, chopped
2 cups cooked brown or white rice

Good: Fiber
Excellent: Potassium
Good: Iron
Excellent: Vitamin C

Diabetic Exchanges: 2 lean meat, 1 1/2 starch, 1 vegetable

In a medium bowl, mix cornstarch, ginger, chicken broth, soy sauce, sherry and chili powder or cayenne pepper. Marinate the turkey in that mixture at least 10 minutes but no more than 2 hours.

In a wok or heavy skillet, heat the oil. Stir-fry mushrooms, snow peas or pea pods, and bell pepper. When vegetables are still firm, add the turkey mixture and cook until heated through, stirring often. Add green onions and cook 1 minute. Serve over hot rice. Makes 4 servings.

Nutrition Information Per Serving

Energy	314 calories
Fat	7 g
Saturated fat	1 g
Cholesterol	49 mg
Sodium	426 mg
Carbohydrate	34 g
Protein	27 g

Heart Smart® Cookbook

Turkey Chili

As we have in this recipe, you can replace red meat in some recipes with turkey. In this chili, we guarantee no one will even know unless you tell them.

1 pound ground turkey
2 tablespoons vegetable oil
3 cloves garlic, peeled, minced
1 1/2 cups onion, peeled, minced
1 1/2 teaspoons dried oregano
1/2 teaspoon dried basil
2 tablespoons chili powder
1/2 teaspoon ground cumin
1/4 teaspoon ground red pepper
2 cups zucchini, washed, unpeeled,
    finely chopped
1 cup carrots, peeled, ends removed,
    finely chopped
1/2 cup green pepper, washed,
    stemmed, seeded, finely chopped
1 can (15 ounces) garbanzo beans,
    drained, rinsed
1 can (14 1/2 ounces) kidney beans,
    drained, rinsed
5 1/2 cups stewed tomatoes
    (44 ounces) drained
4 cups water

Good: Fiber
Excellent: Potassium
Good: Iron
Excellent: Vitamin A
Good: Vitamin C

Diabetic Exchanges: 1 lean meat, 1 starch, 1 vegetable

In a large soup pot, brown ground turkey meat over medium heat. Add oil and saute garlic and onion until tender. Season with oregano, basil, chili powder, cumin and red pepper; mix well. Add zucchini, carrots and green pepper and cook 2 minutes. Add garbanzo and kidney beans, stewed tomatoes and water to mix. Bring to a boil. Reduce heat and simmer 45 minutes. Makes fourteen 1-cup servings.

Nutrition Information Per Serving

Energy .... 154 calories
Fat .... 4 g
Saturated fat .... trace
Cholesterol .... 17 mg
Sodium .... 474 mg
Carbohydrate ...... 19 g
Protein .... 12 g

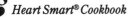

Meats

Beef and Macaroni Casserole

This recipe makes enough that you can divide it and freeze some for quick hearty meals on busy days.

4 pounds lean ground beef
1 bottle (10 ounces) chili sauce
1 package (1.34 ounces) dry onion soup mix
1 package (3/4 ounce) brown gravy mix
4 cans (19 ounces each) stewed tomatoes
4 teaspoons oregano
4 tablespoons chili powder
8 cups or 5 cans (12 ounces each) whole-kernel corn, drained
4 cups (1 pound) elbow macaroni, cooked according to package directions, omitting salt

In a large pot, brown ground beef, stirring and breaking up meat. Drain well. Add chili sauce, onion soup mix, brown gravy mix, stewed tomatoes, oregano, chili powder and corn. Mix well. Add cooked macaroni to beef mixture; stir and cook until heated through, about 10 minutes. (To store in freezer, allow to cool, and freeze in 4 equal portions. Defrost and reheat when ready to use.) Makes 16 servings.

Good: Fiber
Excellent: Potassium
Good: Iron
Good: Vitamin A
Good: Vitamin C

Diabetic Exchanges: 3 starch, 3 lean meat, 2 vegetable, 1/2 fat

Nutrition Information Per Serving

Energy .... 453 calories
Fat .... 13 g
Saturated fat .... 5 g
Cholesterol .... 72 mg
Sodium .... 896 mg
Carbohydrate ...... 58 g
Protein .... 30 g

 Heart Smart® Cookbook

155

Beef Burgundy

This dish is named for the red wine traditionally used in it, but you can substitute nonalcoholic wine.

1 pound boneless top round steak
1 large onion
Vegetable cooking spray
1 tablespoon all-purpose flour
2 cloves garlic, peeled and minced
2 cups dry red wine, preferably a
    Burgundy
1 cup beef broth, defatted
1 teaspoon thyme, crushed
1 small bay leaf
1 small tomato, chopped fine
1 medium carrot, scraped and thinly
    sliced crosswise
1/4 pound fresh mushrooms, thinly sliced
Black pepper to taste

Preheat oven to 350 degrees.

Trim excess fat from steak; cut into cubes and set aside.

Cut onion in half lengthwise (top to bottom, to produce strips, not rings), then put each half flat side down and slice thinly, leaving the onion cut in thin strips. Set aside.

Coat a large nonstick skillet with vegetable cooking spray; place over medium heat. Add meat cubes and cook until browned, about 8 minutes. Add flour and cook until flour is golden brown, stirring often, about 4 minutes more. Remove meat to a 2-quart casserole. Saute onion and garlic in skillet about 1 minute. Add wine, beef broth, thyme, bay leaf and tomato. Bring to a boil, then pour over steak in the casserole.

Bake covered 90 minutes. Remove from oven. Add carrot and mushroom slices, cover and bake an additional 30 minutes. Discard bay leaf and season with pepper. Makes 4 servings.

Excellent: Potassium
Excellent: Iron
Excellent: Vitamin A

Diabetic Exchanges: 3 lean meat, 2 vegetable

Nutrition Information Per Serving

Energy	236 calories
Fat	9 g
Saturated fat	4 g
Cholesterol	76 mg
Sodium	85 mg
Carbohydrate	9 g
Protein	28 g

Beef Stroganoff

Low-fat yogurt pinch-hits for sour cream in this recipe. Sour cream contains 416 calories per cup compared with low-fat yogurt at 125 to 150 calories per cup.

1 clove garlic, peeled, ends removed,
  finely chopped
1 small onion, peeled, ends
  removed, chopped
1 tablespoon vegetable oil
1 pound lean beef tenderloin,
  sliced in thin strips
8 ounces fresh mushrooms, cleaned, sliced
1 1/2 cups beef broth, divided
1 tablespoon Worcestershire sauce
1 teaspoon paprika
3 tablespoons all-purpose flour
1 cup low-fat plain yogurt
6 cups egg-free noodles, cooked
  according to package directions

In a large skillet, lightly brown garlic and onion in oil. Add beef strips and brown quickly over medium high heat. Add mushrooms. Heat until mushrooms are light brown.

In a medium bowl stir together 1 cup of broth, Worcestershire sauce and paprika. Add to skillet. Heat to boiling. Reduce heat, cover and simmer until beef is tender, about 10 minutes.

In a container with a tight lid, shake remaining 1/2 cup of broth and flour. Gradually stir broth-flour mixture into beef mixture. Heat to boiling, stirring constantly. Boil and stir 1 minute. Reduce heat. Stir in

yogurt. Heat thoroughly. Serve over hot cooked noodles. Makes 6 servings.

Good: Iron

Diabetic Exchanges: 2 1/2 lean meat, 2 1/2 starch, 1 vegetable

Nutrition Information Per Serving

Energy	367 calories
Fat	10 g
Saturated fat	3 g
Cholesterol	53 mg
Sodium	170 mg
Carbohydrate	46 g
Protein	27 g

Glazed Pork Loin Roast

Commercial catsup and chili sauce are high in sodium. If your recipe calls for more than 1 or 2 tablespoons, use the low-sodium variety.

1 cup reduced-sodium soy sauce
1/2 cup plus 2 tablespoons water, divided
1/4 cup plus 2 tablespoons brown sugar, divided
1/2 tablespoon dark brown molasses
1 1/2 pounds boneless pork loin, trimmed of fat
3/4 tablespoon dry mustard
1/2 cup catsup (optional, low-sodium catsup)
1/2 cup prepared chili sauce, low-sodium

In a medium saucepan, combine soy sauce, 1/2 cup water, 1/4 cup brown sugar and molasses; bring to a boil. Remove from heat and let cool. Place pork loin in large glass bowl and pour cooled marinade over meat. Cover and marinate in refrigerator for 6 hours, turning occasionally. The pork will absorb the dark color; turning will keep the color even.

Preheat oven to 325 degrees.

Remove pork from marinade and place in baking pan. Cover tightly with foil. Bake about 1 hour or until tender.

In a medium saucepan mix dry mustard, remaining 2 tablespoons water and remaining 2 tablespoons brown sugar. Stir until lump free. Add catsup and chili sauce and bring mixture to a boil. Remove from heat and set aside. When pork loin is tender, remove from oven and pour sauce over. Return to oven for 30 minutes or until lightly glazed. Makes 6 servings.

Excellent: Potassium

Diabetic Exchanges: not appropriate for diabetics

Nutrition Information Per Serving

Energy	258 calories
Fat	4 g
Saturated fat	1 g
Cholesterol	79 mg
Sodium	660 mg
Carbohydrate	26 g
Protein	29 g

Heart Smart® Cookbook

Grilled Marinated Flank Steak

Flank steak usually is a lean cut of meat and, therefore, needs the tenderizing effect of a marinade. This marinade adds great taste and can be used with other cuts of lean meat.

1 cup dry red wine
2 teaspoons sherry
3 cloves garlic, crushed
Dash of sesame hot oil or sesame oil, available at specialty stores
Dash of freshly ground black pepper
Dash of freshly ground ginger
1/8 teaspoon oregano, crushed
1/8 teaspoon marjoram, crumbled
1 1/2 pounds thick flank steak or London Broil

Mix together the wine, sherry, garlic, oil and seasonings. Score the steak (make very thin slashes, about 1 inch apart, diagonally across the grain). Place the steak in a long glass baking dish and pour marinade over the meat. Cover and chill at least 12 to 18 hours, turning at least once.

Preheat gas grill or prepare charcoal.

Grill meat 5 minutes on each side. To serve, cut thin slices diagonally across the grain. Makes eight 3-ounce servings.

Good: Potassium
Excellent: Iron

Diabetic Exchanges: 3 lean meat, 1/2 starch

Nutrition Information Per Serving

Energy	213 calories
Fat	9 g
Saturated fat	3 g
Cholesterol	76 mg
Sodium	60 mg
Carbohydrate	1 g
Protein	26 g

Honey and Mustard Pork Tenderloin

Pork needn't be banned from a Heart Smart® diet, but be sure to use lean cuts of pork, as we do here.

1 pound pork tenderloin (2 tenderloins)
1/8 teaspoon pepper
Vegetable cooking spray
1 teaspoon olive oil
1/4 cup cider vinegar
1 tablespoon honey
1 teaspoon Dijon mustard

Trim fat from tenderloins; sprinkle with pepper. Coat large nonstick skillet with vegetable cooking spray. Add oil and set on medium-high heat until hot. Add tenderloins and brown for about 10 minutes.

Meanwhile, preheat oven to 400 degrees. Place tenderloins on a rack coated with cooking spray; place rack in a shallow roasting pan. Mix together vinegar, honey and mustard in a small bowl and brush over tenderloins.

Insert meat thermometer into thickest part of the tenderloin. Bake 30 to 35 minutes or until meat thermometer reaches 160 degrees. Baste often with vinegar mixture. Makes 4 servings.

Excellent: Potassium

Diabetic Exchanges: 4 lean meat, 1/2 fruit

Nutrition Information Per Serving

Energy	218 calories
Fat	7 g
Saturated fat	2 g
Cholesterol	105 mg
Sodium	93 mg
Carbohydrate	5 g
Protein	32 g

Peppercorn Pork Tenderloin with Cider Gravy

Making effective use of spices means you don't need salt to have flavor. Here we use cracked whole peppercorns and mustard seed.

Vegetable cooking spray
1 1/2 pounds pork tenderloin
1/4 cup water
1 tablespoon soft tub margarine
2 tablespoons all-purpose flour
2 tablespoons Dijon mustard
1 tablespoon dry mustard
1 tablespoon cracked black peppercorns
1 tablespoon cracked white peppercorns
1 tablespoon whole mustard seeds
2 teaspoons brown sugar
2 teaspoons dried thyme, crumbled

Gravy
2 tablespoons pork drippings
1 1/2 cups apple cider
2 tablespoons all-purpose flour
3/4 cup chicken broth
   (low sodium), defatted
1 tablespoon cider vinegar
1 teaspoon Dijon mustard
Pepper to taste

Preheat oven to 400 degrees.
Coat a large skillet with vegetable cooking spray. Add tenderloin and sear until brown. Remove tenderloin from skillet and place on a rack coated with cooking spray. Place rack in a roasting pan. Add 1/4 cup water to pan. In a medium bowl combine margarine with flour, Dijon mustard, dry mustard, black and white peppercorns, mustard seeds, brown sugar and thyme. Spread paste over top and sides of tenderloin. Bake 35 to 45 minutes or until meat thermometer reaches 160 degrees. Transfer tenderloin to cutting board and tent with foil.

TO MAKE GRAVY: Transfer 2 table-spoons pork drippings in pan to heavy small saucepan. Discard remaining drippings. Heat the 2 tablespoons of pan drippings over medium-low heat. Add apple cider and boil until liquid is reduced to 3/4 cup, about 8 minutes. Add flour and stir until golden brown, about 2 minutes. Whisk in chicken broth. Simmer until thickened, stirring occasion-ally, about 2 minutes. Remove from heat. Mix in cider vinegar and mustard. Season with pepper. Carve meat into slices and serve with gravy. Makes 6 servings.

Good: Iron

Diabetic Exchanges: 3 lean meat, 1 starch, 1/2 fat

Nutrition Information Per Serving

Energy	268 calories
Fat	11 g
Saturated fat	4 g
Cholesterol	82 mg
Sodium	171 mg
Carbohydrate	14 g
Protein	26 g

Polynesian Sirloin Steak

This makes a filling and healthful meal served over rice or noodles.

1 1/2 pounds boneless sirloin steak,
    2 inches thick
1/4 teaspoon black pepper
1/4 cup light molasses
1/3 cup orange-pineapple juice, canned,
    bottled or made from concentrate
2 tablespoons reduced-sodium soy sauce
1/2 teaspoon garlic powder

Trim excess fat from steak. Place steak in 9-by-13-inch glass baking dish. Season the steak with pepper. In a small dish, combine the molasses, orange-pineapple juice, soy sauce and garlic powder. Pour over steak. Turn meat once to coat completely. Cover and let stand in refrigerator, turning occasionally, for 2 hours.

Preheat outdoor grill or oven broiler.

Drain meat, reserving marinade. Cook over medium heat, 12 to 15 minutes per side for medium rare. Brush occasionally with the reserved marinade. To serve, slice meat across the grain into thin strips. Makes 6 servings.

Excellent: Potassium
Good: Iron

Diabetic Exchanges: 3 1/2 lean meat, 3/4 fruit (occasional use)

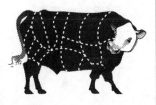

Nutrition Information Per Serving

Energy .... 247 calories
Fat .... 10 g
Saturated fat .... 4 g
Cholesterol .... 76 mg
Sodium .... 140 mg
Carbohydrate ...... 11 g
Protein .... 26 g

Pork Chops with Raisins and Apple Brandy

Lean tenderloin pork chops get a distinctively sweet flavor from the apple brandy and raisins in this recipe.

1/4 cup raisins
2 tablespoons Calvados (also known as
    apple brandy or applejack)
Vegetable cooking spray
4 lean tenderloin pork chops,
    (4 ounces each) trimmed of excess fat
1/4 teaspoon salt
Freshly ground black pepper to taste
1/3 teaspoon dried thyme
1 clove garlic, pressed or minced
1 medium carrot, sliced
1 small onion, chopped
1/2 cup chicken broth, defatted, low sodium
1/2 cup dry white wine

In a small bowl, marinate raisins in Calvados.

Coat a large skillet with vegetable cooking spray. Add chops and saute, turning, until browned on both sides. Sprinkle with salt, pepper and thyme. Add garlic. Reduce heat to moderately low, cover and cook 20 minutes. Add carrot and onion and cook until vegetables are tender, about 20 minutes. Add raisins and Calvados marinade and cook 5 minutes more. Remove chops to a warm serving dish, allowing any excess grease to drain by using a slotted spoon. Arrange vegetables and raisins around chops; cover to keep warm.

Drain excess fat, if any, from pan. Add chicken broth and white wine to skillet. Heat sauce, stirring frequently, until it boils and thickens slightly, approximately 10 minutes. Pour some sauce over meat and vegetables and serve. Makes 4 servings.

Excellent: Potassium
Excellent: Vitamin A

Diabetic Exchanges: 3 lean meat, 1 vegetable, 1/2 starch

Nutrition Information Per Serving

Energy	229 calories
Fat	5 g
Saturated fat	1 g
Cholesterol	79 mg
Sodium	202 mg
Carbohydrate	12 g
Protein	26 g

Ratatouille Round Steak over Rice

Ratatouille is a classic vegetable stew, originally from Nice, France, that is now found all over southeast France and abroad. Here it is combined with round steak.

1 1/2 pounds boneless beef round steak
   (1/2 inch thick, fat trimmed)
2 tablespoon lemon or lime juice
1/2 cup dry sherry or wine
1 tablespoon Worcestershire sauce
1 clove garlic, minced
Dash of pepper
Dash of salt-free seasoning blend
1/2 teaspoon salt
1/4 teaspoon dried basil
1/4 teaspoon dried oregano
1/4 teaspoon dried thyme
Vegetable cooking spray
1 medium onion, chopped
1 teaspoon vegetable oil (optional)
4 medium tomatoes, chopped, peeled
   if desired
3 medium zucchini squash, sliced
1 medium green pepper, seeded and
   chopped
1 cup fresh mushrooms, sliced
3 cups rice, cooked without added
   salt or margarine
1/2 cup (2 ounces) part-skim milk
   mozzarella cheese, shredded

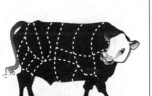

Nutrition Information Per Serving

Energy	373 calories
Fat	9 g
Saturated fat	2 g
Cholesterol	71 mg
Sodium	134 mg
Carbohydrate	36 g
Protein	32 g

Trim excess fat from meat. Combine juice, wine, Worcestershire sauce, garlic, pepper, salt-free seasoning, salt, if desired, basil, oregano and thyme in a shallow dish. Pierce steak with a fork and place the meat in the shallow dish. Cover tightly and refrigerate overnight, turning occasionally to marinate all sides.

Remove meat from marinade; reserve marinade. Coat large skillet with vegetable cooking spray. Brown meat and onion over medium heat, stirring frequently. Add 1/2 the marinade (about 3/4 cup); cover, reduce heat and simmer 20 minutes while you prepare vegetables.

In a saute pan or small skillet, heat oil and saute tomatoes, zucchini squash, green pepper and mushrooms until vegetables are crisp-tender, 3 to 5 minutes. (Or omit oil and cook vegetables in microwave at full setting, covered with plastic wrap, until vegetables are still slightly crisp, about 1 to 2 minutes.)

Add vegetable mixture and the rest of the marinade to beef and simmer, uncovered, 15 minutes or until marinade boils down. Serve immediately over cooked rice. Sprinkle with shredded cheese. Makes 6 servings.

Good: Fiber
Good: Potassium
Excellent: Iron
Excellent: Vitamin A

Diabetic Exchanges: 3 lean meat, 2 1/2 starch, 1 vegetable

Spicy Pork and Asparagus Stir-Fry

This is a wonderful and easy main course, especially in the spring, when asparagus is so plentiful.

1/2 pound pork tenderloin
1 slice (1/4-inch slice) from a medium-size piece fresh ginger root, peeled and `minced
2 cloves garlic, peeled and crushed
1 teaspoon cornstarch plus 1 tablespoon cornstarch, divided
2 teaspoons reduced-sodium soy sauce
1 teaspoon sesame oil (or substitute 1 teaspoon vegetable oil in addition to the 1 teaspoon that follows)
1 teaspoon vegetable oil
1 whole dried pequin chili, available at Asian markets, or a dash of cayenne pepper
1/2 medium green bell pepper, seeded and cut into strips
1/2 medium red bell pepper, seeded and cut into strips
1/2 cup water chestnuts
1 cup asparagus spears and tips, cut into 2-inch pieces
3 green onions, chopped, with green tops
1/2 cup low-sodium chicken broth
1/4 cup water
1 tablespoon sherry
2 medium tomatoes, plunged into boiling water for 30 seconds, then peeled and cut into quarters
4 cups cooked hot rice

Cut pork into very thin (1/4-inch) slices across the grain. Pork cuts better if partially frozen. Mix ginger root, garlic, 1 teaspoon cornstarch and soy sauce in a bowl. Add the pork, stir and allow to marinate at least 5 minutes.

Heat oil or oils in a wok or large skillet over medium-high heat and stir-fry the meat and marinade and pequin chili until meat loses its pink color and begins to brown, about 4 to 5 minutes. (If using cayenne pepper, don't add until you add vegetables.) Do not overcook meat. Remove meat and set aside; discard the pequin chili. Add green and red pepper, water chestnuts, asparagus, onions and cayenne pepper if pequin chili was not used. Add chicken broth and water and stir well. Cover and cook over medium heat for 3 minutes. Dissolve the remaining 1 tablespoon cornstarch in sherry. Add it to wok or skillet, cover and cook for 5 minutes more. Add tomatoes and pork; cover and cook 1 to 2 minutes longer. Serve over hot rice. Makes 4 servings.

Excellent: Potassium

Diabetic Exchanges: 3 starch, 3 vegetable, 1 1/2 lean meat, 1/2 fat

Nutrition Information Per Serving	
Energy	415 calories
Fat	9 g
Saturated fat	3 g
Cholesterol	41 mg
Sodium	114 mg
Carbohydrate	63 g
Protein	18 g

Beef Casserole with Spinach and Rice

The trick to keeping this dish Heart Smart® also can be used on your favorite recipes. After browning ground beef, drain it well and pat it with a paper towel to further reduce fat.

Vegetable cooking spray
1 pound ground round
1/2 cup celery, washed, ends removed, thinly sliced
1/2 cup onion, peeled, ends removed and chopped
1 package (10 ounces) frozen chopped spinach, cooked according to package directions and drained
1 cup long-grain rice (cooked without salt or fat)
3 egg whites (slightly beaten)
1/4 teaspoon garlic powder, or more to taste
1/2 teaspoon thyme, dried, or more to taste
1/4 teaspoon pepper, dried, or more to taste
1/2 cup (2 ounces) low-fat Cheddar cheese, shredded
Sweet red pepper rings (optional)

Preheat oven to 350 degrees.
Spray a large nonstick skillet with vegetable cooking spray. Add ground round, celery and onion. Cook over medium heat until browned, stirring to crumble meat. Drain well, pat dry with paper towels.
In a medium bowl, combine meat mixture, spinach, cooked rice, egg whites, garlic powder, thyme and pepper; mix well. Spray a 1 1/2-quart baking dish with vegetable cooking spray and place mixture in dish. Bake uncovered for 20 minutes. Top with cheese and bake,

uncovered, 5 minutes or until cheese melts. Garnish with red pepper rings, if desired. Makes 6 servings.

Good: Potassium
Excellent: Vitamin A

Diabetic Exchanges: 2 1/2 lean meat, 1 vegetable, 1/2 starch

Nutrition Information Per Serving

Energy	221 calories
Fat	5 g
Saturated fat	2 g
Cholesterol	51 mg
Sodium	145 mg
Carbohydrate	13 g
Protein	20 g

Stir-Fried Beef with Ginger

Fresh ginger is wonderful to have on hand for recipes like these. To keep it longer, pare the skin, cut it into chunks and store in the refrigerator in a tightly covered jar of vodka or sherry. Try fresh when it is available.

1/4 cup dry vermouth
1/4 cup chicken broth
1 tablespoon low-sodium soy sauce
1 teaspoon fresh ginger, peeled, chopped
1 garlic clove, peeled, ends removed,
    minced or pressed
1 pound beef round eye steak, well trimmed
    of visible fat, sliced into 1-inch strips
1 tablespoon peanut oil
1 whole dried hot red chili, or cayenne
    pepper to taste
1 package (6 ounces) frozen Chinese
    pea pods, thawed
1 red bell pepper, washed, cored, seeded,
    sliced into strips
2 green onions, washed, ends removed,
    cut diagonally into 1/4-inch lengths
2 cups fresh mushrooms, cleaned, sliced
1 tablespoon cornstarch mixed with
    3 tablespoons cold water

In a medium bowl, stir together vermouth, chicken broth, soy sauce, ginger and garlic. Toss meat strips in mixture to cover. Cover and refrigerate for at least 1 hour.

Heat wok or skillet over high heat. Add oil to coat bottom. When oil is hot, if using whole dried hot chili, add to oil and cook 30 seconds. Drain meat, reserving marinade.

Add meat to pan and cook, stirring 1 to 2 minutes. If using cayenne pepper, add to meat.

Add pea pods and red pepper and stir-fry until crisp. Add green onions and mushrooms. Add soy sauce marinade and cornstarch mixture. Stir until liquid bubbles. Remove whole red chili, if used, and discard. Makes 4 servings.

Good: Fiber
Good: Potassium
Good: Iron
Excellent: Vitamin C

Diabetic Exchanges: 3 lean meat, 2 vegetable

Nutrition Information Per Serving

Energy	248 calories
Fat	9 g
Saturated fat	3 g
Cholesterol	59 mg
Sodium	223 mg
Carbohydrate	10 g
Protein	28 g

Layered Cabbage–Beef Casserole

This is our lower-fat version of a traditional dish. You can make it ahead and keep it in the refrigerator until you're home from work.

1 pound extra-lean ground beef
1 cup chopped onion
Vegetable cooking spray
1 cup cooked rice
1/2 teaspoon salt (optional)
1/2 teaspoon black pepper
1/2 teaspoon thyme, dried
1/2 teaspoon basil, dried
1/2 teaspoon oregano, dried
1 clove garlic, peeled and pressed
6 cups cabbage, shredded (approximately one small head)
1 tablespoon all-purpose flour
1 can (6 ounces) tomato paste
1 cup skim milk
1 teaspoon sugar

Preheat oven to 350 degrees.

In a plastic microwave-safe colander, placed over a microwave-safe dish, microwave ground beef on high. Stir every 2 minutes, until well done, about 6 minutes, allowing fat and juice to drip out into dish below. Or cook in skillet over medium heat and drain thoroughly. Rinse crumbled meat with hot water in colander to eliminate more fat. Microwave chopped onion until translucent, or saute in vegetable cooking spray. Mix meat and onion with cooked rice, salt if desired, pepper, thyme, basil, oregano and garlic in a large bowl. Spread half the cabbage on the bottom of a 2- to 3-quart baking dish; sprinkle with flour. Layer with meat and rice mixture, followed by the remaining cabbage. Mix tomato paste, skim milk and sugar in a small bowl and pour mixture over casserole. Cover with a lid or foil and bake for 1 hour. Makes 4 servings.

Excellent: Potassium
Good: Iron
Good: Vitamin A
Excellent: Vitamin C

Diabetic Exchanges: 3 lean meat, 2 vegetable, 1 starch, 1/2 fat

Nutrition Information Per Serving

Energy .... 308 calories
Fat .... 12 g
Saturated fat .... 5 g
Cholesterol .... 72 mg
Sodium .... 452 mg
Carbohydrate ...... 24 g
Protein .... 27 g

Heart Smart® Cookbook

Stuffed Peppers

We used lean meat and low-fat cheese in this recipe to provide you with lots of protein and iron.

8 green peppers, washed
Vegetable cooking spray
1 pound extra-lean ground beef
1/3 cup onion, ends removed, peeled, minced
1 stalk celery, washed, chopped
1 small zucchini, washed, ends removed, diced
1 medium tomato, chopped
1 small clove garlic, peeled, ends removed, minced
2 cups cooked brown rice
1/2 teaspoon dried oregano
1 can (15 ounces) tomato sauce, divided
1/2 cup (2 ounces) part-skim milk mozzarella cheese

Preheat oven to 350 degrees.

Cut a slice from the top of each pepper and discard seeds and membranes.

Spray a large nonstick skillet with vegetable cooking spray. Add ground beef. Cook over medium heat, stirring, until browned. Drain well and set aside. Remove from the skillet. Coat skillet again with vegetable cooking spray and over medium heat, saute onion, celery, zucchini and tomato 2 to 3 minutes. Add garlic and saute an additional minute.

Combine rice, ground beef, oregano and all but 1/4 cup of the tomato sauce. Add to the vegetable mixture. Stuff peppers with meat-rice mixture. Top each pepper with remaining tomato sauce, about 1 1/2 teaspoons for each pepper. Place peppers in a 9-by-13-inch or larger baking dish, depending on size of peppers. Bake 20 minutes. Remove from oven and sprinkle each pepper with mozzarella cheese. Bake 10 more minutes to melt cheese. Makes 8 servings

Good: Fiber
Excellent: Potassium
Good: Iron
Good: Vitamin A
Excellent: Vitamin C

Diabetic Exchanges: 1 1/2 lean meat, 2 vegetable, 1 starch, 1/2 fat

Nutrition Information Per Serving

Energy .... 242 calories
Fat .... 9 g
Saturated fat .... 3 g
Cholesterol .... 40 mg
Sodium .... 921 mg
Carbohydrate ...... 27 g
Protein .... 16 g

Veal Oscar Rolls

Veal contains slightly more cholesterol per ounce than beef, but it is usually leaner and contains less saturated fat. So small portions of lean veal can be used in a Heart Smart® diet.

1 1/2 pounds veal cutlets (about 6)
1 teaspoon soft tub margarine
1 tablespoon vegetable oil
1/4 cup finely chopped shallots
6 ounces shredded imitation crab meat
1/4 cup nonfat plain yogurt
1/4 teaspoon dry mustard
1/8 teaspoon pepper
4 tablespoons all-purpose flour
1/2 pound mushrooms, sliced
2 tablespoons chopped parsley
1/4 cup dry white wine
1/4 teaspoon tarragon

Preheat the oven to 350 degrees.
Place cutlets between 2 sheets of wax paper. Using a meat mallet or rolling pin, pound cutlets to 1/4-inch thickness.
In a large skillet heat the margarine and oil. Add the shallots and cook, stirring frequently, until soft. Remove the skillet from heat. Combine 1 tablespoon of shallots, imitation crab, yogurt, mustard and pepper in a small mixing bowl. Place 2 tablespoons of this mixture down the center of each veal cutlet. Roll up the cutlets and secure with toothpicks. Lightly coat each one with flour. Place the veal rolls in the skillet with the remaining shallots and cook over medium heat, about 10 minutes. Stir in the mushrooms, parsley, wine and tarragon. Reduce the heat, simmer 3 to 4 minutes. Place veal and mushrooms in a 9-by-9-inch baking dish. Cover.

Bake for 15 minutes. Makes 6 servings.

Excellent: Potassium
Excellent: Iron

Diabetic Exchanges: 4 lean meat, 1/2 starch

Nutrition Information Per Serving

Energy .... 280 calories
Fat .... 13 g
Saturated fat .... 5 g
Cholesterol .... 94 mg
Sodium .... 322 mg
Carbohydrate 7g
Protein .... 30 g

Venison Stew

Game meats are generally lower in fat than beef, because game animals don't usually become fat.

Marinade
2 cups dry red wine
2 tablespoons lemon juice
2 tablespoons lime juice
2 large bay leaves
2 whole cloves
1 large yellow onion, peeled and sliced
Top leaves, not stalks, of 2 celery stalks
1 large garlic clove, peeled, crushed or minced
1/2 teaspoon dried tarragon
Pinch of dried thyme
1/4 teaspoon black pepper
Dash of gin (optional)

Stew
1 1/2 pounds lean venison (cut in 1-inch cubes)
2 tablespoons vegetable oil
1/2 pound fresh mushrooms, sliced
2 onions, quartered
3 carrots, peeled and sliced
1/4 cup all-purpose flour

TO PREPARE MARINADE: In a large glass bowl, combine red wine, lemon juice, lime juice, bay leaves, whole cloves, onion, celery leaves, garlic, tarragon, thyme, black pepper and gin, if desired; stir well. Add venison cubes, cover and refrigerate for 24 hours. Turn meat once or twice in marinade.

TO PREPARE STEW: Remove meat from marinade and dry thoroughly with paper towels. Reserve marinade. Preheat oven to 300 degrees.

In large skillet over medium heat, brown cubed venison in vegetable oil. Any liquid released from the meat should be added back to the reserved marinade. After meat has browned, about 15 minutes, transfer venison to a 3- to 4-quart ovenproof casserole. Add 1/2 cup of marinade to hot skillet to deglaze, loosening any browned bits on bottom of skillet with a wooden spoon. Cook 1 to 2 minutes, stirring constantly. Add to casserole. Add mushrooms, onions, carrots and remaining marinade to casserole; stir well. Bake covered for 4 hours, stirring once every hour. Remove bay leaves. Sprinkle with flour and toss to coat. Place stew into large skillet and simmer 5 to 10 minutes until flour taste is cooked out and stew is thick. Makes 6 servings.

Good: Fiber
Good: Potassium
Good: Iron
Excellent: Vitamin A

Diabetic Exchanges: 3 lean meat, 2 vegetable, 1 starch

Nutrition Information Per Serving

Energy	289 calories
Fat	7 g
Saturated fat	3 g
Cholesterol	78 mg
Sodium	77 mg
Carbohydrate	28 g
Protein	27 g

Yu-Shiang Pork

This wonderfully spicy dish will convince even the biggest skeptics that eating Heart Smart® does not mean sacrificing taste.

Sauce
1 tablespoon sugar
1 tablespoon vinegar
1 tablespoon dry sherry
2 tablespoons low-sodium soy sauce
3 tablespoons chicken stock, defatted; or water
2 teaspoons cornstarch

Pork
1 teaspoon cornstarch
Dash of white pepper
1 tablespoon dry sherry
3/4 pound trimmed, boneless pork loin, cut into matchstick pieces (1 1/4 pounds with bone trimmed and discarded)
2 tablespoons vegetable oil, divided
2 cloves garlic, peeled, ends removed, minced
1 teaspoon fresh ginger, minced
3-4 dried whole hot red chilies
2/3 cup bamboo shoots, sliced, cut into matchstick pieces
10 green onions (including tops), washed, ends removed, cut into 2-inch lengths
4 cups brown rice, cooked

FOR SAUCE: In a medium bowl mix together sugar, vinegar, dry sherry, soy sauce, chicken stock or water, and cornstarch. Stir until cornstarch and sugar are dissolved. Set aside.

FOR PORK PREPARATION: In a large bowl combine cornstarch, dash of white pepper and sherry. Add pork, stir to coat. Marinate for 15 minutes.

Heat a wok or wide frying pan over high heat. When pan is hot, add 1 tablespoon of the oil. When oil begins to heat, add garlic, ginger and chilies; stir once. Add pork and stir-fry until lightly browned (about 4 minutes); remove from pan. Wipe pan with paper towel. Heat remaining 1 tablespoon oil in pan. Add bamboo shoots and onions and stir-fry for 1 minute. Return pork to pan. Stir in reserved sauce and cook, stirring, until sauce boils and thickens. Serve with rice. Makes 4 servings.

Excellent: Potassium
Good: Iron
Excellent: Vitamin A

Diabetic Exchanges: 3 starch, 2 lean meat, 2 vegetable, 1/2 fat

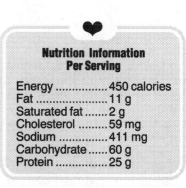

Nutrition Information Per Serving

Energy .... 450 calories
Fat .... 11 g
Saturated fat .... 2 g
Cholesterol .... 59 mg
Sodium .... 411 mg
Carbohydrate ...... 60 g
Protein .... 25 g

172

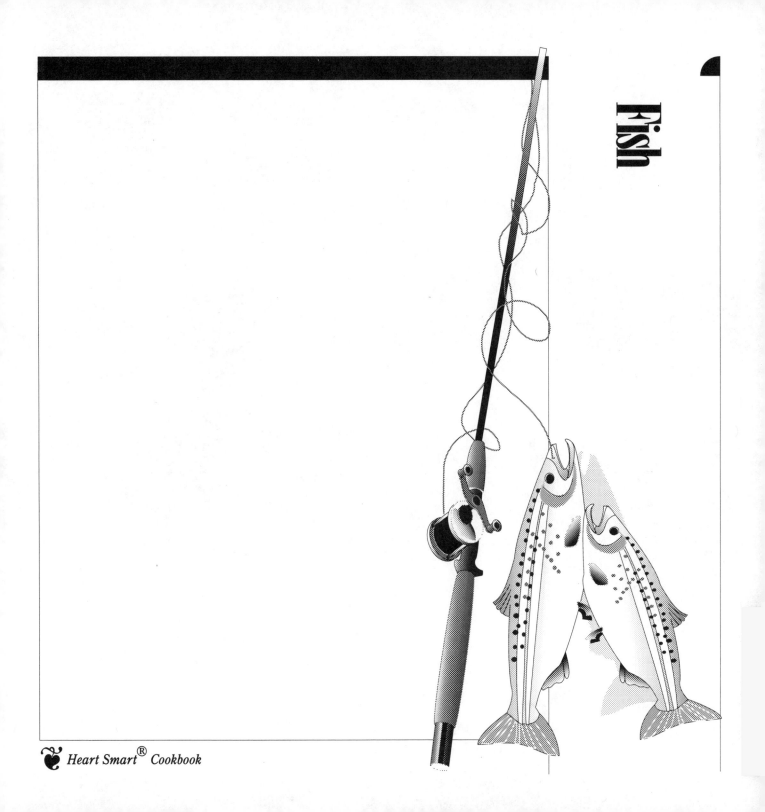

Fish

Bouillabaisse

This fish stew was originally concocted as a way to use up the fish least suitable for market.

1 tablespoon olive oil
1 large onion, chopped
1/2 teaspoon fennel seeds, or anise seeds
2 garlic cloves, peeled and minced
1/4 cup chopped fresh parsley, or
   2 tablespoons dried parsley
1 medium tomato, chopped
1 bay leaf
1/4 teaspoon dried thyme
4 saffron threads
1/4 teaspoon salt
1/2 teaspoon freshly ground pepper
1 bottle (8 ounces) clam juice
2 cups dry white wine
1/2 pound medium shrimp, shelled
   and deveined
1/2 pound thick fish fillets
   (red snapper, cod, scrod or
   orange roughy) cut into 3-inch chunks

In a large kettle, heat oil over moderate heat. Add the onion and cook until softened but not browned, about 3 minutes. Stir in the fennel or anise seeds, garlic, parsley, tomato, bay leaf, thyme, saffron, salt and pepper; cook, covered, for 5 minutes over low heat, stirring often. Add clam juice and white wine. Simmer, covered, for 20 to 30 minutes. Stock can be stored up to a day ahead of time to this point.

When ready to serve, bring the stock to a boil in a large kettle. Reduce heat to moderate and add shrimp and fish. Let simmer, covered, for about 6 minutes. When the soup returns to a boil, the seafood should be done. Do not overcook. Using a slotted spoon, remove the seafood from the cooking pot and place on a large, heated serving platter. Return the broth to a boil, taste and adjust with pepper, if necessary. Strain and pour into a large soup tureen. To serve, place a portion of the seafood in each of 4 wide soup bowls and ladle hot broth over it. Makes 4 servings.

Excellent: Potassium

Diabetic Exchanges: 2 lean meat, 1 1/2 starch, 1 vegetable

Nutrition Information Per Serving

Energy .... 246 calories
Fat .... 6 g
Saturated fat .... trace
Cholesterol .... 60 mg
Sodium .... 432 mg
Carbohydrate ...... 26 g
Protein .... 23 g

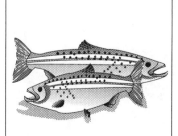

Cajun–Style Catfish

High-fat fish such as catfish still can be a heart-healthy choice. Catfish contains 1.5 grams of fat per ounce—still lower in fat than even the leanest cuts of red meat.

1 1/2 cups fresh orange juice
2 tablespoons fresh lemon juice
3 tablespoons fresh lime juice
1 tablespoon rice vinegar
3 cloves garlic, peeled, ends removed
2 tablespoons jalapeno peppers, seeded,
   cored and diced
1/4 cup chili powder
1/4 teaspoon black pepper
1 pound catfish or red snapper fillets

Preheat grill or broiler.
In a medium bowl combine orange juice, lemon juice, lime juice, rice vinegar, garlic, jalapeno peppers, chili powder and black pepper.
Arrange each fish fillet on a sheet of aluminum foil. Bring edges of foil upwards to form a bowl. Spoon 2 tablespoons of sauce over each fillet. Pinch top edges of foil together (leave a small amount of space for steam to escape). Arrange foil packets on a grill and cook 8 to 10 minutes, or until fish flakes easily when tested with a fork. Heat remaining sauce and serve with fish. Makes 4 servings.

Excellent: Potassium
Excellent: Vitamin A
Excellent: Vitamin C

Diabetic Exchanges: 3 lean meat, 1 fruit

**Nutrition Information
Per Serving**

Energy .... 185 calories
Fat .... 5 g
Saturated fat .... 1 g
Cholesterol .... 45 mg
Sodium .... 126 mg
Carbohydrate ...... 17 g
Protein .... 24 g

Dilled Salmon with Asparagus

This dish marries two of our favorite flavors—salmon and dill. With fresh asparagus, it makes a great main course for entertaining.

1 1/2 pounds fresh asparagus, or
   1 package (10 ounces) frozen
2 tablespoons soft tub margarine
2 teaspoons lemon juice, fresh if possible
2 teaspoons fresh dill, snipped; or
   1 teaspoon dried; divided
Vegetable cooking spray
4 fresh salmon steaks (6 ounces each),
   3/4-inch thick

Rinse asparagus and cut off the tough bottom portion of the stalks. Steam fresh asparagus in a vegetable steamer in a covered saucepan, or cook in boiling water in a saucepan until just tender, about 5 minutes. If using frozen, simply defrost.

In a small saucepan, melt margarine. Add lemon juice and half of the dill, reserving the rest for garnish.

Coat broiler pan or grill with vegetable cooking spray and place salmon steaks, evenly spaced, on broiler pan in oven or on the grill over medium-hot coals. Brush half of the lemon-margarine mixture on the steaks. Broil about 6 inches from the heat source for 5 minutes. Turn, baste with the remaining half of the mixture and broil for 5 or 6 more minutes, or until the salmon meat flakes. Remove salmon to warmed plate. Put asparagus stalks over the salmon and sprinkle lightly with remaining dill. Makes 4 servings.

Good: Fiber
Excellent: Potassium
Good: Iron
Good: Vitamin A
Excellent: Vitamin C

Diabetic Exchanges: 4 lean meat,
2 vegetable

Nutrition Information Per Serving

Energy	278 calories
Fat	11 g
Saturated fat	2 g
Cholesterol	88 mg
Sodium	171 mg
Carbohydrate	8 g
Protein	38 g

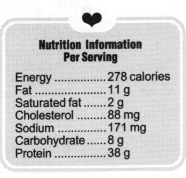

Fish Stew with Pepper, Carrot and Tomatoes

All oils contain the same calories, but olive oil is mostly monounsaturated and, therefore, a good choice.

1 tablespoon olive oil
1 large onion, finely chopped
2 cloves garlic, minced or pressed
1 green bell pepper, seeded and chopped
1 medium carrot, shredded
1 teaspoon paprika
1/2 teaspoon dried basil
1/4 teaspoon ground turmeric
3 medium tomatoes, peeled and chopped
1 cup chicken broth
1/2 cup dry sherry
1 pound firm, mild-flavored fish fillets,
    cut into 1-inch squares
1 can (6 1/2 ounces) crabmeat
1/2 cup plain nonfat yogurt
Chopped parsley for garnish

In a 4-quart Dutch oven, over medium heat, place olive oil, onion, garlic, bell pepper and carrot. Cook, stirring often, until onion begins to brown. Mix in paprika, basil, turmeric, tomatoes, broth and sherry. Bring to boil, then reduce heat. Boil uncovered 15 to 20 minutes. Mix in fish and crab. Continue cooking until fish is opaque and flakes when tested with a fork (3 to 5 minutes). Gradually stir in yogurt. Heat until hot (do not boil). Sprinkle with parsley. Makes 4 servings.

Good: Fiber
Excellent: Potassium
Excellent: Vitamin A
Excellent: Vitamin C

Diabetic Exchanges: 3 lean meat, 1 starch, 1 vegetable

**Nutrition Information
Per Serving**

Energy .... 292 calories
Fat .... 6 g
Saturated fat .... trace
Cholesterol .... 55 mg
Sodium .... 526 mg
Carbohydrate ..... 18 g
Protein .... 30 g

Heart Smart® Cookbook

Gefilte Fish

You'll love our low-fat version of this traditional favorite.

Court bouillon
1 quart water
Bones, heads and skin of assorted fish
1 onion, peeled and sliced
1 carrot sliced
1/2 teaspoon pepper
1 bay leaf
3 or 4 sprigs parsley

Fish
1 1/2 pound uncooked white fish
    (such as trout, pike or pickerel)
1 large onion, peeled and quartered
2 egg whites, lightly beaten
1 tablespoon matzo meal
1/4 teaspoon salt
Pepper to taste
1/2 teaspoon sugar
1/4 cup ice water

TO MAKE COURT BOUILLON: Combine water, fish bones, heads and skin with onion, carrot, pepper, bay leaf and parsley in a large, heavy soup kettle. Bring to a boil, reduce heat and simmer, covered, for 30 minutes.

TO PREPARE FISH: As bouillon is cooking, cut fish in large chunks, in a food processor with steel blade in place. Add onion and process until finely chopped and well mixed.

Mix in beaten egg whites, matzo meal, salt, pepper and sugar until well blended. Add ice water gradually, mixing constantly until water is absorbed. Set aside.

To finish: Remove skin, heads, bones, onion and carrot from court bouillon. Skim off foam from broth. Bring stock to a boil. Meanwhile, moisten hands with cold water and shape fish mixture into 16 two-inch balls. Drop into boiling stock. Partially cover, reduce heat and simmer 30 minutes. Remove fish balls carefully with slotted spoon and place on a serving platter. Cool completely. Serve at room temperature with horseradish sauce. Makes 4 servings, 4 balls per serving.

Diabetic Exchanges: 4 lean meat, 1 vegetable, 1/2 fat

Nutrition Information Per Serving

Energy	278 calories
Fat	14 g
Saturated fat	trace
Cholesterol	81 mg
Sodium	258 mg
Carbohydrate	5 g
Protein	32 g

Grilled Red Snapper

Red snapper is a mild-tasting low-fat fish great for people who do not like a strong, fishy flavor.

Vegetable cooking spray
1/2 red onion, peeled, ends removed,
   thinly sliced
4 red snapper fillets (6 ounces each),
   washed and patted dry
1 lime, peeled, removing the membrane
   with the skin, thinly sliced
1 tomato, chopped
Black pepper (optional)
4 sprigs of thyme, or 1/2 teaspoon dried

Cut 4 pieces of foil each about twice the size of 1 fillet and apply cooking spray to the center of each. Scatter 1/4 of the onions over the sprayed area of each piece of foil. Add a fillet. Top each fish with 1/4 of the lime slices, the chopped tomato, and the pepper, if desired, and with a sprig of thyme or sprinkle of dried thyme. Seal foil tightly, folding twice.

Grill over hot coals or in oven for 7 to 12 minutes. Snapper should flake when touched with a fork. Makes 4 servings.

Excellent: Potassium

Diabetic Exchanges: 4 lean meat, 1 vegetable

Nutrition Information
Per Serving

Energy .... 140 calories
Fat .... 2 g
Saturated fat .... trace
Cholesterol .... 40 mg
Sodium .... 89 mg
Carbohydrate ...... 5 g
Protein .... 26 g

Sole Fillets en Papillote

"En papillote" is used to describe a preparation cooked and served in a wrapping of grease-proof paper or aluminum foil. The wrapping swells in the oven during cooking and the dish is served piping hot, before the wrapping collapses.

4 sole fillets (6 ounces each)
2 ripe tomatoes peeled, cored and chopped
2 green onions, chopped
2 tablespoons dry white wine
2 tablespoons fresh lemon juice
Freshly ground pepper
2 tablespoons snipped fresh chives

Preheat oven to 400 degrees.

Cut parchment or foil into 4 rectangles 12 by 14 inches each. Arrange each fillet in the center of one half of the foil or parchment, along with 1/4 the tomato and green onion. Mix wine and lemon juice. Pour 1 tablespoon of wine-lemon mixture over each fish and sprinkle with freshly ground pepper to taste. Then fold the remaining half of the foil or parchment over the fish and seal the package by folding in the edges. Cook the packages in the oven for 10-15 minutes. Serve in open pouches sprinkled with fresh chives. Makes 4 servings.

Excellent: Potassium
Good: Vitamin A
Good: Vitamin C

Diabetic Exchanges: 3 lean meat, 1 vegetable

Nutrition Information Per Serving

Energy	141 calories
Fat	1 g
Saturated fat	trace
Cholesterol	86 mg
Sodium	92 mg
Carbohydrate	4 g
Protein	26 g

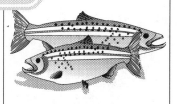

Sole Fillets with Curry Sauce

If you're in a hurry, you'll love cooking fish using the microwave method in this recipe because it's so fast and flavorful.

Fish
1 1/2 pounds sole fillets, cut into
   6-ounce servings
2 tablespoons lemon juice
1/4 teaspoon paprika
Parsley, to taste

Curry Sauce
1 tablespoon soft tub margarine
1 tablespoon all-purpose flour
1/8 teaspoon curry powder
Dash of pepper
1/2 cup skim milk

TO PREPARE FISH: Arrange fish in a 9-by-13-inch microwave-safe dish. Drizzle with lemon juice. Sprinkle with paprika. Cover tightly and microwave on high 5 minutes, rotating dish 1/2 turn in middle of cooking. Microwave until fish flakes easily with a fork, 2 to 4 minutes longer. Let stand 3 minutes. Remove and place on platter; keep warm.

TO MAKE CURRY SAUCE: Place margarine in a microwave-safe 2-cup measure. Microwave uncovered on high until margarine is melted, 15-30 seconds. Stir in flour, curry powder and pepper. Gradually stir in milk. Microwave uncovered on high, stirring every minute until thickened, 2 to 3 minutes. Pour sauce over fish. Sprinkle with parsley. Makes 4 servings.

Good: Potassium

Diabetic Exchanges: 2 1/2 lean meat

Nutrition Information Per Serving

Energy	109 calories
Fat	3 g
Saturated fat	trace
Cholesterol	57 mg
Sodium	93 mg
Carbohydrate	2 g
Protein	18 g

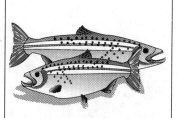

Whitefish with White Wine and Peppercorns

Fresh-cracked peppercorns are what give this dish its distinctive flavor. Once you enjoy the flavor of fresh pepper, you'll want to buy a pepper mill and grind your own.

1/4 cup lemon juice
1/2 cup white wine vinegar
2 garlic cloves, peeled, ends
   removed, crushed
1 1/2 tablespoons sugar
1/4 teaspoon salt
1 1/2 pounds whitefish fillets, skinned
2 tablespoons cracked black peppercorns
   (or to taste)
1/2 cup fish stock
1/2 teaspoon dried thyme leaves
1 lemon, sliced

In a large plastic bag or bowl big enough to hold the fillets in a single layer, stir together lemon juice, vinegar, garlic, sugar and salt. Place fillets in bag or bowl. Seal plastic bag or cover bowl and let the fish marinate in the refrigerator at least 4 hours, turning the fillets after 2 hours.
   Preheat broiler.
   Remove fillets from marinade and pat dry with paper toweling. Strain marinade through sieve into small saucepan. Sprinkle both sides of fillets with pepper. Broil the fillets about 4 inches below broiler about 3 minutes on each side or until fish flakes when tested with a fork. While fish is cooking, add stock and thyme to marinade and cook over medium heat about 5 minutes. When fillets are cooked, transfer them to a serving platter. Pour marinade over the fillets. Garnish with lemon slices. Makes 6 servings.

Excellent: Potassium

Diabetic Exchanges: 3 lean meat, 1/2 fat

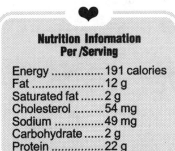

**Nutrition Information
Per /Serving**

Energy .... 191 calories
Fat .... 12 g
Saturated fat .... 2 g
Cholesterol .... 54 mg
Sodium .... 49 mg
Carbohydrate ...... 2 g
Protein .... 22 g

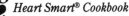

Whitefish Sesame Dijon

We use mustard sparingly in this dish because prepared mustard contains 204 milligrams of sodium per tablespoon.

1 1/2 pounds whitefish fillets
1/4 cup Dijon mustard
2 tablespoons low-sodium soy sauce
1/2 cup dry white wine
2 tablespoons sesame seeds, toasted

Place fillets in shallow dish. Mix together mustard, soy sauce and wine. Pour evenly over fish. Marinate, covered with plastic wrap, for 3 to 4 hours in the refrigerator.

When ready to cook, prepare charcoal grill or preheat oven to a broil.

Remove fish from marinade and discard marinade. Place fillets on foil-covered hot grill or broiler pan about 4 inches from heat or coals, with grill covered. Top with sesame seeds. Cook for approximately 10 minutes or until fish flakes easily, turning once during cooking. Makes 6 servings.

Good: Potassium

Diabetic Exchanges: 3 lean meat

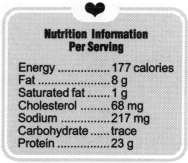

**Nutrition Information
Per Serving**

Energy .... 177 calories
Fat .... 8 g
Saturated fat .... 1 g
Cholesterol .... 68 mg
Sodium .... 217 mg
Carbohydrate ...... trace
Protein .... 23 g

Marinated Scallop Kabobs

Either bay scallops or sea scallops can be used in this recipe, which offers a change from chicken and beef kabobs. Remember that bay scallops are smaller than sea scallops.

1/4 cup vegetable oil
1/2 cup white wine vinegar
2 tablespoons lemon juice
2 teaspoons reduced-sodium soy sauce
1/2 teaspoon garlic powder
1/4 teaspoon thyme
1/2 teaspoon pepper
1 1/2 pounds fresh sea scallops
18 cherry tomatoes
1 green pepper, cut into 1-inch pieces
3 medium yellow onions, peeled,
   ends removed, quartered

In a medium deep bowl, combine oil, vinegar, lemon juice, soy sauce, garlic powder, thyme and pepper and mix well. Add scallops and marinate in refrigerator for at least 1 hour.
  Preheat broiler or grill.
  Thread scallops, tomatoes, green pepper and onions on 6 skewers. Brush with marinade. Place on broiler pan or an outdoor grill, 3 inches from heat. Cook for 10 minutes, turning occasionally, until scallops are firm. Remove the scallops and vegetables from skewers to serve. Makes 6 servings.

Excellent: Potassium
Good: Iron
Good: Vitamin A
Excellent: Vitamin C

Diabetic Exchanges: 3 lean meat, 1 vegetable, 1/2 starch

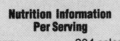

Nutrition Information Per Serving

Energy	204 calories
Fat	8 g
Saturated fat	1 g
Cholesterol	60 mg
Sodium	354 mg
Carbohydrate	14 g
Protein	28 g

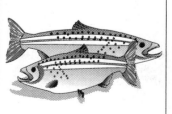

 Heart Smart® Cookbook

Scallops with Red Pepper and Snow Peas

This makes a colorful dish for entertaining because of the white, red and green of the main ingredients.

Water to cook linguine
8 ounces linguine (uncooked)
1 tablespoon olive oil
3 cloves garlic
1 tablespoon cornstarch
2 tablespoons cold water
1/2 cup dry white wine
1 teaspoon black pepper
1 pound scallops (about 20 large scallops), defrosted and drained if frozen
1/4 cup grated Parmesan cheese
1/2 cup red bell peppers, cut into julienne strips
1/2 cup snow peas
1/4 cup chopped parsley

Bring water to boil. Add linguine and cook according to package directions, without adding fat or salt. Stir frequently to prevent sticking.

Meanwhile, in a large skillet or wok, heat olive oil over medium heat. When hot, saute garlic until golden, but do not burn. In a small bowl mix cornstarch and cold water until smooth. Add cornstarch mixture, wine and black pepper to skillet. Bring mixture to a boil. Add scallops and Parmesan cheese; simmer slowly 1 to 2 minutes. Add pepper strips and snow peas and simmer 1 to 2 minutes more, stirring gently. Remove garlic from scallop mixture. Drain linguine and toss with hot scallops. Sprinkle with parsley. Makes 4 servings.

Excellent: Potassium
Excellent: Iron
Good: Vitamin C

Diabetic Exchanges: 3 lean meat, 2 1/2 starch, 1 vegetable

Nutrition Information Per Serving

Energy .... 396 calories
Fat .... 9 g
Saturated fat .... 2 g
Cholesterol .... 100 mg
Sodium .... 350 mg
Carbohydrate ...... 49 g
Protein .... 30 g

Shrimp Creole

Shrimp are moderately high in cholesterol. But they are low in fat and if cooked appropriately are acceptable on a Heart Smart® diet.

12 medium ripe tomatoes
Boiling water and ice water to prepare
    tomatoes
2 pounds medium-sized shrimp
3 tablespoons vegetable oil
2 cups onions, peeled, ends removed,
    coarsely chopped
1 cup green pepper washed, seeds and
    stems removed, coarsely chopped
1 cup celery, washed, ends removed,
    coarsely chopped
2 teaspoons garlic, peeled, ends removed,
    finely chopped
1 cup water
2 bay leaves
1 tablespoon paprika
1/2 teaspoon ground hot red pepper
2 tablespoons cornstarch mixed with
    1/4 cup water
6 cups cooked long-grain white rice

Place tomatoes, 3 to 4 at a time, into a pan of boiling water and remove them with tongs or slotted spoon after 15 seconds. Plunge them into a bowl of ice water and peel with a sharp knife. Cut out the stems, then slice the tomatoes in half and squeeze the halves gently to remove the seeds and juice. Chop coarsely.

Shell the shrimp. Devein them by making a shallow incision down the back with a knife and lifting out the black-and-white intestinal vein with the point of the knife. Wash the shrimp in a colander set under cold running water and spread them out on paper towels to drain.

In a 4- to 5-quart dutch oven or large skillet, heat the oil over medium heat. Add the onions, green pepper, celery and garlic and cook for 5 minutes, stirring frequently. Next stir in the tomatoes, 1 cup water, bay leaves, paprika and red pepper; bring to a boil. Reduce heat to low, cover and simmer for 20 minutes, stirring occasionally. Stir in the shrimp and continue to simmer, partially covered. After the shrimp have cooked 2 minutes, stir the cornstarch-and-water mixture and pour it into the Creole mix. Continue cooking shrimp for about 5 minutes total, or until shrimp are pink and firm to the touch and sauce thickens slightly. Remove the bay leaves and serve the Creole alongside the cooked rice. Makes 8 servings.

Excellent: Potassium
Good: Iron
Excellent: Vitamin A
Excellent: vitamin C
Good: Fiber

Diabetic Exchanges:
3 starch, 2 lean meat,
2 vegetable

Nutrition Information Per Serving

Energy	387 calories
Fat	7 g
Saturated fat	1 g
Cholesterol	75 mg
Sodium	36 mg
Carbohydrate	53 g
Protein	27 g

Shrimp Fajitas

This spicy south-of-the border dish gets its flavor from fresh lime juice and jalapeno peppers.

12 6-inch flour tortillas
2 tablespoons vegetable oil
2 medium onions, chopped
2 large garlic cloves, minced
2 tomatoes, chopped
2 fresh jalapeno peppers, seeded and minced
1 pound medium shrimp, fresh
 or frozen, deveined, uncooked
1/3 cup lime juice
1/4 cup chopped fresh cilantro or 1/3 cup
 chopped fresh parsley plus a pinch
 of ground cumin
4 scallions, sliced, including green tops
1/2 cup plain low-fat yogurt
2 limes, cut into wedges, for garnish

Preheat oven to 300 degrees. Wrap stack of tortillas in aluminum foil. Put them in the oven and let them heat 20 to 30 minutes while you prepare the filling.

In a skillet, heat oil over medium heat and saute onions and garlic in hot oil until tender, about 7 minutes. Add tomatoes, jalapeno peppers and shrimp. Cook, stirring gently, until shrimp turns pink and opaque, about 10 minutes. Mix in lime juice and cilantro (or parsley and cumin) and stir. When well mixed, remove from stove and drain to remove excess liquid. Remove tortillas from oven. Fill each with about 1/3 cup shrimp mixture. Top each with about 1 tablespoon scallions and 2 teaspoons yogurt. Fold shrimp-filled tortilla in half and then fold it again to form a triangle. Garnish with a lime wedge. Makes 6 servings, 2 fajitas per serving.

Good: Potassium
Good: Iron
Excellent: Vitamin C

Diabetic Exchanges: 2 lean meat, 2 starch, 2 vegetable, 1/2 fat

Nutrition Information Per Serving

Energy .... 346 calories
Fat .... 10 g
Saturated fat .... 1 g
Cholesterol .... 51 mg
Sodium .... 23 mg
Carbohydrate ...... 44 g
Protein .... 21 g

188

Pasta, Beans and Rice

Pasta with Broccoli, Carrot, Pepper and Zucchini

All sweet peppers—green, yellow and red—are good sources of Vitamin C. Mixed in a dish they look so attractive, too.

Vegetable cooking spray
1 cup broccoli florets, washed
1 cup carrots, peeled, ends removed, thinly sliced
1 cup zucchini, washed, ends removed, sliced
1/4 cup onion, peeled, ends removed sliced
1 sweet yellow pepper, cored, seeded, cut into thin strips
1 green pepper, cored, seeded, cut into thin strips
1/2 cup fresh mushrooms, cleaned, sliced
1/2 pound pasta (cooked and drained)
1 small tomato, cored, washed, cut into wedges
2 tablespoons dry vermouth
1/4 cup plus 2 tablespoons grated Parmesan cheese
1 tablespoon fresh parsley, washed, dried, minced
1/4 teaspoon sweet red pepper flakes (optional)

Spray a large nonstick skillet with cooking spray and place over medium heat until hot. Add broccoli, carrots, zucchini and onion; saute 4 minutes. Add yellow and green pepper strips and mushrooms; saute 4 minutes. Add cooked pasta, tomato and vermouth and toss gently. Cook until thoroughly heated. Sprinkle with cheese, parsley and pepper flakes, if desired; toss gently. Serve immediately. Makes 4 servings.

Excellent: Potassium
Excellent: Vitamin A
Excellent: Vitamin C

Diabetic Exchanges: 2 1/2 starch, 2 vegetable, 1/2 fat

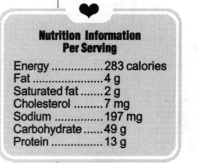

**Nutrition Information
Per Serving**

Energy ....283 calories
Fat ....4 g
Saturated fat ....2 g
Cholesterol ....7 mg
Sodium ....197 mg
Carbohydrate ......49 g
Protein ....13 g

Spinach Lasagna

When using Parmesan cheese, try to use freshly grated. You can use less and still have the great Parmesan flavor.

1 package (10 ounces) frozen spinach
Vegetable cooking spray
1 large onion, peeled and finely chopped
2 or 3 cloves garlic, peeled and minced
1 teaspoon dried oregano
1 teaspoon dried basil
1/2 teaspoon dried rosemary
1 can (15 ounces) low-sodium tomato
    puree
1/4 cup tomato paste, low-sodium variety if
    possible
1/2 cup dry red wine
12 lasagna noodles (white, green or whole
    wheat, but not egg noodles)
        1 egg white
        2 cups (1 pound) part skim-milk
          ricotta cheese
        Freshly ground pepper to taste
        1/4 teaspoon ground nutmeg
        1 cup shredded part-skim
          mozzarella cheese
        1/2 cup grated Parmesan cheese

Cook spinach according to package directions. Drain well and let cool. Press to remove as much water as possible. Set aside.

Spray vegetable cooking spray in a large skillet (nonstick is best). Over medium heat, cook onion, garlic, oregano, basil and rosemary, stirring often, until onion is soft, about 10 minutes. Add tomato puree, tomato paste and wine. Cover and simmer for about 10 minutes. Uncover and cook until sauce thickens and is reduced to about 2 1/2 cups, about 10 minutes.

Meanwhile, cook noodles according to package directions. Drain and set aside. When cool enough to handle, carefully separate noodles.

Preheat oven to 350 degrees. Spoon about 1/4 of the sauce into a 9-by-13-inch baking dish. Arrange 4 noodles lengthwise on the bottom and sides of the dish, overlapping as needed and bringing noodles up the sides of the dish. Spread half of the spinach over the noodles.

In a small bowl, lightly beat the egg white, then blend in the ricotta cheese, pepper and nutmeg. Spread half of this mixture over the spinach. Sprinkle with 1/3 of the mozzarella cheese and 1/3 of the Parmesan cheese. Add another 1/4 of the tomato sauce. Top with 4 more noodles, remaining spinach, remaining ricotta mixture and another 1/3 of mozzarella and Parmesan cheese. Then layer in order remaining 4 noodles, tomato sauce, mozzarella and Parmesan cheeses. Bake uncovered for 25-35 minutes or until hot and bubbly. Let cool about 10 minutes before cutting. Makes 8 servings.

Excellent: Potassium ;
Good: Iron
Excellent: Vitamin A , Vitamin C, Calcium

Diabetic Exchanges: 1 1/2 starch,
1 1/2 medium-fat meat, 2 vegetable

Nutrition Information Per Serving

Energy	296 calories
Fat	10 g
Saturated fat	6 g
Cholesterol	32 mg
Sodium	611 mg
Carbohydrate	32 g
Protein	19 g

Fettuccine Parmesan with Vegetables

Fettuccine noodles like those in this recipe usually are made with egg yolks and contain 50 milligrams of cholesterol per cup. You can reduce the cholesterol in this recipe even further by using the new eggless fettuccine.

1 pound ripe tomatoes, peeled and chopped, seeds and juice reserved
1 cup onion, chopped
1 carrot, peeled, quartered lengthwise and cut into 1/4-inch strips
1 teaspoon fresh thyme, or 1/4 teaspoon dried thyme
1 tablespoon fresh parsley, or 1 teaspoon dried parsley
1/8 teaspoon black pepper
1 1/2 cups fresh asparagus, cut into 1-inch pieces
2 tablespoons red wine vinegar
8 ounces fettuccine
1/4 cup grated Parmesan cheese

Place chopped tomatoes, onion, carrot, thyme, parsley and pepper in a large saucepan over a medium-high heat. Bring mixture to a boil, reduce heat to low and simmer 5 minutes. Add asparagus pieces to saucepan. Pour in vinegar and simmer mixture, uncovered, for 15 minutes. Add reserved tomato seeds and juice, and continue cooking until most of the liquid has evaporated and asparagus is tender, about 15 minutes.

About 15 minutes before vegetables are done, cook fettuccine according to package directions. Drain fettuccine and add it immediately to the sauce. Sprinkle cheese over top, toss lightly and serve. Makes 4 servings.

Excellent: Potassium
Good: Iron
Excellent: Vitamin A
Excellent: Vitamin C

Diabetic Exchanges: 3 starch, 2 vegetable

Nutrition Information Per Serving

Energy .... 305 calories
Fat .... 5 g
Saturated fat .... 2 g
Cholesterol .... 55 mg
Sodium .... 206 mg
Carbohydrate ...... 56 g
Protein .... 14 g

Pasta Primavera

Noodles are not naturally a good source of iron; however, most commercial noodles are enriched with iron.

1 tablespoon olive oil
3 medium cloves garlic, minced
1 1/2 cups cauliflower florets
1/2 cup carrots, sliced in julienne strips
1 cup broccoli florets
1/2 cup yellow squash, sliced
1/2 of a red bell pepper, seeded and sliced in
    julienne strips
2 scallions, diced, including green tops
1 1/2 cups mushrooms, sliced
1/2 cup water
1 tablespoon soft tub margarine
2 teaspoons cornstarch
1 cup skim milk
1/4 cup grated Parmesan cheese
        1/4 cup grated Romano cheese
        1/4 teaspoon white pepper
        1/2 pound linguine or other pasta
        1/2 cup fresh parsley, chopped
without stems

Heat oil in large skillet or wok over medium high heat until hot but not smoking. Add vegetables one at a time and saute each a few seconds, starting with garlic, cauliflower, carrots, broccoli, yellow squash, red pepper, scallions and mushrooms. Saute until vegetables soften a little and turn golden, about 3 minutes total. Add 1/2 cup water and cover. Steam vegetables until just tender, approximately 2 to 3 minutes, depending on how crisp you like vegetables. Drain vegetables and set aside. Keep them warm, but stop cooking so they don't get mushy.

Melt margarine in a small saucepan over medium heat. Add cornstarch and milk and stir with a wire whisk until smooth. Sprinkle in cheeses and white pepper and stir. Bring mixture to a gentle boil over medium low heat, stirring constantly. Reduce heat and simmer until mixture lightly thickens, about 2 to 3 minutes.

Meanwhile, cook linguine or other pasta to al dente stage (tender but firm to the teeth) in boiling water, following package directions but omitting any salt or oil. Stir frequently to prevent sticking. Drain and put in a large serving bowl. Immediately add cooked vegetables, sauce and parsley to pasta and gently toss until thoroughly mixed. Makes 4 servings.

Good: Fiber
Excellent: Potassium
Good: Iron
Excellent: Vitamin A
Excellent: Vitamin C
Good: Calcium

Diabetic Exchanges: 2 3/4 starch,
2 vegetable, 1 1/2 fat, 1/2 medium-fat meat

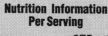

Nutrition Information Per Serving

Energy	375 calories
Fat	12 g
Saturated fat	2 g
Cholesterol	63 mg
Sodium	296 mg
Carbohydrate	50 g
Protein	17 g

Heart Smart® Cookbook

Spinach Noodles with Vegetable Stir-Fry

Egg noodles contain 50 milligrams of cholesterol per cup. Try these spinach noodles using egg whites for a tasty low-cholesterol noodle.

Vegetable cooking spray
1 medium onion, peeled, ends removed, coarsely chopped
1 clove garlic, peeled, ends removed, crushed
2 cups yellow squash, washed, ends removed, thinly sliced
2 cups zucchini squash, washed, ends removed, thinly sliced
1 small red bell pepper, washed cored, seeded, thinly sliced
1 carrot, peeled, ends removed, sliced in julienne strips
1 tablespoon fresh parsley, washed, chopped
3/4 teaspoon dried basil
3/4 teaspoon oregano
1/4 teaspoon freshly ground pepper
1 cup mushrooms, cleaned, sliced
2 medium tomatoes, cored, peeled, chopped
4 cups cooked Spinach Noodles (recipe follows)
4 teaspoons sesame seeds

Coat a large skillet or wok with vegetable cooking spray; place over medium heat until hot. Add onion and garlic. Saute for 3 minutes, or until tender. Add yellow squash, zucchini squash, red bell pepper, carrot, parsley, basil, oregano and pepper.

Saute 4 minutes or until vegetables are tender. Do not overcook. Add mushrooms; saute 1 minute. Stir in tomatoes and heat through, about 20 seconds. Serve vegetables over warm Spinach Noodles. Sprinkle with sesame seeds. Makes 4 servings.

Good: Fiber
Excellent: Potassium
Excellent: Iron
Excellent: Vitamin A
Excellent: Vitamin C

Diabetic Exchanges:
4 vegetable, 3 starch, 1/2 fat

Nutrition Information Per Serving

Energy	356 calories
Fat	4 g
Saturated fat	trace
Cholesterol	trace
Sodium	92 mg
Carbohydrate	67 g
Protein	15 g

Spinach Noodles

2 1/4 cups flour, divided
3 egg whites
1 tablespoon nonfat dry milk
1 teaspoon vegetable oil
1/4 cup spinach, cooked, drained, minced,
    squeezed of all juices
2 to 3 tablespoons water

In a large bowl, place 2 cups flour and make a deep well in center. Set aside.

In medium bowl, mix egg whites, dry milk, vegetable oil and spinach. Pour spinach mixture into flour well. Using a circular motion, begin to draw flour from sides of well, adding water one tablespoon at a time, mixing until flour is moistened. When dough becomes stiff, use hands to finish mixing. Pat dough into a ball and knead to help flour absorb liquid. Using remaining 1/4 cup flour, lightly flour the work surface. Knead dough, sprinkling with flour as needed for 10 minutes or until dough is smooth and elastic. Cover and let dough rest for 20 minutes.

With a rolling pin, roll out 1/4 of the dough (keep remaining dough covered) to 1/16-inch thick. Using pasta cutter, pasta machine or knife, cut strips about 1/4-inch wide. Repeat for remaining dough. Place pasta on pasta rack or towel until stiff and dry, about 2 hours. Cook in 3 quarts boiling water until tender, 5 to 7 minutes. Rinse. Makes four 1-cup servings.

Diabetic Exchanges: 3 starch, 1 vegetable

**Nutrition Information
Per Serving**

Energy .... 272 calories
Fat .... 2 g
Saturated fat .... trace
Cholesterol .... trace
Sodium .... 75 mg
Carbohydrate ...... 52 g
Protein .... 11 g

Pasta, Beans and Rice

Meatballs with Marinara Sauce

Pasta is high in carbohydrates, low in fat and a wonderful Heart Smart® entree with this sauce. But be careful of other sauces—many are high in fat. Serve with Marinara Sauce over noodles or simply as an appetizer.

1 pound extra-lean ground beef
Freshly ground black pepper to taste
1 teaspoon fresh, peeled, garlic, chopped, minced or pressed (about 2 cloves)
1 cup dry bread crumbs
1/2 cup egg substitute
1/2 cup skim milk
1/2 cup chopped, fresh parsley, or 1/4 cup dried
Vegetable cooking spray
1 1/2 cup cooked pasta per person
Marinara Sauce (recipe follows)
1 teaspoon grated Parmesan cheese per person

Preheat oven to 350 degrees.

In large mixing bowl combine ground beef, pepper, garlic and bread crumbs until mixed. Add egg substitute, milk and parsley. Knead; form into 32 firm meat balls, 1 1/2 inch in diameter.

CONVENTIONAL OVEN METHOD: Spray broiler pan and rack with vegetable cooking spray. Place meatballs on the rack of the broiler pan. Bake in preheated oven for 20 to 25 minutes.

MICROWAVE METHOD: Cook in 2 batches. Place meatballs in microwave. Cover with wax paper. Bake on high (100 percent or full power) for 8 to 10 minutes for each batch, turning one-quarter turn halfway through.

Cook pasta according to package directions. Serve 1 1/2 cups pasta per serving, with 1/2 cup marinara sauce on the top, and two to three meatballs with the sauce or on the side. Sprinkle Parmesan cheese on top. Meatballs can be added to marinara sauce and refrigerated up to 3 days. Makes 10 servings.

Diabetic Exchanges:
1 1/2 lean meat, 1/2 starch

Nutrition Information
Per Serving

Energy .... 125 calories
Fat .... 5 g
Saturated fat .... 2 g
Cholesterol .... 27 mg
Sodium .... 119 mg
Carbohydrates .... 8 g
Protein .... 11 g

Marinara Sauce

8 cups peeled, seeded and chopped tomatoes
    (preferably plum tomatoes)
Boiling water for preparing tomatoes
2 tablespoons olive oil
3 cups peeled, chopped onions
1 cup peeled, finely sliced carrots
1 tablespoon peeled, finely chopped garlic
1/2 cup dry red wine (optional)
1/2 teaspoon salt
Freshly ground pepper to taste
2 tablespoons freshly chopped basil, or
    2 teaspoons dried
1 tablespoon fresh oregano, or 1 teaspoon
    dried
1 tablespoon fresh rosemary, or 1 teaspoon
    dried
1/3 cup fresh chopped parsley, or 1 tablespoon
    dried

Cut a cone shape in each tomato to remove the stem and core. Drop tomatoes into boiling water, and let cook for 10 seconds. Remove from the water, cool for a minute under cool water. When cool enough to handle, pull off the skin with a small paring knife. If skin still sticks, return to hot water for 10 seconds more. To seed, halve the tomatoes parallel to their stem and gently squeeze out the jelly-like juice and seeds. The flesh that is left is the "pulp" or "meat" of the tomato.

In a heavy-bottomed large skillet, heat the oil and saute the onions and carrots over medium-high heat until onions are translucent and golden, about 8 minutes. Add the garlic, tomatoes and wine if desired; simmer covered for 20 minutes. Process in a food processor with steel blade inserted, or a blender, or chop by hand until very fine, about 2 minutes in a food processor or blender. Return sauce to pan and add salt, pepper, basil, oregano and rosemary. Simmer covered for 30 minutes. Stir in parsley. Makes approximately 10 cups. You may freeze the sauce for up to 6 months.

Good: Potassium
Excellent: Vitamin A

Diabetic Exchanges: 1 vegetable, 1/2 fat

Nutrition Information Per Serving

Energy .... 46 calories
Fat .... 2 g
Saturated fat .... trace
Cholesterol 0
Sodium 61mg
Carbohydrate ...... 8 g
Protein .... 1 g

Mostaccioli

Choose your ground meats wisely. Ground sirloin tip at 55 calories and 2.7 grams of fat per ounce is a good low-fat choice. You can substitute ground turkey in this recipe as well.

3/4 pound ground sirloin tip
1 large onion, peeled, ends removed, minced
1 tablespoon vegetable oil
2 cloves garlic, peeled, ends removed, minced
1/8 teaspoon pepper
1 can (22 ounces) tomato sauce
1 can (6 ounces) tomato paste
1/2 teaspoon basil
1/2 teaspoon oregano
3 cups uncooked mostaccioli

Excellent: Potassium
Good: Iron

Diabetic Exchanges: 3 starch, 1 1/2 lean meat, 1 vegetable

In large skillet, cook ground meat over medium heat until well done, about 5 minutes, stirring occasionally. Drain excess fat, set meat aside.

Over medium heat in same skillet, cook onion in vegetable oil until golden, about 5 minutes. Do not let onion turn brown. Add garlic, pepper, tomato sauce, tomato paste, basil and oregano. Add the browned meat. Cover and simmer over low heat 25 minutes.

Meanwhile, cook noodles according to package directions, omitting any salt and oil. Drain noodles, toss with tomato sauce. Serve immediately. Makes 8 servings.

Nutrition Information Per Serving

Energy	322 calories
Fat	7 g
Saturated fat	2 g
Cholesterol	29 mg
Sodium	220 mg
Carbohydrate	48 g
Protein	18 g

Spaghetti Squash with White Clam Sauce

Spaghetti squash is a unique squash that becomes very stringy when a fork is run through the flesh. Cover it with your favorite sauce for a tasty, low-fat, no-cholesterol noodle.

2 dozen fresh littleneck clams, or 16 standard-size fresh clams
1/3 cup dry white wine
1 tablespoon olive oil
3 to 4 cloves garlic, peeled and minced
1/4 teaspoon salt
Freshly ground pepper to taste
6 to 8 cups cooked, shredded squash (see directions below)
1/4 cup chopped parsley
2 tablespoons grated Parmesan cheese

Scrub clams. Steam them in wine in a saucepan over medium heat until they open (about 8 to 10 minutes). Remove flesh, discard shells, strain broth and reserve one cup broth.

Heat oil in a large skillet and saute garlic until softened but not browned, about 5 minutes. Add wine-clam broth to oil, add salt and pepper, then bring to a boil. Lower heat and simmer 5 minutes. Add clams and stir. Pour over hot spaghetti squash (cooking methods follow) and toss with parsley and Parmesan cheese. Makes 4-6 servings.

FOR BAKED WHOLE SPAGHETTI SQUASH: Prick a spaghetti squash with fork so skin will not burst while cooking. Bake in preheated 350-degree oven for 40 to 90 minutes, depending on size. It is done when a fork goes easily into the flesh.

FOR BOILED WHOLE SPAGHETTI SQUASH: Boil a large kettle of water in a pot large enough to hold the whole squash. When water is boiling, place squash in pot and cook 20 to 30 minutes, depending on size. When a fork goes easily into the flesh, the squash is done. Remove from water and let cool.

FOR MICROWAVE WHOLE SPAGHETTI SQUASH: Prick skin all over with a fork. Place uncovered on a paper towel and cook in microwave oven on medium high 6 to 8 minutes per pound (about 15 to 25 minutes total for a small to average-size squash) or until fork goes easily into the flesh. Remove from oven and let cool (squash will continue to cook).

Regardless of how it's cooked, the squash will cool faster if you split it in half lengthwise with a sharp knife. When it is cool enough to handle, remove the seeds and stringy portion and discard. With a fork, comb the squash flesh; the flesh will pull off in long spaghetti-like strands.

Good: Fiber
Excellent: Potassium
Good: Iron
Good: Vitamin A
Excellent: Vitamin C

Diabetic Exchanges: 2 lean meat, 2 vegetable

Nutrition Information Per Serving

Energy	189 calories
Fat	6 g
Saturated fat	2 g
Cholesterol	45 mg
Sodium	289 mg
Carbohydrate	17 g
Protein	15 g

Turkey Lasagna

This recipe uses Turkey Breakfast Sausage (see recipe on page 72) for extra flavor. Compare this to regular lasagna, which contains about 500 calories and 45 grams of fat per serving.

3/4 pound uncooked Turkey Breakfast
    Sausage (Use half of recipe)
1 can (15 ounces) tomato sauce (2 cups)
1/2 teaspoon garlic powder
1/4 teaspoon black pepper
1/2 teaspoon crushed, dried basil leaves
1/2 cup water
1 package (7 ounces) macaroni, cooked and
    drained
1 1/2 cups cream style 1-percent lowfat
    cottage cheese
1 1/2 cups processed low-fat American
    cheese, shredded

Preheat oven to 375 degrees.
Brown turkey sausage. Add tomato sauce, garlic powder, pepper, basil and 1/2 cup water. Cover; simmer 15 minutes, stirring occasionally.
In a 2-quart casserole layer half each of macaroni, cottage cheese, shredded cheese and meat sauce. Repeat. Bake for 30 minutes. Remove from oven and let stand 10 minutes. Makes 6 to 8 servings.

Excellent: Potassium
Good: Calcium

Diabetic Exchanges: 4 lean meat, 1 starch, 1 vegetable

Nutrition Information Per Serving	
Energy	282 calories
Fat	9 g
Saturated fat	5 g
Cholesterol	56 mg
Sodium	774 mg
Carbohydrate	19 g
Protein	31 g

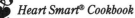

Turkey Stuffed Shells

The jumbo shells and turkey make this recipe an attractive, Heart Smart® main course for entertaining. Pasta has taken many forms since it was first brought to Europe. In Italian, pasta means "paste." It is actually a pasty mixture of ground grain and liquid.

Nutrition Information Per Serving

Energy	287 calories
Fat	9 g
Saturated fat	2 g
Cholesterol	35 mg
Sodium	208 mg
Carbohydrate	33 g
Protein	20 g

Vegetable cooking spray
16 jumbo macaroni shells
1 1/2 cups finely chopped celery
1/4 cup water
2 tablespoons soft tub margarine
1 cup finely chopped onion
1 clove garlic, minced
3 tablespoons all-purpose flour
1 3/4 cups skim milk
1/2 cup chicken broth
1 tablespoon Dijon mustard
1/8 teaspoon thyme
1/8 teaspoon pepper
2 1/2 cups diced cooked turkey
1 tablespoon mayonnaise-like salad dressing
2 tablespoons non-fat plain yogurt
1/3 cup raisins
1/3 cup finely chopped walnuts
1 tablespoon chopped parsley for garnish (optional)

Preheat oven to 375 degrees. Spray an 11-by-7-inch or 9-by-9 inch baking dish with vegetable cooking spray and set aside.

In a small soup pot, cook shells according to package directions, omitting salt. Drain in a colander. Rinse the shells thoroughly in cold water to prevent sticking, then set aside.

Meanwhile, in a small saucepan over medium-high heat, steam the celery in 1/4 cup water.

Cook 5 minutes or until soft, stirring often. In a small saucepan, melt margarine and saute onion and garlic; cook, stirring often, 2 to 5 minutes.

Add the celery to the onion mixture. Mix to combine. Place 3/4 cup of the steamed and sauteed vegetables in large bowl. Sprinkle flour over the remaining onion-celery mixture in skillet, stirring constantly for 30 seconds. Gradually stir in milk and broth. Stir in mustard, thyme and pepper. Cook, stirring often, 5 minutes or until thickened mixture comes to a boil. Reduce heat and simmer 2 minutes. Remove from the heat.

Add turkey to reserved onion-celery mixture in the bowl. Stir in the salad dressing, yogurt and 1/2 cup of the white sauce mixture from the skillet. Add raisins and chopped nuts. Fill each shell with turkey mixture from the bowl. Place turkey-filled shells in prepared baking dish and pour the contents of the skillet over the shells. Sprinkle with the parsley. Bake 20 minutes or until heated through. Makes 8 servings.

Excellent: Potassium

Diabetic Exchanges: 2 lean meat, 2 starch

Brown Rice Pilaf

Brown rice has the bran, or outer coating, still intact. This provides lots of fiber and a nuttier flavor than white rice.

1/2 cup diced onion
1/2 cup low-sodium chicken broth, defatted
1 cup water
3/4 cup brown rice, uncooked
1/2 cup chopped, seeded red pepper
1/8 teaspoon dried whole thyme

Preheat oven to 350 degrees.
Combine onion and chicken broth in a 1-quart, ceramic, ovenproof dish; cover and cook over medium heat on top of the stove for about 3 minutes or until onion is translucent, stirring frequently. Stir in remaining ingredients. Bring to a boil. Remove from heat. Cover and bake for 40 minutes or until liquid is absorbed. Makes four 1/2-cup servings.

Excellent: Fiber

Diabetic Exchanges: 2 starch

Nutrition Information Per Serving

Energy	144 calories
Fat	trace
Saturated fat	0
Cholesterol	0
Sodium	7 mg
Carbohydrate	30 g
Protein	3 g

Rice Florentine

Long-grain rice (and the name means exactly that — the grains are longer than medium-grain or short-grain rice) tends to cook up fluffier and lighter than the short-grain kind.

1/4 cup chopped onion
1 1/2 teaspoons olive oil
1/2 cup long-grain rice
1/4 teaspoon salt
1 1/4 cups water
1/2 cup chopped spinach
1 tablespoon fresh lemon juice
1/4 cup chopped sweet red pepper

In a small saucepan, saute onion in olive oil until soft. Mix in the rice and salt. Add water and bring to a boil. Reduce heat to low and cover saucepan. After 15 minutes, stir spinach and lemon juice into rice. Cook 10 minutes more or until liquid is completely absorbed. Mix in red pepper and serve. Makes four 1/2-cup servings.

Diabetic Exchanges: 1 starch, 1 vegetable

Nutrition Information Per Serving

Energy	106 calories
Fat	2 g
Saturated fat	trace
Cholesterol	0
Sodium	130 mg
Carbohydrate	20 g
Protein	2 g

Heart Smart® Cookbook

Risotto Parmesan with Asparagus

Risotto is a short-grain rice simmered in a flavorful liquid. It is creamy and delicious. To defat the canned broth you'll need, put it in the refrigerator before use; then skim the fat off after opening.

Risotto Parmesan (recipe follows)
1/2 pound asparagus
1/2 cup nonfat plain yogurt

Prepare basic risotto, but decrease broth to about 3 cups and add 1/8 teaspoon white pepper.

While risotto is cooking, snap off tough ends of asparagus. Cut stems diagonally into 1/2-inch slices. Set tips aside. About 10 minutes before rice is done, mix in sliced asparagus stems. About 5 minutes later, mix in tips. When rice is almost done, stir in yogurt. Makes six 1/2-cup servings.

Good: Potassium

Diabetic Exchanges: 2 starch, 1 fat, 1/2 vegetable

**Nutrition Information
Per Serving**

Energy ....224 calories
Fat ....6 g
Saturated fat ....2 g
Cholesterol ....7 mg
Sodium ....221 mg
Carbohydrate ......30 g
Protein ....9 g

Risotto Parmesan

1 tablespoon soft tub margarine, divided
1 tablespoon olive oil
1 small onion, peeled and finely chopped
1 small clove garlic, peeled and minced
1 cup imported Italian rice (short-grain or long-grain rice)
2 cans (14 1/2 ounces each) low-sodium chicken or beef broth, defatted
1/2 cup shredded or grated Parmesan cheese

Place half of the margarine (1 1/2 teaspoons) with the olive oil in a heavy 2-quart pan over medium heat. When margarine is melted, add onion and cook, stirring until soft and golden. Add garlic and rice, and stir until rice looks milky and opaque (about 3 minutes). Mix in broth; cook, stirring occasionally, until mixture comes to a boil. Adjust heat so rice boils gently; cook uncovered, stirring occasionally until rice is tender and most of the liquid has been absorbed. (20 to 25 minutes). Toward end of cooking time, stir rice often to prevent sticking. Remove from heat and add 1/2 Parmesan cheese and remaining 1 1/2 teaspoons of margarine; mix gently. Turn into a warm serving bowl and top with remaining cheese. Makes 6 servings.

Diabetic Exchanges:
2 starch, 1 fat

Nutrition Information Per Serving

Energy .... 205 calories
Fat .... 6 g
Saturated fat .... 2 g
Cholesterol .... 7 mg
Sodium .... 205 mg
Carbohydrate ...... 28 g
Protein .... 8 g

Sauteed Mushrooms and Rice

Try substituting wild mushrooms for a deep, rich, woodsy flavor.

1 1/2 cups water
1/2 cup dry white wine
1 teaspoon low-sodium instant beef broth
1 cup enriched white rice
1 tablespoon soft tub margarine
12 ounces sliced fresh mushrooms, cleaned
1 finely chopped garlic clove

In a medium saucepan, heat water, wine and instant broth to boiling over high heat. Stir in rice and simmer, covered, over low heat until rice is tender and all the liquid is absorbed, about 20 to 25 minutes.

While rice is simmering, melt margarine in a medium skillet over medium heat. Saute mushrooms and garlic in the margarine until tender and slightly browned, about 10 minutes; set aside.

When rice is done, remove saucepan from heat and stir in sauteed garlic and mushrooms. Makes 6 servings.

Good: Potassium

Diabetic Exchanges: 1 1/2 starch, 1 vegetable

Nutrition Information Per Serving

Energy .... 161 calories
Fat .... 2 g
Saturated fat .... trace
Cholesterol 0
Sodium .... 31 mg
Carbohydrate ...... 28 g
Protein .... 3 g

Heart Smart® Cookbook

Tex-Mex Beans and Rice

Beans and rice together provide all the amino acids necessary for the body to use as a complete protein.

Beans
1 cup red kidney beans, dried (not canned)
Water to cover beans for soaking
1 1/2 quarts warm water for cooking beans
1 cup diced onion
1/2 cup diced green pepper
2 large tomatoes, chopped
2 cloves garlic, peeled and minced
1/4 teaspoon cayenne pepper
1/2 teaspoon dried oregano
1/2 teaspoon dried thyme
1 bay leaf
1/4 teaspoon black pepper
1/4 teaspoon cumin

Rice
1 cup uncooked rice
2 cups water

TO MAKE BEANS: Sort and wash beans; place in Dutch oven. Add water to cover 2 inches above beans. Let soak overnight. Drain and rinse beans, discarding water. Return beans to Dutch oven. Add 1 1/2 quarts warm water and bring to a boil over high heat. Add onions, green pepper, tomatoes, garlic, cayenne pepper, oregano, thyme, bay leaf, black pepper and cumin. Reduce heat to medium low. Cook uncovered for 1 hour. Add additional water if necessary. Cook an additional hour, or until beans are tender.

TO MAKE RICE: Meanwhile, combine rice and water in saucepan and bring to a boil, uncovered, over high heat. Cover, reduce heat and simmer 15 to 20 minutes or until rice is tender.

Discard bay leaf from beans; serve beans over hot rice. Makes 4 servings.

Excellent: Fiber
Good: Iron
Good: Vitamin C

Diabetic Exchanges:
2 1/2 starch, 2 vegetable

Nutrition Information Per Serving

Energy	247 calories
Fat	trace
Saturated fat	trace
Cholesterol	0
Sodium	11 mg
Carbohydrate	53 g
Protein	8 g

 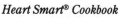

Vegetables

Apple and Parsnip Puree

For a special presentation of this dish, place the puree in a pastry bag fitted with a star tip and pipe onto the serving plate in an attractive pattern.

1/4 cup lemon juice
1/4 cup water
4 large Granny Smith or other tart apples, peeled, seeded, cored, cut into eighths
2 pounds parsnips, peeled, ends removed, coarsely chopped
1/4 cup chicken broth
1 tablespoon soft tub margarine
2 tablespoons light brown sugar
1/4 teaspoon ground nutmeg
Black pepper to taste
Parsley for garnish

Preheat oven to 375 degrees.

In a large bowl, combine lemon juice and water. Place apple pieces in lemon juice mixture. Toss to coat.

Place parsnips in a 9-by-13-inch baking pan. With slotted spoon, add the apples and 1/4 cup of lemon juice mixture. Add chicken broth. Dot the parsnips and apples with margarine and sprinkle with brown sugar, nutmeg and pepper. Cover dish, bake 1 1/2 hours, stirring a few times during the baking. Remove parsnips and apples from oven and cool at least 20 minutes, stirring occasionally for faster cooling.

Reduce oven temperature to 350 degrees. Transfer the cooled parsnips and apples with their cooking liquid to a food processor and puree until smooth, working in batches if necessary. Reheat in a covered ovenproof dish for 15 minutes. Serve garnished with parsley. Makes 8 servings.

Excellent: Fiber
Excellent: Potassium
Good: Vitamin C

Diabetic Exchanges: 1 vegetable, 1 fruit, 1 starch

Nutrition Information Per Serving

Energy .... 162 calories
Fat .... 2 g
Saturated fat .... trace
Cholesterol .... trace
Sodium .... 56 mg
Carbohydrate ...... 37 g
Protein .... 2 g

Eggplant Italiano

Eggplant is best when it is very, very fresh. A truly fresh eggplant will begin to lose its flavor after just 3 or 4 days. This dish is much heart-healthier than eggplant Parmesan, which contains 570 calories per serving and 44 grams of fat, almost 10 teaspoons.

6 round, 1/2-inch thick slices eggplant, peeled
1/4 cup egg substitute
1/2 cup Italian bread crumbs
Vegetable cooking spray
1 cup tomato sauce
1/2 teaspoon oregano
1/2 teaspoon basil
5 ounces part-skim milk mozzarella cheese, grated or sliced

Preheat oven to 450 degrees.

Using mallet, pound eggplant slices to 1/4-inch thickness. Dip eggplant slices in egg substitute, then in bread crumbs. Saute breaded eggplant in skillet sprayed with nonstick vegetable spray.

Place cooked eggplant in bottom of 10-by-10-inch baking dish. Top with tomato sauce, oregano and basil. Arrange cheese over top. Bake at 450 degrees for 15 to 20 minutes. Finish browning cheese under broiler if necessary. Makes 6 servings.

Excellent: Potassium

Diabetic Exchanges: 2 vegetable, 1 medium-fat meat, 1/4 starch

Nutrition Information Per Serving	
Energy	140 calories
Fat	5 g
Saturated fat	3 g
Cholesterol	14 mg
Sodium	439 mg
Carbohydrate	16 g
Protein	9 g

Grilled Marinated Vegetables

These make an easy and unusual side dish, perfect if you've got the barbecue fired up for the main course.

2 tablespoons lemon juice
1/2 cup orange juice
1 tablespoon olive oil
2 cloves garlic, peeled, ends removed, crushed
1 tablespoon fresh rosemary or other herb of choice, washed, dried, finely chopped
1 cup new potatoes (small)
3/4 cup fresh mushrooms, cleaned, sliced
3/4 cup cherry tomatoes, stemmed, washed, dried
3/4 cup red, green or yellow peppers, seeded, cored, ends removed, cut into 1 1/2-inch square pieces
3/4 cup zucchini, washed, ends removed, sliced

Preheat grill.

In a jar, combine lemon juice, orange juice, olive oil, garlic, and fresh rosemary or other herb of choice; mix well.

In a small bowl, place 1 tablespoon of marinade. Add potatoes to bowl. Let potatoes marinate about 1 to 2 hours.

In separate medium bowl, place 3 tablespoons of marinade, reserving remaining marinade for another time. Add mushrooms, tomatoes, red, green or yellow peppers and zucchini. Marinate 1 to 2 hours.

After marinating, place the potatoes on a square of heavy-duty foil. Place marinated mushrooms, tomatoes, red, green or yellow peppers and zucchini on a separate piece of heavy duty foil. Bring the edges of the foil together and fold to close. Cook the potatoes on the grill for about 20 to 30 minutes, turning once. Cook mushrooms, tomatoes, peppers and zucchini for 6 to 8 minutes, turning once. Makes eight 1/2-cup servings.

Excellent: Potassium
Excellent: Vitamin C

Diabetic Exchanges:
2 vegetable, 1/2 starch

Nutrition Information Per Serving

Energy	88 calories
Fat	1 g
Saturated fat	trace
Cholesterol	0
Sodium	8 mg
Carbohydrate	18 g
Protein	2 g

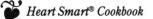

Hash Brown Potatoes

Hash browns don't have to be dripping in fat to have flavor. Ours aren't. And these hash browns include potato skin. The flavor is great, and they contain lots of fiber.

3 medium baking potatoes, washed, cooked,
    grated with skins on
2 tablespoons grated onion
1/4 teaspoon salt
Pepper to taste
1 tablespoon vegetable oil
1 tablespoon parsley, washed, chopped

In a large bowl, mix grated potatoes, grated onion, salt and pepper.

In a nonstick pan, heat oil over medium-high heat. Put potatoes in skillet. Cover and cook over medium-low heat until bottom is brown. Turn and brown on other side. Sprinkle parsley on top and serve. Makes 4 servings.

Good: Fiber
Excellent: Potassium
Good: Iron

Diabetic Exchanges: 2 starch, 1/2 fat

**Nutrition Information
Per Serving**

Energy .... 197 calories
Fat .... 4 g
Saturated fat .... trace
Cholesterol 0
Sodium .... 135 mg
Carbohydrate ...... 39 g
Protein .... 4 g

Oven–Baked French Fries

A same-size serving of french fries at a fast-food restaurant contains about 23 grams of fat. This recipe has just a trace. Also, you can season these fries before baking by sprinkling the potato strips with chili powder or salt-free spice.

6 large russet or other baking potatoes, scrubbed
Vegetable cooking spray

Preheat oven to 475 degrees.

Cut each potato into 1/2-inch strips, or make them thicker if you prefer more of a potato wedge.

Lightly spray a baking pan with vegetable cooking spray. Working in two batches, arrange potato strips in a single layer on baking sheet. Spray strips with vegetable cooking spray before placing pan in oven. Bake the strips 15 to 20 minutes, turn them and continue baking until crisp and browned, approximately 15 to 20 more minutes (more for thicker wedges). Makes 6 servings.

Good: Fiber
Excellent: Potassium
Good: Vitamin C
Good: Iron

Diabetic Exchanges: 2 1/2 starch

**Nutrition Information
Per Serving**

Energy .... 222 calories
Fat .... trace
Saturated fat .... trace
Cholesterol 0
Sodium .... 16 mg
Carbohydrate ...... 51 g
Protein .... 5 g

Potato and Parsnip Mash

Ricotta cheese can be made from whole milk or skim milk. Read the label to be sure you choose a carton made from skim milk.

1 1/2 pounds parsnips, peeled, ends removed, diced
2 to 3 cups water, divided
1 1/2 pounds boiling potatoes, peeled, diced
3/4 cup part-skim milk ricotta cheese
3/4 cup skim milk
1 tablespoon soft tub margarine
Black pepper to taste
1 green onion (white bulb and 3 inches of greens) for garnish, washed, ends removed, sliced very thin along the diagonal (optional)

In a wide skillet, cover parsnips in 1 to 1 1/2 cups water and cook 10 to 15 minutes. Drain parsnips and return to the pan. Shake over medium heat for 30 seconds to remove excess moisture. Set aside.

Place potatoes in a sauce pan with remaining 1 to 2 cups water, and bring to a boil. Reduce the heat slightly and cook uncovered until very tender, 20 to 30 minutes. Drain potatoes and return them to the saucepan. Shake over medium heat for 30 seconds to remove excess moisture.

Transfer parsnips and potatoes to mixing bowl.

Beat with electric mixer on medium speed until lump-free, gradually adding ricotta cheese, milk, margarine and pepper. Beat until smooth. Garnish with green onion if desired. Makes 8 servings.

Diabetic Exchanges: 1 starch, 1 vegetable, 1/2 milk, 1/2 fat

Nutrition Information Per Serving

Energy .... 172 calories
Fat .... 3 g
Saturated fat .... 1 g
Cholesterol .... 8 mg
Sodium .... 70 mg
Carbohydrate ..... 31 g
Protein .... 6 g

Potato Latkes

Latkes are pancakes made in many Jewish kitchens, usually using eggs and butter. Try this lighter version.

6 medium potatoes, grated (about 3 cups)
1 onion, chopped
2 egg whites, or 1/4 cup egg substitute
1/4 cup bread crumbs
Black pepper to taste
1/2 teaspoon salt
2 tablespoons vegetable oil
Vegetable cooking spray

Mix grated potatoes and chopped onion in bowl. Stir in egg whites or egg substitute and mix well. Add bread crumbs, pepper and salt and combine well.

Preheat oven to 350 degrees.

Heat vegetable oil in a large nonstick skillet over medium heat. To make each pancake, drop about 1/4 cup of the potato mixture into the skillet and flatten into a rounded rectangle about 2 by 3 inches, just under 1/2-inch thick. Lightly brown pancakes on one side, then turn and brown on the other side (pancakes will fall apart if they are not cooked enough on first side before turning). Transfer to a baking sheet that has been lightly coated with vegetable cooking spray, stacking pancakes on top of each other. Bake pancakes about 15 minutes. Turn once and bake another 10 minutes. Transfer to a platter and blot with paper towels before serving. (If you prefer crisper latkes, use enough baking sheets to have a single layer of latkes. Reduce baking time to 8 to 10 minutes on each side.) Makes 12 two-pancake servings.

Diabetic Exchanges:
1 starch, 1/2 fat

**Nutrition Information
Per Serving**

Energy .... 96 calories
Fat .... 3 g
Saturated fat .... trace
Cholesterol 0
Sodium .... 108 mg
Carbohydrate ...... 16 g
Protein .... 2 g

Southern Black-Eyed Peas

Southern tradition says black-eyed peas bring good luck if served on New Year's Day. Our low-fat version of them surely will.

2 cups shelled fresh or frozen black-eyed
     peas (half of an 18-ounce bag), defrosted
2 cups water
Vegetable cooking spray
1 medium onion, chopped
1/2 teaspoon beef-flavored bouillon granules
1/4 teaspoon ground savory
1/4 teaspoon crushed red pepper flakes

If you use fresh peas, wash and drain them well. Combine peas and water in a medium saucepan; bring to a boil. Cover, reduce heat and simmer for 10 minutes.

Meanwhile, spray a medium nonstick skillet with vegetable cooking spray. Saute onion in the pan until soft, about 3 minutes. Add bouillon granules, savory and red pepper flakes and stir to combine. Add onion mixture to beans, cover and let simmer 50 minutes more or until tender. Makes 4 servings.

Good: Fiber
Excellent: Potassium

Diabetic Exchanges: 1 starch, 1 vegetable

Nutrition Information Per Serving

Energy .... 104 calories
Fat .... 1 g
Saturated fat 0
Cholesterol .... trace
Sodium .... 154 mg
Carbohydrate ...... 17 g
Protein .... 7 g

Squash and Potato Bake

Butternut squash is a sweet-tasting winter squash very high in Vitamin A.

8 teaspoons soft tub margarine
4 egg whites
1/2 teaspoon salt
1/4 teaspoon basil
1/4 teaspoon thyme
1/8 teaspoon pepper
1 onion, peeled, ends removed
1 clove garlic, peeled, and minced or
  pressed
1 butternut squash (about 1 pound)
2 medium russet potatoes
1/4 cup fine dry bread crumbs
Vegetable cooking spray

Melt margarine in small pan over low heat; pour into a large mixing bowl. Let cool, then beat in egg whites, salt, basil, thyme and pepper. Insert metal blade into food processor work bowl. Finely chop onion and add onion and garlic to egg mixture.

Change blade to shredding disc. Cut squash in half. Scoop out and discard seeds and fiber. Peel and cut into pieces to fit feed tube. Shred squash and add it to egg mixture. Peel potatoes, then shred. (Or shred squash and potatoes in a cheese grater.) Add to egg mixture with bread crumbs; stir well. Spread mixture evenly in a 10-inch quiche dish or pie pan that has been lightly sprayed with vegetable cooking spray. Bake uncovered in a 350-degree oven until lightly browned, about 1 hour. Makes 8 servings.

Good: Potassium
Excellent: Vitamin A

Diabetic Exchanges: 1 starch, 1/2 fat

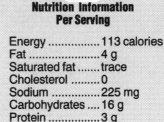

**Nutrition Information
Per Serving**

Energy .... 113 calories
Fat .... 4 g
Saturated fat .... trace
Cholesterol 0
Sodium .... 225 mg
Carbohydrates .... 16 g
Protein .... 3 g

 Heart Smart® Cookbook

Stuffed Tomatoes with Herbs

Try sprinkling a small amount of Parmesan cheese on top of the tomatoes before baking for variety. Instead of baking them, you can microwave on medium in a microwave-safe dish until tomatoes are soft and warm, 1 to 2 minutes.

4 medium tomatoes
2 green onions, diced, green tops included
1 medium zucchini, diced
1/4 teaspoon dried dill
1/4 teaspoon dried oregano
1/4 teaspoon basil
Freshly ground pepper to taste
1/2 cup bread crumbs
Chopped fresh parsley for garnish

Preheat oven to 350 degrees.

Remove top of each tomato and discard. Scoop inner pulp and seeds into a bowl. Mix pulp and seeds with green onions, zucchini, dill, oregano, basil and pepper.

Put tomatoes in an 8- or 9-inch square baking dish. Fill each with one-quarter of the mixture and top with one-quarter of the bread crumbs. Bake 20 minutes. Garnish with chopped parsley. Makes 4 servings.

Good: Potassium
Excellent: Vitamin A
Excellent: Vitamin C

Diabetic Exchanges: 1 vegetable, 1/4 starch

Nutrition Information Per Serving

Energy .... 47 calories
Fat .... trace
Saturated fat .... trace
Cholesterol 0
Sodium .... 41 mg
Carbohydrate ...... 10 g
Protein .... 2 g

Stuffed Winter Squash

You can microwave this dish using the same instructions for combining ingredients. Then cover with wax paper and cook on high 8 minutes per pound.

1 cup cooked brown or white rice
1 tablespoons walnuts, shelled, coarsely
   chopped
3/4 cup bread crumbs
1 medium onion, peeled, finely chopped
1 egg white or 1/4 cup egg substitute
1/8 teaspoon thyme
2 teaspoons chopped fresh parsley, washed,
   dried
1/4 teaspoon salt
1/4 teaspoon pepper
2 acorn squash, washed, dried, cut in half,
   seeds removed

Preheat oven to 350 degrees.
 In a medium bowl combine the rice,
walnuts, bread crumbs, onion, egg white or
egg substitute, thyme, parsley, salt and
pepper. Place mixture loosely in squash
halves. Bake stuffed squash in a pan covered
with foil for one hour or until squash is easily
pierced with fork. Makes 4 servings.

Good: Fiber
Excellent: Potassium
Excellent: Vitamin A
Good: Vitamin C

Diabetic Exchanges: 2 starch

Nutrition Information
Per Serving

Energy .... 152 calories
Fat .... 2 g
Saturated fat .... trace
Cholesterol 0
Sodium .... 182 mg
Carbohydrate ...... 31 g
Protein .... 5 g

Cakes, Cookies

Rich Chocolate Cake with Frosting

Compare regular chocolate cake with frosting to this Heart Smart® cake with frosting: The usual cake has 303 calories, 12 grams of fat, 7 grams of saturated fat, 56 milligrams of cholesterol and 233 milligrams of sodium per serving.

1 1/4 cups sugar, divided
1/2 cup cocoa, sifted
1 cup buttermilk or yogurt, divided
1/2 cup soft tub margarine
4 egg whites
2 cups cake flour, sifted, plus 1 teaspoon for pan
1 teaspoon baking soda
1/8 teaspoon salt
1 teaspoon vanilla
Vegetable cooking spray

Preheat oven to 350 degrees.
In a medium bowl, beat 3/4 cup sugar, cocoa and 1/2 cup buttermilk or yogurt until well blended. Set aside. In a large bowl, beat margarine, gradually adding remaining 1/2 cup sugar. Add egg whites and beat until blended. Beat in cocoa mixture. Re-sift 2 cups of cake flour with baking soda and salt. Add the flour in three parts to the margarine mixture, alternating with remaining buttermilk or yogurt and vanilla. Beat batter after each addition until smooth.
Spray tube pan with vegetable cooking spray and flour well. Pour batter into pan and bake about 1 hour in preheated oven. Let cake cool 10 minutes on wire rack, then remove from pan. Frost with icing (optional, see below). Makes one 9-inch tube cake, about 16 slices.

Chocolate Frosting

2 tablespoons soft tub margarine
4 tablespoons cocoa, sifted
1 cup powdered sugar, sifted
1/2 teaspoon vanilla
2 tablespoons skim milk

Combine margarine and cocoa in a small mixing bowl; beat at medium speed with electric mixer until smooth. Add powdered sugar and vanilla; mix well. Gradually add milk, one teaspoon at a time; beat until smooth. Spread mixture over top of cake.

Diabetic Exchanges: Not appropriate for diabetics

Nutrition Information Per Serving	
Energy	218 calories
Fat	8 g
Saturated fat	1 g
Cholesterol	trace
Sodium	172 mg
Carbohydrate	35 g
Protein	3 g

Chocolate Valentine Cake with Raspberry Filling

Your Valentine will love you for making this Heart Smart® cake.

1 1/4 cups sugar, divided
1/2 cup cocoa, sifted
1 cup buttermilk, divided
1/2 cup soft tub margarine
4 egg whites
2 cups cake flour, sifted, plus one teaspoon for pan
1 teaspoon baking soda
1/8 teaspoon salt
1 teaspoon vanilla
Vegetable cooking spray
Raspberry Filling (recipe follows)

Preheat oven to 350 degrees.

In a medium bowl, beat until well blended: 3/4 cup sugar, cocoa and 1/2 cup buttermilk. Set aside.

In a large bowl, beat margarine, gradually adding remaining 1/2 cup sugar. Add egg whites and beat until blended. Beat in cocoa mixture. Re-sift 2 cups cake flour with baking soda and salt. Add 2 cups of cake flour in 3 parts to the margarine mixture, alternating with remaining buttermilk and vanilla. Beat batter after each addition until smooth.

Spray bundt or tube pan with vegetable cooking spray and dust with remaining 1 teaspoon of flour. Pour batter into pan and bake 40 to 45 minutes.

Let cake cool in pan about 10 minutes on wire rack, then remove from pan. Let cake continue to cool an additional 30 minutes. With a sharp knife, slice cake horizontally though center so you will be able to spread raspberry filling inside the cake. Spread filling evenly on bottom half of the cake and carefully replace top half. Be sure to line up ridges if you are using a bundt pan. Makes 1 cake, about 16 slices.

Raspberry Filling

2 containers (10 ounces each) frozen red raspberries (sugar added)
2 tablespoons cold water
1 tablespoon cornstarch

Defrost berries according to instructions on container. Reserve 1/4 cup juice and discard remaining juice from berries. In a small saucepan, combine berries and 1/4 cup juice; cook on low heat until slightly thickened. While berries heat, mix cold water with cornstarch and stir until cornstarch is dissolved. Add cornstarch to berries and continue heating until mixture becomes the consistency of jam. Remove from heat; refrigerate until ready to spread, at least 20 minutes.

Diabetic Exchanges: Not appropriate for diabetics

Nutrition Information Per Serving

Energy .... 217 calories
Fat .... 6 g
Saturated fat .... 1 g
Cholesterol .... trace
Sodium .... 172 mg
Carbohydrate ...... 39 g
Protein .... 3 g

Golden Angel Food Cake with Fresh Strawberries

This is a healthy option in place of traditional strawberry shortcake, which can be loaded with fat.

1 cup cake flour
1 cup sugar, plus 6 teaspoons (optional) for strawberries
1/4 teaspoon salt
10 egg whites
1 teaspoon cream of tartar
1/2 teaspoon vanilla
1/2 teaspoon grated lemon zest
3 pints fresh strawberries
12 sprigs of fresh mint

Pre-heat oven to 375 degrees.

Sift the flour twice, the second time adding 1 cup sugar and salt. Set aside. Beat egg whites until foamy. Add cream of tartar and continue to whip until stiff but not dry. Gently fold in flour mixture, vanilla and lemon zest. Pour into an ungreased tube pan, preferably with removable rim. Bake about 45 minutes in the lower part of the oven.

When cake springs back lightly when touched, it is done. Remove from oven and invert the pan onto a rack. Let it rest 1 to 1 1/2 hours until it is thoroughly cooled.

While cake is cooling, pick over strawberries and place in a colander. Rinse berries with cool water, using your hand to break the force of the water. Drain well, remove hulls (leafy caps), slice strawberries and refrigerate until ready to serve. Add sugar if added sweetness is desired.

Cake should come down out of the pan on its own when cool; if it does not after 1 1/2 hours of cooling, gently run a knife around the edge to remove it. Cut with a pronged cake divider or saw gently with a serrated knife. (Cut it into 12 pieces.)

To serve, place a piece of cake on a dessert plate and arrange strawberry slices on top, about 1/2 cup per serving. Garnish each with a sprig of mint. Makes 12 servings.

Excellent: Vitamin C

Diabetic Exchanges: Not appropriate for diabetics

Nutrition Information Per Serving

Energy	116 calories
Fat	trace
Saturated fat	0
Cholesterol	0
Sodium	141 mg
Carbohydrate	25 g
Protein	4 g

Holiday Fruitcake

Dried fruits are high in calories because they contain little water. Ten dates contain 200 calories. Use them sparingly in holiday baking.

1 package (8 ounces) pitted dates or figs, chopped
1 package (8 ounces) chopped, dried apricots
1/2 cup dark rum
1 cup cranberries, chopped
1 can (6 ounces) frozen orange juice concentrate, thawed, undiluted
1 cup chopped pecans
1 tablespoon grated orange rind
1 teaspoon vanilla
2 eggs, lightly beaten
1 can (8 ounces, or 1 cup) unsweetened pineapple chunks, drained
2 cups all-purpose flour
1 1/4 teaspoons baking soda
1/4 teaspoon salt
1 teaspoon cinnamon
1/2 teaspoon mace
Vegetable cooking spray

Combine dates or figs, apricots and rum in a medium bowl and allow to sit at room temperature overnight.

The next day, add cranberries and orange juice concentrate and let stand 1 hour. Add pecans, orange rind, vanilla, eggs and pineapple, and stir well.

In separate bowl, combine flour, baking soda, salt, cinnamon and mace. Add to fruit mixture and stir well.

Preheat oven to 325 degrees. With vegetable cooking spray, lightly coat a bundt pan or two 9-by-5-inch loaf pans. Pour batter into pan and bake 45 minutes or until wooden pick comes out clean. Cool in pan 20 minutes; remove and let cool completely on a rack. Makes 16 servings.

Excellent: Potassium
Good: Vitamin A
Good: Vitamin C

Diabetic Exchanges: 1 1/2 fruit, 1 starch, 1 fat

Nutrition Information Per Serving

Energy .... 223 calories
Fat .... 6 g
Saturated fat .... 1 g
Cholesterol 27mg
Sodium .... 106 mg
Carbohydrate ...... 38 g
Protein .... 4 g

Marbled Angel Food Cake

Egg whites at room temperature will beat into a froth more easily than cold eggs.

1/2 cup plus 5 tablespoons unbleached all-purpose flour
1 1/4 cups sugar, divided
3 tablespoons unsweetened cocoa powder
10 egg whites, at room temperature
1 teaspoon cream of tartar
1/2 teaspoon almond extract
1/2 teaspoon vanilla
1 tablespoon confectioners' sugar

Sift 1/2 cup of flour and 2 tablespoons of sugar into a medium bowl. Sift the mixture three more times and set it aside.

Sift the remaining 5 tablespoons of flour, the cocoa powder and 2 more tablespoons of sugar into a medium bowl. Sift the cocoa mixture 3 more times and set it aside.

Preheat the oven to 350 degrees. Rinse out a tube pan and shake—do not wipe it—dry.

With an electric mixer, beat the egg whites until soft peaks form when the beater is lifted. Add the cream of tartar, then blend in the remaining cup of sugar a little at a time, beating the mixture until it forms stiff peaks. With the mixer set on the lowest speed, blend in the almond extract, then the vanilla.

Transfer half the beaten egg whites to a clean bowl. Fold the dry mixture without cocoa into half the beaten egg whites. Fold the cocoa mixture into the other beaten egg whites, then pour the chocolate batter into the moistened tube pan. Spoon the white batter over the chocolate batter in the tube pan. Plunge a spatula down thorough both layers of batter, then bring it back to the surface with a twisting motion. Repeat this step in 1-inch intervals around the cake to marble the batter thoroughly. Bake for 45 minutes. Invert the pan and let the cake cool for 90 minutes. Run a knife around the sides of the pan, if necessary, to loosen the cake before turning it out. Sift the confectioners' sugar over the cake. Makes 12 servings.

Diabetic Exchanges: Not appropriate for diabetics

Nutrition Information Per Serving	
Energy	123 calories
Fat	trace
Saturated fat	trace
Cholesterol	0
Sodium	61 mg
Carbohydrate	28 g
Protein	4 g

Apricot-Oatmeal Bars

These fruit bars provide 21 grams of carbohydrates per bar, making them a good energy source.

Fruit bars
Flour baking spray
1 cup all-purpose flour
1/2 cup whole wheat flour
1/2 teaspoon baking soda
1/2 teaspoon ground cinnamon
1/4 cup packed brown sugar
1/2 cup plain nonfat yogurt
1/3 cup water
1/4 cup molasses
1/4 cup vegetable oil
1 egg white, beaten
1 cup quick-cooking rolled oats
3/4 cup dried apricots, chopped
1/2 cup raisins

Glaze
3/4 cup powdered sugar, sifted
1 to 2 tablespoons orange juice or skim milk

TO MAKE FRUIT BARS: Preheat oven to 350 degrees. Spray a 9-by-13-inch pan with flour baking spray.

In a large bowl, combine the all-purpose flour, whole wheat flour, baking soda and cinnamon.

In a medium mixing bowl, combine brown sugar, yogurt, water, molasses, oil and egg white. Mix yogurt mixture into flour mixture. Stir in oats, apricots and raisins. Spread stiff batter into baking pan. Bake for 20 to 25 minutes or until a wooden pick inserted comes out clean. Remove from oven and cool.

TO MAKE GLAZE: In a medium bowl, stir together powdered sugar and enough orange juice or milk to make it drizzling consistency. Drizzle over bars. Makes 24 one-bar servings.

Diabetic Exchanges: 3/4 starch, 1/2 fruit, 1/2 fat (occasional use)

**Nutrition Information
Per Serving**

Energy .... 111 calories
Fat .... 3 g
Saturated fat .... trace
Cholesterol 0
Sodium .... 25 mg
Carbohydrate ...... 21 g
Protein .... 2 g

Gingerbread Cookies

These cookies make a great low-fat Halloween treat.

1 1/2 cups whole wheat flour
1 1/2 cups unbleached all-purpose flour,
   plus flour for rolling out dough
2 1/2 teaspoons ground ginger
1 teaspoon cinnamon
1/4 teaspoon cloves
1/2 teaspoon nutmeg
1/2 teaspoon baking soda
1/2 cup dark or light molasses
1/4 cup soft tub margarine
1/2 cup brown sugar
2 egg whites or 1/4 cup egg substitute
Vegetable cooking spray
Icing (recipe at right)

In large bowl, sift together whole wheat flour, all-purpose flour, ginger, cinnamon, cloves, nutmeg and baking soda. Set aside.

In a small saucepan, heat molasses over low heat until bubbles form around sides, about 1 minute. Remove from heat and stir in margarine until completely incorporated. Scrape molasses-margarine mixture into another large bowl. Add brown sugar and stir until well blended. Beat in egg whites or egg substitute.

Make a well in the center of the dry ingredients; pour in molasses mixture. Stir, gradually mixing dry ingredients with molasses mixture. Turn dough onto floured surface and knead lightly until smooth. Pat dough into a 6-inch disk, cover with plastic wrap and refrigerate overnight.

When ready to bake, preheat oven to 350 degrees. Lightly coat a cooking sheet with vegetable cooking spray.

Roll out half of dough to about 1/4-inch thickness, keeping remaining dough well wrapped and chilled until ready to use. Using a 5-inch gingerbread man shape (or other favorite shapes), cut out cookies. Place cookies about 1/2 inch apart on prepared cookie sheet and bake 10 to 12 minutes. Let cookies cool. Repeat with remaining dough. Decorate cookies with icing. Makes 24 one-cookie servings.

Icing

1/4 cup confectioners' sugar
Few drops (no more than 1/4 teaspoon) water

In a small bowl, stir together the confectioners' sugar and water into a paste-like consistency. Apply icing with a small knife or pastry tube in desired design. Makes enough to frost 24 gingerbread cookies.

Diabetic Exchanges: Not appropriate for diabetics

♥ Nutrition Information Per Serving	
Energy	111 calories
Fat	2 g
Saturated fat	trace
Cholesterol	0
Sodium	50 mg
Carbohydrate	21 g
Protein	2 g

Oat Chocolate Chip Cookies

This chocolate chip cookie is high in fiber, and the kids will love it.

Vegetable cooking spray
1/4 cup brown sugar
2 tablespoons vegetable shortening
1/4 cup light corn syrup
3 egg whites whipped to stiff peaks
3 tablespoons water
1 teaspoon vanilla
1/3 cup plus 3 tablespoons sifted, enriched, all purpose flour
1/4 cup instant nonfat dry milk powder
1/4 cup plus 1 tablespoon (most of a .9-ounce package) reduced-calorie vanilla pudding mix
1/2 teaspoon baking soda
2 cups quick-cooking rolled oats
1/4 cup All-Bran cereal (other bran cereal may be substituted)
1/2 cup semisweet chocolate pieces

Preheat oven to 350 degrees. Spray two cookie sheets with vegetable cooking spray.

In a 1 1/2-quart bowl, cream brown sugar and shortening with an electric mixer on low speed until mixture is smooth and creamy. Add corn syrup and continue beating until well mixed. Add beaten egg whites, water and vanilla. Mix on medium speed for 1 minute or until smooth.

Stir together flour, non-fat dry milk, reduced-calorie pudding and baking soda. Add to egg white mixture and mix 2 minutes on low speed or until thick and fluffy. Stir in oats, bran cereal and chocolate chips until well mixed.

Place rounded teaspoons of dough about 1 inch apart on prepared cookie sheets. Slightly flatten cookies with a fork. Bake 10 to 12 minutes. Cookies will be full and puffy. Makes 40 to 48 cookies, each one serving.

Good: Fiber

Diabetic Exchanges: 1/2 starch, 1/4 fat

Nutrition Information Per Serving

Energy	46 calories
Fat	2 g
Saturated fat	trace
Cholesterol	trace
Sodium	36 mg
Carbohydrate	7 g
Protein	1 g

Oat Drops

Sunflower seeds are high in fat and calories. Even though it is mostly monounsaturated fat—good fat—they should be used sparingly.

1 1/2 cups quick cooking rolled oats (uncooked)
1/2 cup all-purpose flour
1/2 cup toasted wheat germ
1/4 cup sugar
1/4 cup packed brown sugar
1/4 teaspoon cinnamon
1/8 teaspoon nutmeg
5 tablespoons soft tub margarine
2 tablespoons sunflower seeds
1/4 cup plus 3 tablespoons orange juice
Vegetable cooking spray

Blend oats in a covered blender 1 minute or until evenly ground. Transfer oats to a mixing bowl and add flour, wheat germ, sugar, brown sugar, cinnamon and nutmeg. Stir to mix well. Cut in margarine until mixture forms coarse crumbs. Mix in sunflower seeds. Stir in juice to moisten dough, and form dough into a ball. Cover and chill 1 hour or longer. Preheat oven to 375 while dough is chilling and spray nonstick cookie sheets with vegetable cooking spray. Divide dough into 3 pieces. Roll each piece of dough into twelve 3/4- to 1-inch balls and place on cookie sheets. Flatten dough ball with thumb, cookie press or glass. Bake 10 to 12 minutes. Makes 36 one-cookie servings.

Diabetic Exchanges: 1/2 starch, 1/2 fat

Nutrition Information Per Serving	
Energy	53 calories
Fat	2 g
Saturated fat	trace
Cholesterol	0
Sodium	19 mg
Carbohydrate	8 g
Protein	1 g

Pumpkin Cookie Sticks

A great fun way to put Vitamin A in your diet.

1/2 cup soft tub margarine
1/3 cup sugar
1 cup canned pumpkin
1/3 cup maple syrup
1 teaspoon vanilla
1/4 cup egg substitute or 2 egg whites
2 cups all-purpose flour
1 teaspoon baking powder
1/2 teaspoon baking soda
1 teaspoon ground cinnamon
1 teaspoon nutmeg
1/2 teaspoon ginger
Vegetable cooking spray
31 Popsicle sticks
31 almond slivers
3 tablespoons raisins

Preheat oven to 350 degrees.

Cream margarine and sugar together until blended in large bowl; add pumpkin, syrup, vanilla, and egg substitute or egg whites; beat well.

Into a separate bowl, sift flour, baking powder, baking soda, cinnamon, nutmeg and ginger. Add to creamed mixture and mix well.

Drop dough by 2 level tablespoonfuls onto cookie sheets sprayed with vegetable cooking spray. Insert a stick into one side of cookie. Gently press almond and raisins into dough to make mouth, noses and eyes. Bake 15 to 20 minutes. Cool completely on wire racks. Store in a tightly covered container. Makes 31 cookie sticks, each 1 serving.

Good: Vitamin A

Diabetic Exchanges: 3/4 starch, 1/2 fat (occasional use)

Nutrition Information Per Serving

Energy	79 calories
Fat	3 g
Saturated fat	trace
Cholesterol	0
Sodium	73 mg
Carbohydrate	11 g
Protein	1g

Melon Sorbet

Melons are a great low-calorie fruit. They have a very sweet taste and are only 50 to 60 calories per cup.

3 cups chopped melon (honeydew,
    cantaloupe or watermelon)
1/2 cup sugar
2/3 cup dry white wine
Mint sprigs for garnish

Puree chopped melon in a blender or food processor; set aside. Combine sugar and wine in saucepan and simmer until sugar is dissolved. Mix in melon puree. Pour into loaf pan and freeze 4 hours or until hard.

Puree again 30 minutes before serving. Return to freezer until time to serve. Garnish serving dishes with mint sprigs. Makes four 1-cup servings.

Good: Potassium
Good: Vitamin A
Excellent: Vitamin C

Diabetic Exchanges: Not appropriate for diabetics

Nutrition Information Per Serving

Energy	154 calories
Fat	trace
Saturated fat	0
Cholesterol	0
Sodium	11 mg
Carbohydrates	34 g
Protein	1 g

Strawberry Fruit Ice

This fruit ice can be made in advance and makes a refreshing summer alternative to high-fat ice creams.

1 cup orange juice
6 tablespoons lemon juice
4 tablespoons sugar
1 cup strawberries, washed and sliced
3 bananas, mashed
1 cup plain low-fat yogurt

Mix the juices, sugar, fruits and yogurt; place in the freezer until almost set. Beat with an electric mixer on high speed until creamy and fluffy. Cover and return to the freezer. If fruit ice is made ahead of time, it must be rebeaten, then returned to the freezer for a brief period. Makes 8 servings.

Good: Potassium
Excellent: Vitamin C

Diabetic Exchanges: 1 1/2 fruit, 1/4 milk (occasional use)

Nutrition Information Per Serving

Energy	104 calories
Fat	trace
Saturated fat	trace
Cholesterol	2 mg
Sodium	21 mg
Carbohydrate	24 g
Protein	2 g

Heart Smart® Cookbook

Banana–Pineapple Pudding Pops

A great low-fat treat for kids. Some commercial pudding contains 7.4 grams of fat, most saturated.

1 ripe banana
1 can (20 ounces) unsweetened pineapple
    chunks, with liquid
1 cup lemon-flavored nonfat yogurt
1 box (.9 ounces) instant vanilla pudding,
    sugar free

Mix banana, pineapple and yogurt in a blender or food processor until smooth, about 30 seconds. Gradually add the powdered instant vanilla pudding; blend thoroughly. Freeze in freezer-pop containers or small paper cups. Makes about 8 servings, 2 pops or 1 paper cup per serving.

Good: Potassium

Diabetic Exchanges: 1 fruit, 1/4 milk

Nutrition Information Per Serving

Energy	73 calories
Fat	trace
Saturated fat	trace
Cholesterol	trace
Sodium	183 mg
Carbohydrate	17 g
Protein	2 g

Heart Smart® Cookbook

Cherry Blintzes

If you do not have a crepe pan for this recipe, a small frying pan will work just as well.

Crepes
2 egg whites or 1/4 cup egg substitute
2 tablespoons all-purpose flour
1/2 teaspoon vegetable oil
1/4 cup skim milk
1/2 teaspoon lemon rind
1/2 teaspoon sugar
Vegetable cooking spray

Filling
1 1/2 cups low-fat cottage cheese
1 teaspoon vanilla

Cherry sauce
2 teaspoons cornstarch
3 tablespoons lemon juice
3/4 cup water
3 tablespoons sugar
1 cup fresh cherries, pitted, sliced in half; or
    10 ounces drained, frozen cherries

TO MAKE CREPES: Beat egg whites or egg substitute until frothy; gradually stir in flour. Mix in oil, followed by the milk. Do not overbeat. Add lemon rind and sugar. Let stand at least 40 minutes.

Spray a small crepe pan with vegetable cooking spray. Place pan over medium-high heat. When pan is hot, add 2 tablespoons of batter, tilting pan to coat bottom evenly. Cook crepe until lightly brown. Flip and cook the other side. Repeat, making 6 crepes total. As crepes are finished, cool on a rack, stacking with a layer of wax paper between crepes.

TO MAKE FILLING: Mix cottage cheese and vanilla in blender or food processor until smooth. Set aside.

TO MAKE CHERRY SAUCE: Dissolve cornstarch in lemon juice. Combine water, sugar and lemon juice mixture in a sauce pan. Bring to a moderate boil. Boil uncovered 5 minutes, stirring vigorously. Remove from heat. Mix in cherries.

TO ASSEMBLE: Spoon 1/6 of the cheese filling onto each crepe. Roll and place on dessert plate. Serve topped with 1/6 of the warm cherry sauce. Makes 6 Servings.

Diabetic Exchanges: 1 lean meat, 1/2 starch, 1/2 fruit (occasional use)

Nutrition Information Per Serving

Energy	118 calories
Fat	1 g
Saturated fat	1 g
Cholesterol	3 mg
Sodium	252 mg
Carbohydrate	18 g
Protein	9 g

240

Chocolate-Covered Strawberries

Put a mound of these on a buffet table, and your guests won't even know they're eating Heart Smart®. Cocoa powder itself is Heart Smart® because the cocoa butter—the fat— is removed when making it.

3/4 cup sugar
1/3 cup water
1/2 teaspoon lemon juice
1/3 cup plus 1 tablespoon unsweetened
    cocoa powder, sifted
1 tablespoon vegetable oil
1 tablespoon orange liqueur, such as Grand
    Marnier (optional)
32 whole strawberries, washed and dried

In a small saucepan, combine sugar, water and lemon juice. Cook over medium heat, stirring with a wooden spoon until sugar dissolves, about 2 minutes. Increase heat to high and boil for 1 minute. Remove from heat. Stir in cocoa powder and oil until well blended and slightly thickened, about 2 minutes. Let sauce cool to room temperature for 15 to 20 minutes, stirring occasionally. Pour into small bowl or cup and stir in orange liqueur.

Holding each strawberry by the leafy stem, dip in cooled chocolate sauce. Invert and place on plate covered with wax paper. Chill in refrigerator until hard, about 20 minutes. Makes 1 cup of chocolate sauce, enough to coat about 32 large strawberries, each one serving.

Diabetic Exchanges: 1/2 fruit
(occasional use)

**Nutrition Information
Per Serving**

Energy .... 30 calories
Fat .... trace
Saturated fat .... trace
Cholesterol 0
Sodium .... trace
Carbohydrate ...... 6 g
Protein .... trace

Cran-Apple Cobbler

This colorful cobbler is low in fat and high in fiber. The cranberries give it an added kick.

Vegetable cooking spray
3 cups (12 ounces) raw cranberries, stems removed
2 apples, cored and cubed (about two cups)
1 cup apple juice, divided
3/4 cup sugar
2/3 cup raisins
1/4 teaspoon cinnamon
2 tablespoons cornstarch
3/4 cup all-purpose flour
3/4 cup rolled oats
3 tablespoons brown sugar
1 1/2 teaspoons baking powder
3 tablespoons soft tub margarine
2 egg whites
1/4 cup skim milk
1/4 teaspoon vanilla

Preheat oven to 400 degrees. Prepare an 8-inch-square baking pan or dish with vegetable cooking spray.

In a 3-quart saucepan, combine cranberries, apples, 3/4 cup apple juice, sugar, raisins and cinnamon. Cover and bring to a boil over medium heat. Boil 6 minutes or until the cranberries have popped. Stir in cornstarch and remaining 1/4 cup apple juice. Cook, stirring constantly, 2 to 3 minutes more until mixture boils and thickens. Pour batter into prepared pan. Set aside.

In a large bowl, stir together flour, rolled oats, brown sugar and baking powder. With a pastry blender or two knives used scissor-fashion, cut in margarine until the mixture resembles coarse crumbs.

In a small bowl, combine egg whites, skim milk and vanilla. Fold into crumb mixture until blended.

With a tablespoon, drop topping mixture onto cranberry mixture in baking pan. Bake 20 minutes or until topping is lightly browned. Let stand for 10 minutes before serving. Makes 8 servings.

Good: Fiber
Good: Potassium

Diabetic Exchanges: Not appropriate for diabetics

Nutrition Information Per Serving

Energy	252 calories
Fat	3 g
Saturated fat	trace
Cholesterol	trace
Sodium	122 mg
Carbohydrate	50 g
Protein	7 g

Heart Smart® Cookbook

Fresh Peach Crisp

You can use canned peaches in this recipe, but use fruit canned in its own juice to reduce sugar. If you use canned peaches for fresh peaches, use 2 cans (16 ounces) of sliced peaches, drained.

4 cups peeled, pitted, sliced fresh peaches
1 tablespoon soft tub margarine
1/4 cup rolled oats, instant or regular
2 tablespoons brown sugar, packed
2 tablespoons wheat germ
1/8 teaspoon nutmeg
1/2 teaspoon ground cinnamon

In an 8-inch-square microwave-safe baking dish, arrange peach slices end-to-end in a row. Set aside.

Melt margarine in small, microwave-safe bowl in microwave on high for 45 to 60 seconds, or until melted. Add oats, brown sugar, wheat germ, nutmeg and cinnamon to margarine; mix well.

Sprinkle mixture over peaches. Cook uncovered in microwave 10 minutes for fresh peaches (7 to 8 minutes for canned), turning dish once during cooking. Serve warm. Makes four 1/2-cup servings.

Excellent: Potassium
Excellent: Vitamin A

Diabetic Exchanges: 1 starch, 1 fruit, 1/2 fat (occasional use)

Nutrition Information Per Serving

Energy	156 calories
Fat	3.5 g
Saturated fat	trace
Cholesterol	0
Sodium	90 mg
Carbohydrate	30 g
Protein	3 g

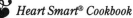

Fruit and Cream Tapioca

Tapioca, from the root of a tropical plant, gives this fruit and cream dessert a great flavor.

1/3 cup sugar
3 tablespoons quick-cooking tapioca
2 3/4 cups skim milk
1 egg white, slightly beaten
3/4 teaspoon vanilla
1 1/2 cups strawberries, washed, stems
    removed, sliced; if frozen are used, defrost,
    drain and pat dry
1 1/2 cups blueberries, washed, stems
    removed; if frozen are used, defrost, drain
    and pat dry
1 tablespoon orange rind, grated
1 cup frozen light whipped topping, thawed

Diabetic Exchanges: 1 fruit, 1/2 milk
(occasional use)

In a medium saucepan, combine sugar and tapioca. Blend in skim milk and egg white and let stand 5 minutes. Stir over medium heat until mixture comes to a full boil and is slightly thickened, about 6 to 8 minutes. Mixture thickens as it cools. Remove from heat. Stir in vanilla and pour into bowl. Let cool for 20 minutes on the counter. Stir, cover and chill thoroughly in refrigerator.

Remove from refrigerator. Spoon about 1 cup of tapioca mixture into a serving bowl or 8 individual dessert dishes. Add strawberries and top with 1 cup tapioca. Add blueberries and remaining tapioca. Chill.

Just before serving, in a medium bowl, fold together orange rind and whipped topping. Dollop whipped topping mixture evenly among 8 individual servings or into large serving bowl. Makes 8 servings.

Nutrition Information
Per Serving

Energy .... 110 calories
Fat .... 1 g
Saturated fat .... trace
Cholesterol .... 1 mg
Sodium .... 52 mg
Carbohydrate ...... 22 g
Protein .... 4 g

Heart Smart® Cookbook

Meringue Cups with Strawberry Almond Topping

One cup of whole strawberries contains only 45 calories and about as much Vitamin C as an average-size orange.

3 egg whites
1/4 teaspoon cream of tartar
3/4 cup sugar
2 cups strawberries, washed, stemmed, sliced
2 teaspoons sugar
3 tablespoons slivered almonds
2 cups low-fat frozen yogurt or ice milk (vanilla or flavor of choice)

Excellent: Vitamin C

Diabetic Exchanges: Not appropriate for diabetics

Preheat oven to 275 degrees. Cover cookie sheet with parchment or heavy brown paper.

In a medium mixing bowl beat 3 egg whites until foamy. Add cream of tartar and sugar, a tablespoon at a time. Beat until stiff and glossy and sugar is totally absorbed into the mixture. Drop meringue mixture 1/3 cup at a time onto parchment or brown paper. Using a spoon, shape into circles, building up the sides. You should have 8 meringues. Bake 1 hour (do not open oven door), then turn oven off. Leave meringues in oven with doors closed for 1 1/2 hours. Remove from oven and finish cooling meringues at room temperature.

Place sliced strawberries in a small bowl. Sprinkle with sugar and almonds. Toss gently. Fill baked meringues with 1/4 cup frozen yogurt or ice milk and top with strawberry almond mixture. Makes 8 Servings.

Nutrition Information Per Serving

Energy .... 106 calories
Fat .... 2 g
Saturated fat .... 1 g
Cholesterol 0
Sodium .... 34 mg
Carbohydrate ...... 19 g
Protein .... 4 g

Berry Peach Shortcake

When choosing stick margarines, look for one that lists a liquid oil as the first ingredient. They're usually the most Heart Smart®.

1 pint blueberries, fresh, washed; or frozen, defrosted and drained
2 pints raspberries or 2 pints hulled strawberries, fresh, washed; or frozen, defrosted and drained
2 peaches, fresh, washed, pits removed, sliced; or canned with no sugar, drained
20 biscuits (see recipe for shortcake, below)
Sprigs of mint for garnish (optional)
Yogurt Sauce (recipe at right)

Layer blueberries and raspberries or strawberries, peaches and biscuits in large serving bowl. Garnish with sprigs of mint if desired. Spoon into 10 individual serving bowls; spoon yogurt sauce over shortcake. Makes 10 servings.

Shortcake
Vegetable cooking spray
1 cup sifted all-purpose flour, plus 1/3 cup for board
1 1/4 teaspoons baking powder
1/8 teaspoon baking soda
3 tablespoons stick margarine
1/2 cup buttermilk
1 teaspoon sugar

Preheat oven to 450 degrees. Prepare a cookie sheet with vegetable cooking spray. Sift 1 cup flour, baking powder and baking soda into a medium bowl; cut in margarine with a pastry blender until mixture is crumbly. Add buttermilk all at once; mix lightly until evenly moist.

Flour pastry cloth on board with 1/3 cup flour. Turn out dough onto board; knead gently 30 seconds; pat into round 1/4-inch thick piece. Cut into small rounds with a floured 1 1/2-inch cutter; place on prepared cookie sheet. Prick tops with a floured fork; sprinkle with sugar. Bake 12 to 15 minutes, or until golden; remove from cookie sheet; cool on wire racks. Makes 20 small biscuits.

Yogurt Sauce
1/2 cup plain nonfat yogurt
1 1/2 teaspoons brown sugar
1/8 teaspoon vanilla

Combine yogurt, brown sugar and vanilla in a bowl, and mix well. Makes 10 servings.

Good: Fiber
Good: Potassium
Good: Vitamin A

Diabetic Exchanges: 1 starch, 3/4 fruit, 1 fat

Nutrition Information Per Serving

Energy	150 calories
Fat	4 g
Saturated fat	trace
Cholesterol	trace
Sodium	116 mg
Carbohydrate	26 g
Protein	3g

Heart Smart® Cookbook

Strawberry–Rhubarb Crisp

Instant rolled oats are high in sodium, with 351 milligrams per cup of cooked cereal. Old-fashioned quick rolled oats contain less than 2 milligrams per cup.

Vegetable cooking spray
2 cups strawberries, washed, hulled and
    sliced
2 cups rhubarb, cleaned, diced, leaves
    discarded (about 4 small stems or 1 to 2
    large stems)
3/4 cup granulated sugar (vary amount
    with berry sweetness and preference)
1 tablespoon cornstarch
1/4 cup cold water
1/2 cup rolled oats
1/2 cup all-purpose flour
1/4 cup light or dark brown sugar
1 teaspoon cinnamon
2 tablespoons soft tub margarine

Good: Potassium
Excellent: Vitamin C

Diabetic Exchanges: Not appropriate for diabetics

Preheat oven to 350 degrees. Prepare an 8- or 9-inch square baking dish with vegetable cooking spray.

Toss strawberries, rhubarb and sugar in prepared baking dish. Dissolve cornstarch in water in small bowl. Add to fruit and toss to coat.

Mix rolled oats, flour, brown sugar and cinnamon in mixing bowl. Set aside. Melt margarine. Add to oat mixture and mix with a fork until crumbly. Spread topping evenly over fruit. Bake until top is golden brown, approximately 45 minutes. Makes 6 servings.

Nutrition Information Per Serving

Energy	224 calories
Fat	4 g
Saturated fat	1 g
Cholesterol	0
Sodium	58 mg
Carbohydrate	47 g
Protein	2 g

Cheesecake with Blueberry Sauce

This is a real health bargain compared with regular cheesecake, which has 450 calories and 25 grams of fat per serving.

1 graham cracker pie crust, unbaked, chilled (recipe follows)
2 envelopes (1/4 ounce each) unflavored gelatin
1/2 cup cold water
1/3 cup egg substitute
3/4 cup skim milk
5 tablespoons sugar
1/4 teaspoon salt
1 cup 1-percent low-fat cottage cheese
2 tablespoons grated orange rind
1 teaspoon vanilla
3 tablespoons honey
2 egg whites
1/3 cup nonfat instant dry milk
1/3 cup ice water
Blueberry Sauce (recipe follows)

While pie crust is chilling, make filling. Sprinkle gelatin over 1/2 cup of cold water in a large bowl and set aside. In the top of a double broiler, beat egg substitute until fluffy; add skim milk, sugar and salt. Place over simmering hot water in double broiler and cook, stirring constantly, until it thickens (about 5 minutes). Add gelatin mixture, stir until dissolved. Remove from heat, let cool slightly and pour into blender. Add cottage cheese, orange rind, vanilla and honey. Blend until smooth. Chill until thickened (about 40 minutes).

In a small, clean bowl with clean beaters, beat egg whites until stiff but not dry. In a large bowl, beat nonfat instant dry milk with 1/3 cup ice cold water until creamy. Gently fold egg whites into the whipped milk mixture. Fold into cooled, thickened cheese mixture. Spoon cheesecake mixture into prepared crust. Chill at least 3 hours until set, overnight if possible. Spoon about 2 1/2 tablespoons of Blueberry Sauce over each portion. Makes 12 servings.

Diabetic Exchanges: Not appropriate for diabetics

Nutrition Information
Per Serving

Energy .... 156 calories
Fat 3g
Saturated fat .... 1 g
Cholesterol .... 1 mg
Sodium .... 194 mg
Carbohydrate ...... 26 g
Protein .... 6 g

Heart Smart® Cookbook

Blueberry Sauce

1/3 cup sugar
1 tablespoon cornstarch
2 cups fresh or frozen blueberries,
    defrosted
2 tablespoons lemon juice
1/3 cup water

In small saucepan, combine sugar and cornstarch. Add berries, lemon juice and water. Cook over medium heat, stirring, until mixture thickens, about five minutes. Makes about 2 cups.

Graham Cracker Crust

3 tablespoons soft tub margarine
3/4 cup plain graham cracker crumbs
    (about 10 squares)

Preheat oven to 400 degrees.
Blend softened or slightly heated margarine with graham cracker crumbs. Press mixture firmly and evenly into the bottom and sides of an 8- or 9-inch pie pan. Bake 5 minutes. Cool on cooling rack while preparing pie filling. Makes 1 pie crust.

Kugel

Kugel resembles a souffle. It is served as accompaniment to meat or poultry or even as a dessert.

Vegetable cooking spray (not available kosher for Passover)
8 Passover matzo wafers, broken in pieces
4 cups water
3 eggs, beaten
6 egg whites
1/2 teaspoon salt
3/4 cup sugar
1/2 cup soft tub margarine, melted, cooled to room temperature (not available kosher for Passover)
2 teaspoons cinnamon
3/4 cup chopped walnuts
4 apples, peeled, cored, finely chopped
1 cup raisins

Preheat oven to 350 degrees. Spray a 9-by-13-inch baking dish with vegetable cooking spray.

Soak matzos in water in large bowl and set aside. In another large bowl combine eggs, egg whites, salt, sugar and margarine; mix well. Drain water from matzos, but do not squeeze them. Add cinnamon, nuts, apples and raisins to matzos and gently mix. Combine matzo mixture with egg mixture and gently mix. Pour into prepared baking dish. Bake 45 minutes. Serve hot or at room temperature. Makes 12 servings.

Good: Potassium

Diabetic Exchanges: 2 starch, 1 1/2 fruit, 2 fat (occasional use)

Nutrition Information Per Serving

Energy	333 calories
Fat	12 g
Saturated fat	2 g
Cholesterol	69 mg
Sodium	228 mg
Carbohydrate	51 g
Protein	7 g

Pumpkin Mousse

Pumpkin is an excellent source of Vitamin A. One serving of this dessert provides 100 percent of the Recommended Daily Allowance of Vitamin A.

1 can (16 ounces) pumpkin
1 can (12 ounces) evaporated skim milk
5 egg whites, divided
1/3 cup sugar
1/2 teaspoon ground cinnamon
1/4 to 1/2 teaspoon ground nutmeg, to taste
1/8 to 1/4 teaspoon ground cloves, to taste
1 envelope (1/4 ounce) unflavored gelatin
1/4 cup cold water
1/4 teaspoon cream of tartar
1 teaspoon vanilla
32 almond slivers for garnish (4 per serving)

Good: Potassium
Excellent: Vitamin A

Diabetic Exchanges: 1 starch, 1/2 milk (occasional use)

In a large saucepan, mix pumpkin, milk, 2 egg whites and sugar. Beat well. Add cinnamon, nutmeg and cloves. Cook over medium heat until mixture is evenly heated, about 10 minutes. Remove from heat and set aside.

In a small saucepan, add the gelatin to the cold water and let sit for 1 minute. Cook on low heat until gelatin is dissolved, approximately 3 to 5 minutes, stirring constantly. Add gelatin to the pumpkin mixture and allow to cool.

In a mixing bowl, whip remaining 3 egg whites and cream of tartar until soft peaks form. Add vanilla and continue beating until stiff peaks form. Fold the egg white mixture into the pumpkin mixture, mixing carefully. Spoon into 8 dessert dishes, garnish with almond slivers and chill mousse until set. Makes 8 servings.

Nutrition Information Per Serving

Energy .... 104 calories
Fat .... 1 g
Saturated fat .... trace
Cholesterol .... 2 mg
Sodium .... 98 mg
Carbohydrate ...... 18 g
Protein 7g

Rice Pudding

Regular rice puddings can be high in cholesterol because egg yolks are used; this one uses one egg white and one whole egg. This is also a great way to use leftover rice.

1 egg white
1 whole egg
1 2/3 cups skim milk
1/3 cup nonfat dry milk
1/4 cup sugar
1/2 teaspoon vanilla
1 1/3 cups cooked rice
1/3 cup raisins
1/8 teaspoon nutmeg
1/3 teaspoon cinnamon

Preheat oven to 300 degrees.
In a 1-quart casserole, beat the egg white and egg slightly with a fork. Add the skim milk, dry milk, sugar and vanilla, mixing well. Stir in the cooked rice and raisins. Sprinkle the mixture with nutmeg and cinnamon.
Set casserole in baking pan; fill pan halfway up side of casserole with boiling water. Place on oven rack. Bake for 15 minutes. Stir the pudding, and bake for another 35 minutes or longer until the milk is absorbed. Serve the pudding warm or chilled. Makes four 1/2-cup servings.

Good: Potassium

Diabetic Exchanges: 1 starch, 1 milk, 1 fruit (occasional use)

Nutrition Information
Per Serving

Energy .... 231 calories
Fat .... 2 g
Saturated fat .... 1 g
Cholesterol .... 56 mg
Sodium .... 114 mg
Carbohydrate ...... 45 g
Protein .... 9 g

252

Chocolate Mint Frozen Yogurt Pie

Frozen yogurt can be made from whole milk with cream or from skim milk. Read the label for ingredients, so you buy the yogurt from skim, and remember that ingredients are listed in order of concentration.

1 1/4 cups graham cracker crumbs
(8 rectangles)
1 1/2 teaspoons sugar
2 tablespoons soft tub margarine
1 quart (32 ounces) chocolate low-fat frozen
    yogurt
1 teaspoon mint extract

Preheat oven to 375 degrees.
Using blender or food processor, crush graham crackers into fine crumbs. Combine sugar and crumbs in mixing bowl. Melt margarine and combine with crumb mixture. Press crumbs into 9-inch pie plate to form a crust. Bake 8 minutes, until lightly brown, or microwave on high, 100 percent power, 2 to 2 1/2 minutes, turning halfway through (be sure to use a microwave-safe pie plate). Cool on rack.
Place yogurt into medium-sized bowl. With mixer, cream mint extract into yogurt. Scoop yogurt mixture into cooled pie crust. Place pie in freezer for approximately 30 to 60 minutes, or until frozen. Makes 8 servings.

Diabetic Exchanges: 1 starch, 1 fat, 1/2 fruit, 1/2 milk

Nutrition Information Per Serving

Energy .... 190 calories
Fat .... 5 g
Saturated fat .... trace
Cholesterol .... 7 mg
Sodium .... 184 mg
Carbohydrate ...... 32 g
Protein .... 4 g

Pumpkin Pie

Here's something to be thankful for: A piece of traditional pumpkin pie contains 300 to 400 calories and 15 to 20 grams of fat; ours contains a fraction of that.

2/3 cup sugar
1/2 teaspoon cinnamon
1/2 teaspoon ginger
1/2 teaspoon nutmeg
1/4 teaspoon ground cloves
1 1/2 cups canned pumpkin
1 teaspoon vanilla
1 1/2 cups canned evaporated skim milk
1/2 teaspoon orange rind (optional)
3 egg whites, beaten
1 8- or 9-inch pie shell with a graham
   cracker crust (recipe at right)

Preheat oven to 450 degrees.
   In a large mixing bowl, combine sugar, cinnamon, ginger, nutmeg and ground cloves. Stir in pumpkin. Add vanilla, evaporated skim milk, orange rind if desired and egg whites. Mix until smooth. Pour into pie shell and bake 10 minutes. Reduce heat to 325 degrees and bake until a knife inserted into the filling comes out clean, about 45 minutes. Serves 8.

Good: Potassium
Excellent: Vitamin A

Graham Cracker Crust

3 tablespoons soft tub margarine
3/4 cup plain graham cracker crumbs
   (about 10 squares)

Preheat oven to 400 degrees.
   Blend softened or slightly heated margarine with graham cracker crumbs. Press mixture firmly and evenly into the bottom and sides of an 8- or 9-inch pie pan. Bake 5 minutes. Cool on cooling rack while preparing pie filling. Makes 1 pie crust.

   Diabetic Exchanges: Not appropriate for diabetics

Nutrition Information Per Serving

Energy .... 187 calories
Fat .... 5 g
Saturated fat .... 1 g
Cholesterol .... 2 mg
Sodium .... 175 mg
Carbohydrate ..... 30 g
Protein .... 6 g

Part III

Appendix

Using the Cookbook

The recipes included in this cookbook are appropriate for use in a Heart Smart® diet. However, if you wish to decrease the fat in your diet even further, you may find ways to modify them. In the average American diet 38 percent fat of daily calories come from fat. The current guidelines established by the American Heart Association recommend 30 percent or less of your daily calories come from fat. However, the health benefits of lowering the percent of fat in your diet to 20 percent or even lower are worth considering.

The nutrition information included with each recipe was derived from computer analysis, based primarily on information from the United States Department of Agriculture. The values are as accurate as possible and are based on these assumptions.

1. Garnishes and optional ingredients were omitted from the nutrition analysis.

2. Statistics on meat recipes were based on lean meat trimmed of fat.

Each serving of food must provide the following amount of each nutrient to qualify as either a good or excellent source in this cookbook.

	Good source	Excellent source
Vitamin A	1000 IU	2000 IU
Vitamin C	15 mg	30 mg
Calcium	240 mg	360 mg
Potassium	300 mg	400 mg
Iron	2.5 mg	3.5 mg
Dietary Fiber	2 g	3 g

Diabetic exchanges are included with each recipe; however, this does not mean that all recipes are appropriate for use by diabetics. If you question the use of some recipes in your diet please discuss it with your dietitian.

Grain Group

(6 - 11 servings per day)

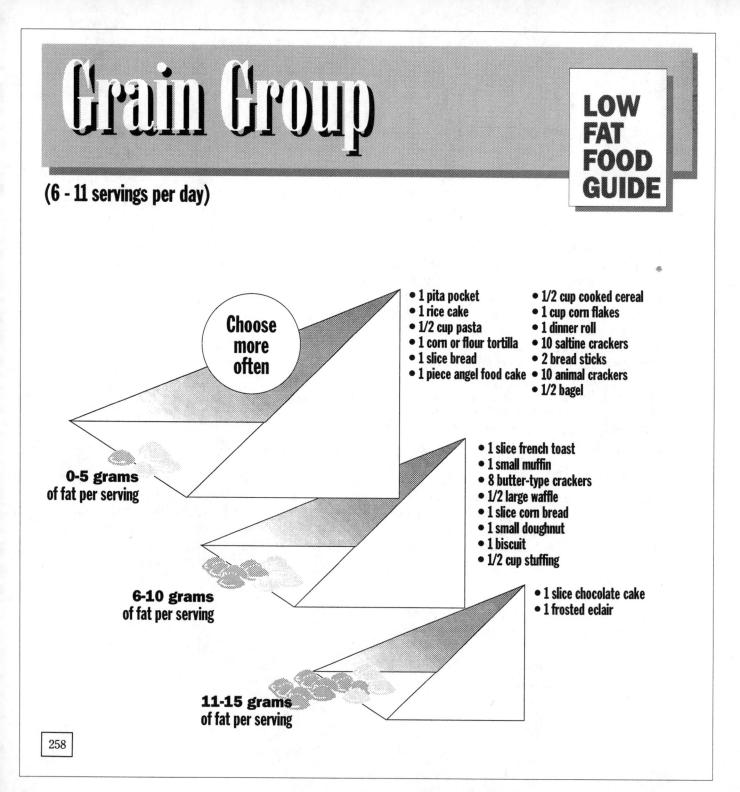

Choose more often

0-5 grams of fat per serving

- 1 pita pocket
- 1 rice cake
- 1/2 cup pasta
- 1 corn or flour tortilla
- 1 slice bread
- 1 piece angel food cake
- 1/2 cup cooked cereal
- 1 cup corn flakes
- 1 dinner roll
- 10 saltine crackers
- 2 bread sticks
- 10 animal crackers
- 1/2 bagel

6-10 grams of fat per serving

- 1 slice french toast
- 1 small muffin
- 8 butter-type crackers
- 1/2 large waffle
- 1 slice corn bread
- 1 small doughnut
- 1 biscuit
- 1/2 cup stuffing

11-15 grams of fat per serving

- 1 slice chocolate cake
- 1 frosted eclair

258

Vegetable Group

(3 - 5 servings per day)

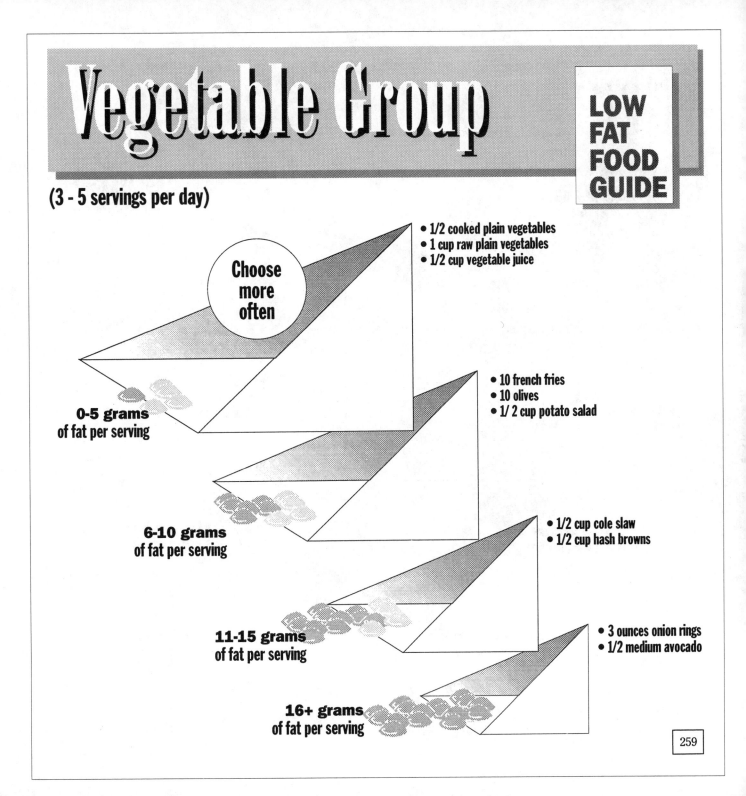

Choose more often

• 1/2 cooked plain vegetables
• 1 cup raw plain vegetables
• 1/2 cup vegetable juice

0-5 grams of fat per serving

• 10 french fries
• 10 olives
• 1/ 2 cup potato salad

6-10 grams of fat per serving

• 1/2 cup cole slaw
• 1/2 cup hash browns

11-15 grams of fat per serving

• 3 ounces onion rings
• 1/2 medium avocado

16+ grams of fat per serving

259

Fruit Group

(2 - 4 servings per day)

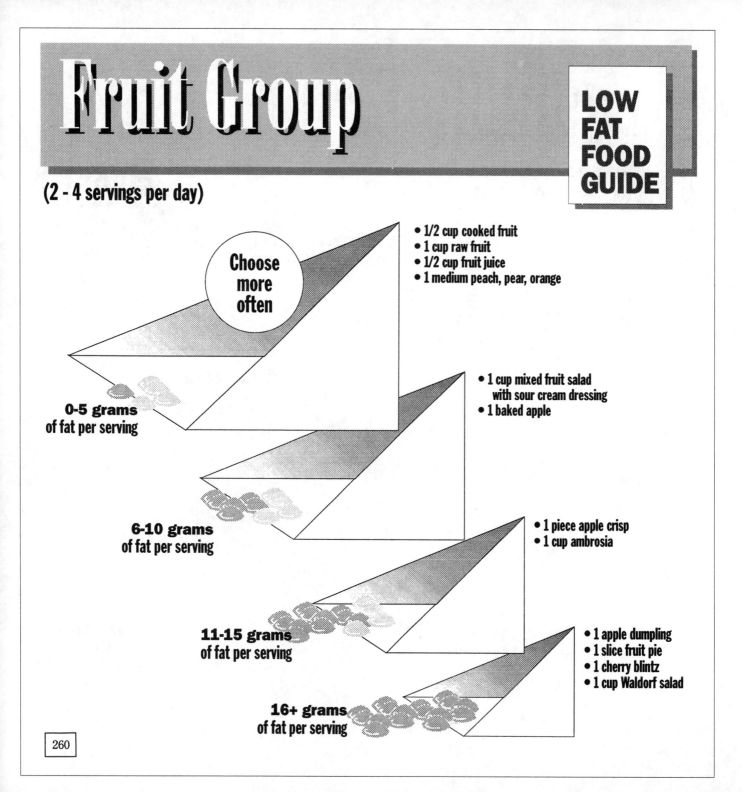

Choose more often

- 1/2 cup cooked fruit
- 1 cup raw fruit
- 1/2 cup fruit juice
- 1 medium peach, pear, orange

0-5 grams of fat per serving

- 1 cup mixed fruit salad with sour cream dressing
- 1 baked apple

6-10 grams of fat per serving

- 1 piece apple crisp
- 1 cup ambrosia

11-15 grams of fat per serving

- 1 apple dumpling
- 1 slice fruit pie
- 1 cherry blintz
- 1 cup Waldorf salad

16+ grams of fat per serving

Dairy Group

(2 - 3 servings per day)

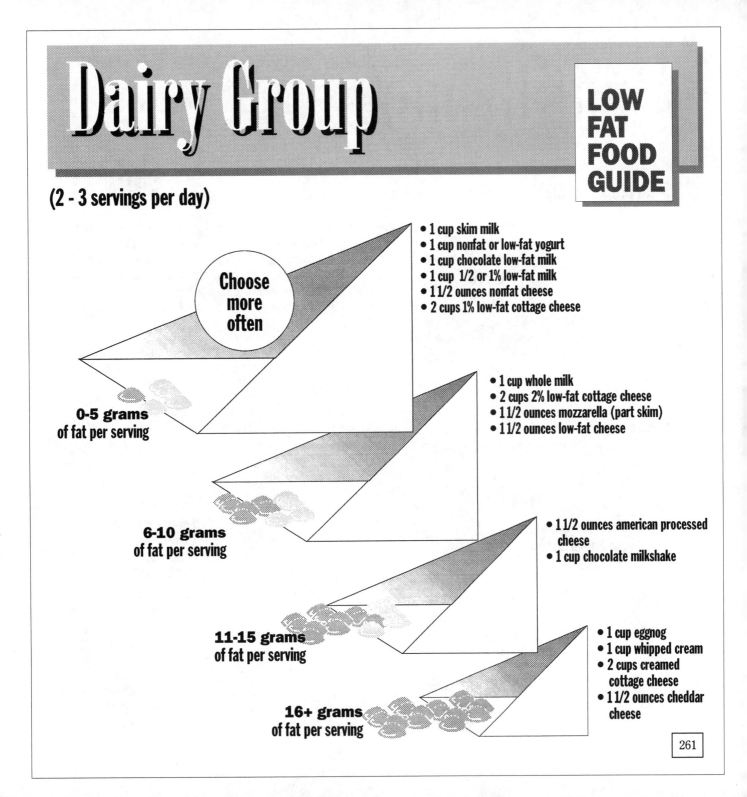

Choose more often

- 1 cup skim milk
- 1 cup nonfat or low-fat yogurt
- 1 cup chocolate low-fat milk
- 1 cup 1/2 or 1% low-fat milk
- 1 1/2 ounces nonfat cheese
- 2 cups 1% low-fat cottage cheese

0-5 grams of fat per serving

- 1 cup whole milk
- 2 cups 2% low-fat cottage cheese
- 1 1/2 ounces mozzarella (part skim)
- 1 1/2 ounces low-fat cheese

6-10 grams of fat per serving

- 1 1/2 ounces american processed cheese
- 1 cup chocolate milkshake

11-15 grams of fat per serving

- 1 cup eggnog
- 1 cup whipped cream
- 2 cups creamed cottage cheese
- 1 1/2 ounces cheddar cheese

16+ grams of fat per serving

261

Meat Group

(2 - 3 servings per day)

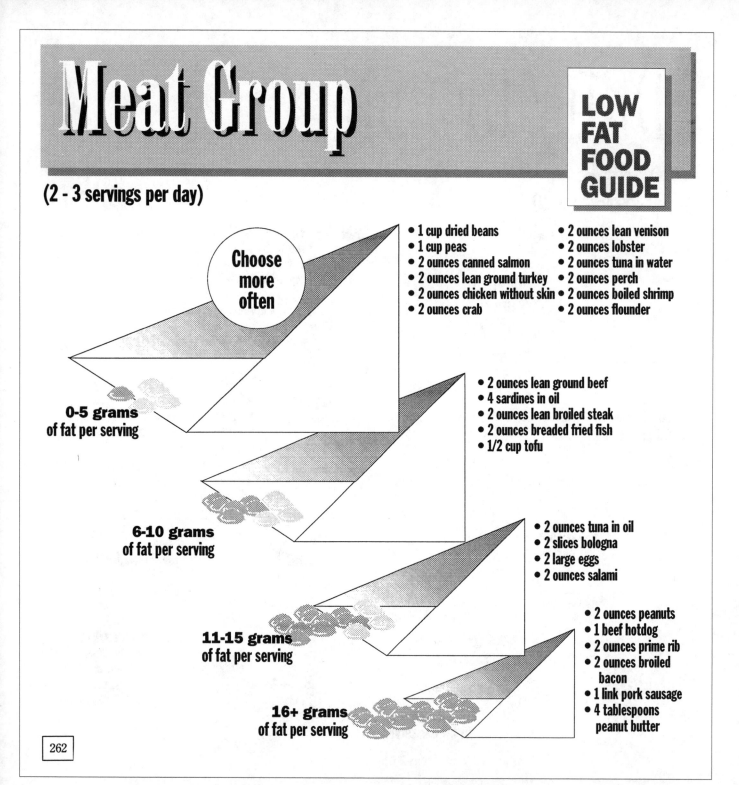

Choose more often

0-5 grams of fat per serving

- 1 cup dried beans
- 1 cup peas
- 2 ounces canned salmon
- 2 ounces lean ground turkey
- 2 ounces chicken without skin
- 2 ounces crab
- 2 ounces lean venison
- 2 ounces lobster
- 2 ounces tuna in water
- 2 ounces perch
- 2 ounces boiled shrimp
- 2 ounces flounder

6-10 grams of fat per serving

- 2 ounces lean ground beef
- 4 sardines in oil
- 2 ounces lean broiled steak
- 2 ounces breaded fried fish
- 1/2 cup tofu

11-15 grams of fat per serving

- 2 ounces tuna in oil
- 2 slices bologna
- 2 large eggs
- 2 ounces salami

16+ grams of fat per serving

- 2 ounces peanuts
- 1 beef hotdog
- 2 ounces prime rib
- 2 ounces broiled bacon
- 1 link pork sausage
- 4 tablespoons peanut butter

Dietary Fiber

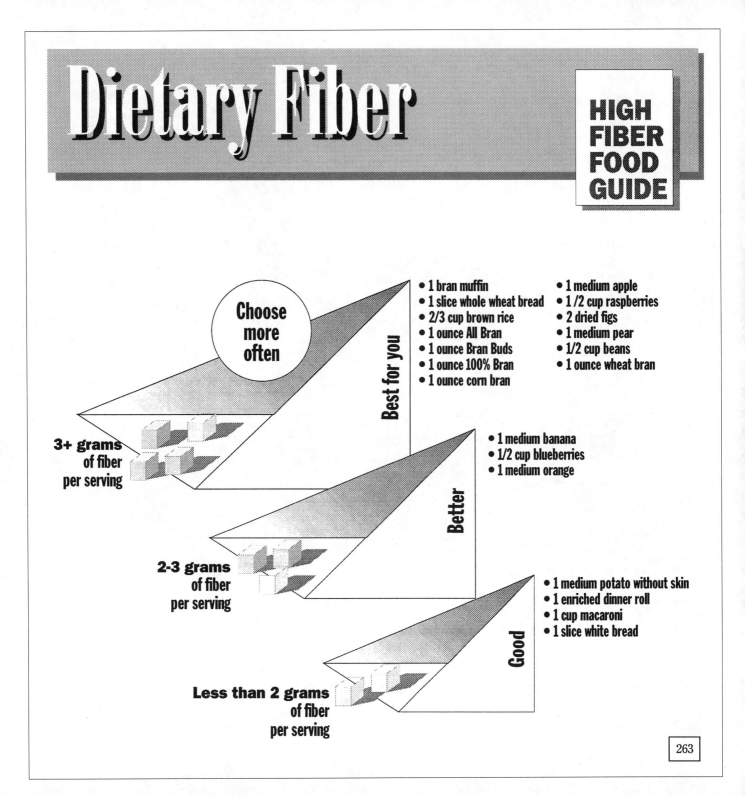

Choose more often

Best for you
- 1 bran muffin
- 1 slice whole wheat bread
- 2/3 cup brown rice
- 1 ounce All Bran
- 1 ounce Bran Buds
- 1 ounce 100% Bran
- 1 ounce corn bran
- 1 medium apple
- 1/2 cup raspberries
- 2 dried figs
- 1 medium pear
- 1/2 cup beans
- 1 ounce wheat bran

3+ grams of fiber per serving

Better
- 1 medium banana
- 1/2 cup blueberries
- 1 medium orange

2-3 grams of fiber per serving

Good
- 1 medium potato without skin
- 1 enriched dinner roll
- 1 cup macaroni
- 1 slice white bread

Less than 2 grams of fiber per serving

Index

Index

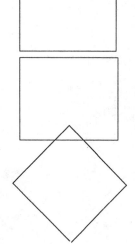

Index

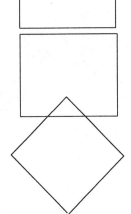

Index

Index

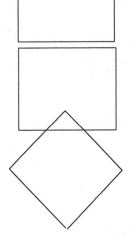

Index

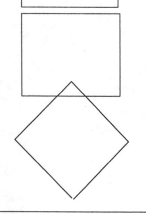